Jiu-Jitsu University

Saulo Ribeiro

with Kevin Howell

Victory Belt Publishing
Las Vegas

First Published in 2008 by Victory Belt Publishing.

ISBN 13: 978-0-9815044-3-8

ISBN 10: 0-9815044-3-4

This book is for educational purposes. The publisher and authors of this instructional book are not responsible in any manner whatsoever for any adverse effects directly or indirectly as a result of the information provided in the book. If not practiced safely and with caution, martial arts can be dangerous to you and to others. It is important to consult with a professional martial arts instructor before beginning training. It is also very important to consult with a physician prior to training due to the intense and strenuous nature of the techniques in this book.

Victory Belt ® is a registered trademark of Victory Belt Publishing.

Printed in Canada.

TC 0116

Cover design by: Haley Woods

Cover photo by: Catarina Monnier

Photographs by: Erich Krauss

Layout & design by: Haley Woods

Technical Editor: John Danaher

CONTENTS

THE GUARD

GUARD PASSING

SUBMISSIONS

ACKNOWLEDGEMENTS

First of all, I would like to thank God for bringing me into the world strong, healthy, and into a family like mine.

To my mom for spoiling me in a good way and being my first example of a great woman and mother,

To my father for building in me all the values that a man should have in order to survive in the modern world,

To my brother for being my other half and going through all the pain and learning together, all battles that made us strong with blood, sweat, and tears.

To my sister and niece for all the unconditional love that I feel in my heart,

To Royler Gracie, my mentor, friend, older brother, sensei and everything in the martial arts world,

To all my students that I've been teaching all over the world, especially the ones in Gracie Tijuca,

To Chris Blanke and Lucas Beddow for being my American older brothers and helping me in my decisions,

To all of you that love the art that means the world to me: Jiu-Jitsu.

—Saulo Ribeiro

To Haley, for the hours and hours of hard work, redesigns, and brainstorming sessions to make sure this book became a reality.

To John Danaher, for being a gentleman and a scholar. Without your guidance and mentorship, this book would not be what it is.

To Billie Hunt, for dotting the "i"s and crossing the "t"s. Thank you so much for everything.

To all my friends and family, thanks for enabling my dream.

—Kevin Howell

Introduction to Jiu-Jitsu

"Technical knowledge is not enough. One must transcend techniques so that the art becomes an artless art, growing out of the unconscious."
—Daisetsu Suzuki

LEVERAGE

Rickson Gracie seeded and molded all my philosophy and thinking regarding jiu-jitsu. I am thankful not only for his technique and competition strategy, but for all his knowledge. This is what I teach today. My jiu-jitsu is based on his knowledge of leverage.

Everybody talks about leverage, but few people use it in their jiu-jitsu. Everything I show in this book relates to the efficiency of the lever and the fulcrum. How can I lift a man twice as heavy as myself? How can I armlock someone who is three times as strong? The answer is always the same – leverage. Keep this in mind when grappling. Always look for positions that multiply your perceived strength while minimizing that of your opponent. These are the leverage points that must be sought.

FEELING JIU-JITSU

"If you think, you are late. If you are late, you use strength. If you use strength, you tire. And if you tire, you die."

This is one of my favorite quotes, and it means that all jiu-jitsu must be based on how you feel your opponent. The timing to make a decision is not based on what you think you should be doing. It is about your body recognizing the move and automatically doing it. It's about muscle memory. For example, when someone is passing your guard, you *feel* he is passing so you cannot wait to decide what to do. There is no time for thought – only reaction.

This is one thing I developed a long time ago

from my teachers – my jiu-jitsu would be based on reaction. When you react, you don't give your mind the time to get filled with emotions. You are devoid of anger, fear, and frustration; you are simply moving. If your opponent is pushing your elbow and you're tired and almost hurt, it doesn't matter because you are reacting already; you haven't given yourself time to get upset. That's why I follow this motto: no mind. If you do not think, you must feel your opponent and react accordingly.

THE BELT SYSTEM

The jiu-jitsu belt system serves to indicate the level of a practitioner's experience. The belts range from the novice levels of white and blue belt to the intermediate level of purple to the advanced levels of brown and black. The following is an indication of what a student should look for at each level.

WHITE BELT

I compare the white belt to the beginning of the life cycle, from birth to socialization. Just as the child must trust his mother, the white belt must believe in the good will of his instructor. There will be time for questioning, but for now he must focus and train. I believe white belts should be exposed to all the possible attacks, moves, and positions that jiu-jitsu entails because I want them to become aware of how to do everything correctly to progress.

Many think that some moves are too advanced for white belts. I disagree. I think that part of a white belt's foundation is to know all the aspects of jiu-jitsu. Although the white belt cannot dive into the intricacies of every little thing but must start with proper fundamentals, knowledge of what those intricacies are is necessary for progress to happen. If you are going to be attacked by it, you might as well know it. It's a matter of learning survival. White belts won't be able to perfect any of it until they have learned to survive.

As a journey, the duration of the white belt is between six to eighteen months, depending on the student's background. Because the transition from white to blue belt is the most important process that an individual must go through in jiu-jitsu, I make sure each student is ready for his promotion.

Some people feel that talent or athleticism should result in an instant promotion to a higher belt. You may be a good wrestler and can beat a few guys, but what about your principles and fundamentals? I will not promote someone because he can use strength; I must see more than that. This is why I must know all my white belts, and I will accompany them as they grow as people and practitioners of jiu-jitsu.

BLUE BELT

Aside from black belt, blue belt is probably the rank in which students will spend most of their time. This is because here they start to develop their own ways of doing things after they have learned the fundamentals of jiu-jitsu. Blue belts start to develop different games and options and they will test everything they see until they build their own game. Therefore, the blue belt is the belt of experimentation. Students will experiment with all kinds of guards and techniques until they see what works for them. These discoveries take considerable time, and this is why a blue belt is often one of the longest processes in jiu-jitsu.

PURPLE BELT

The purple belt is the level where a student starts to refine his technique while mentoring others. As he reflects on his own journey as a blue belt, the purple belt assists lower ranking students by teaching them to avoid the pitfalls that he experienced. In this way, purple belts need contact with blue belts.

Meanwhile, brown belts will sharpen him, work on his speed, and push his defense. In this way, the brown belt will push a purple belt in a way that the blue cannot. It is a back and forth learning experience.

This is also the level where a student begins to get more access to black belts. A black belt can really challenge the purple belt, and the purple belt reminds the black belt of his time spent in the toughest stage of learning. From the beginning of the purple belt to the end, the student should be getting closer to the black belt level of knowledge. This knowledge is what I look for in my higher purple belts.

To become a brown belt, the purple belt must believe in his skill level. He doesn't let the blue and white belts interfere with his confidence. Also, he must be respectful of his fellow students and have the ability to connect defense and offense. Once he has fulfilled this, he is ready for a brown belt.

BROWN BELT

A brown belt is almost a black belt. A brown belt's focus is on polishing the rough edges to tighten his game. This is the belt where helpful tips take a student to the next level. These tips are the only difference between brown and black belts. For a brown belt the important lessons sound like, "Move a little more to this side when you do this..." These small alterations will make all the difference in becoming a black belt. This is why it is important to have black belts around. They are veterans who have already been there and have seen everything students will see.

BELIEVING IN YOUR YOUR RANK

If you worry about the time and speed of your promotions, you lose yourself. Remember, before you are a blue, purple, or brown belt, you want to feel like one. You must feel that your skills are there. You cannot fool yourself. Attaining a belt is just proof that your teacher is connected with you. You will know when you deserve it. My role as an instructor is to be there to say, "It's time." But you should already realize this on your own.

Jiu-jitsu is not math, and promotion is not based on attendance or calendar dates. A regimented promotion schedule based on dates or attendance is the worst way to gauge development. Jiu-jitsu is more complex than this.

There is no sense in chasing a belt and getting it as fast as possible. Often, people do not see that black belt will be their longest belt. Remember, it doesn't matter if you get it in four years or fifteen. Either way, you will have the rest of your life with a black belt around your waist. Building the black belt is what matters.

THE BELT SYSTEM AS USED IN THIS BOOK

This book uses the belt system differently than other instructional manuals on jiu-jitsu. Although the belts should not be used dogmatically (of course there will be opportunities for white belts to use submissions) they are a frame of reference for the skills that you should absorb in each level of your jiu-jitsu journey. For example, the purple belt should understand the guard before moving on to the brown belt. If the student achieves the brown belt rank and does not know the guard, it will be much more difficult learning to pass! The purpose of this system is to create a solid foundation for the student and to promote technical growth and confidence. Therefore, the white belt will start in a position that he must become accustomed to – the bottom. On the other side of the scale, the black belt will be at the top of the food chain sharpening his top game submissions, just as he would in reality.

JIU-JITSU AND THE INDIVIDUAL

Jiu-jitsu is an individual sport where you need partners in order to progress. However, comparing yourself with your partners only hinders your experience. I'm going to treat you as an isolated individual. When I see you grapple, I am not impressed if you win or lose. What I want to see is your use of the fundamentals of jiu-jitsu. It does not matter how it ends. I do not care if you tap five times as long as you try to use technique.

REACHING A HIGH LEVEL IN JIU-JITSU

Ego is the biggest hindrance in reaching a high level in jiu-jitsu. Often, it is difficult to compartmentalize your ego, especially when you have to perform in front of the class. It is natural to worry about how good you look, but to be good you cannot have that mentality. Don't try to look good! It is not important that others are watching while you are failing. It only matters that you try.

Practice jiu-jitsu with a child-like mind. Have you ever considered why children have such an accelerated learning curve? Part of the reason is that they are more concerned with enjoyment than ego. Try to envelop yourself in a child's naivety. Today, all the white belts will mount you. Tomorrow, everybody catches you in armbars. How often do you see a higher-ranked student allow a lower-ranked one to catch a submission? Few people do it and this all comes back to ego.

LEARNING OUTSIDE THE ACADEMY

Everything that is good for your body is good for the practice of jiu-jitsu. This includes surfing, hiking, a healthy diet, and a host of other activities. Besides keeping you nimble and strong, these activities can relax your mind and body, leaving you rejuvenated and ready for jiu-jitsu practice. You can sharpen skills with meditation, physical conditioning, and a stretching system. Ginnastica Natural, an exercise and stretching method that incorporates mechanics from, yoga and jiu-jitsu, is one way of doing this. Every Ginnastica Natural exercise can be done without a partner, which is a great way to learn jiu-jitsu's many body movements. This allows you to develop sport specific conditioning and flexibility that go hand in hand with your technical development.

You can also boost your learning curve if you

take the time to learn from various media sources such as books and videos. However, in the end you will have to train with a partner to commit the techniques to muscle memory.

Kettlebells are a great complement to jiu-jitsu.

As you train with an instructor, keep an open mind so that you are not dependant on that one instructor's techniques and opinions. I tell my students not to be stuck to me! If I see somebody doing something interesting, I will introduce it to my students. Marcelo Garcia, Fernando "Terere" Augusto, Eduardo Telles, and Demian Maia all do particular things that make me wonder, "How did he do that?" I want all my students to learn from them and grow. It's important to learn from more than one source because no one can have all the answers to everything. I don't want to limit you to the weapons I have. As an instructor, I must try to expose you to all the weapons – *everything*!

COMPETITION AND JIU-JITSU

It is not necessary for every student of jiu-jitsu to enter into competitions. Some may do jiu-jitsu simply because they enjoy gaining the knowledge. Others perhaps dislike the limelight or just don't want to compete in this particular sport. I love to do other sports, but I don't have the desire to compete in those sports. Some people don't like to compete because they don't know how to deal with loss. If you win, you are happy, and if you lose, your world gets turned upside down. That is a problem. This fear of losing scares some people from competition.

Then there are those who live and die by competition, but fail to realize it is just a game. It is a game where you mix knowledge, strategy, timing, health, and attitude. Like any game, the best jiu-jitsu practitioner doesn't always win. Take the World Championship for example. Thirty guys sweat

blood in their training, and there is only one winner. What about the twenty-nine who worked so hard? Is the champion really better than all of them? It depends. Sometimes, the person with the best technique gets eliminated in the first round.

If you decide to compete, realize that competition is the art of dealing with pressure. Some people face pressure early in life and others not until much later, but in every case, where there is pressure there is competition. The student who doesn't compete at the tournament is still competing if the pressure is there. Perhaps he even feels more pressure than one who does go to tournaments. He fights against himself. He competes against his feelings. He competes against his choices. This is the toughest opponent you can have – yourself. Ultimately the opponent you will face in the ring is you, because you cannot compete successfully if you do not address internal issues that will affect your performance. When competing, you will not even be able to think about overcoming your opponent if you are too worried about yourself. However, if you are comfortable with your preparation, you will have the confidence to perform. Becoming the champion is not about your opponent. It's about you.

Finally, if you want to learn something about someone's jiu-jitsu, you should learn it in the academy. Many people enter competition with hopes that it will be a fast track to getting better. However, the quality of training partners actually has a much greater impact on skill level than competition does. Though competition can be a part of training, it alone will not improve technique. Competition shows such a small part of any given competitor's knowledge that it masks what he really knows. In the academy, you can see him for who he really is. You will see him relaxed and in the proper environment to exhibit his understanding of jiu-jitsu and educate you and others of its benefits. This is what will keep jiu-jitsu evolving. Competition will always be a window to show the world how professional the sport can be. But the growth of the sport over the coming generations will not be reliant on the competitive aspect.

The Goal of the White Belt: SURVIVAL

"A warrior is tuned to survive, and he survives in the best of all possible ways."
— Carlos Castaneda

1-1 WHAT DOES IT MEAN TO SURVIVE?

Everyone has fears, and every beginning jiu-jitsu practitioner at every academy will be accompanied by those fears when first stepping onto the mats. It may be the nightmare of claustrophobia, pain, or suffocation. In each situation, the student defeats these fears by facing them over and over again. At any moment, the student can tap to signal an end to the fight and start again and give it another try, over time he gradually liberates himself from the cycle of fear. This is a natural process of mental conditioning and it is the law for every student. Through this evolution, the grappler not only overcomes fear but also the instinctive tendencies to fight and waste energy. In place of his fear he develops confidence, fortitude, and peace in stressful times. In other words, he liberates himself from insecurity.

Survival on a physical level is simply an extension of this mental conditioning. Although there are physical techniques that I will show you how to use for survival, you must also make sure to become accustomed to the nature of being physically attacked, and specifically to pressure and to the claustrophobic feeling of crushing weight. In this way you will be mentally prepared to relax and let yourself go into these trying situations. Therefore, survival will depend on the mental aspect of becoming comfortable while under duress as well as physical techniques.

1-2 SURVIVAL AS THE FOUNDATION OF GRACIE JIU-JITSU

It is important to realize that survival is the aspect that brings us closest to the founder of jiu-jitsu, Helio Gracie (See Case Study 1.0). Due to his smaller stature, Helio was forced to learn how to survive against much larger and stronger opponents. Realizing that he would not be able to out-muscle these opponents, Helio instead looked for ways to survive. He was aware that it took much less energy to thwart his opponents' advances than it took to escape. His goal was simple, he may not win the fight, but he would not die. He would definitely survive.

The result of Helio's adaptations was astonishing; by focusing on the use of leverage as a tool for survival, Helio Gracie evolved jiu-jitsu into an art that could benefit a smaller person in a fight against a much larger opponent.

1-3 SURVIVAL POSITIONING

I am going to tell you something that goes against the current dogma of jiu-jitsu instruction. Survival is not based on escaping submissions; it is about putting yourself into a position where you do not need to use muscle to protect yourself. If it were based solely on escaping the submission, then how could we expect Helio Gracie at 130 pounds to be able to escape the tightest armlock or the deepest choke?

Survival is about assuming a position that impedes your opponent's offense, eliminating the chance of his submission. It is about changing the situation to one that favors the defensive player. In doing so, you force your opponent out of his comfort area. As a result, all of his actions become predictable because as he fights for offense from an uncomfortable position there are only certain movements he can make.

Survival is not about escaping, but it becomes easier to escape when you can get to a stronger defensive position that forces your opponent into

Introduction

an awkward one.

Technically speaking, you have to master every defensive aspect of a position, for example, hiding your elbows for protection, getting to your side to create the proper angle, and, if necessary, preventing the cross face to inhibit being controlled. You also have to be able to execute them all at once. I cannot overstate the importance of this. If you fail to become comfortable doing all these things at once, you will be at the mercy of your opponent.

The key to mastering all these aspects is being able to feel what it is your opponent wants. Intuition is vital to your survival, and it will take a considerable amount of time to develop.

To return to the question: How could Helio, or anyone for that matter, escape the deepest choke? The answer is to first seek to avoid the position completely. Of course students need to train, learn submission defense, and get caught several times, and this will occur naturally throughout their involvement in jiu-jitsu, but they must also realize that the best defense is the one that avoids the danger altogether. For example, if I get stuck in a deep triangle position, the longer I remain caught, the less likely it is that I will escape. Even with the knowledge of many triangle escapes, I am still reacting to my opponent and this places him in control of the situation. In the end, my best defense may be to tap. This is why all students need to know how to use positioning to avoid the submission.

1-4 SURVIVAL AND THE WHITE BELT

The theme of the white belt is survival, nothing more and nothing less. After all, this is what the white belt has to do from the first day of class. He is not going to arrive in class and beat the best. He has no one to whom he can compare himself because he is still an empty vessel. Although one often takes up jiu-jitsu to learn submissions, the first lesson for the beginner is survival. Before he moves on, the white belt must become a survivor.

Beyond this, the white belt is the level where I will first test a student's insecurity and patience. There have been countless professionals who have walked into my academy beaming with confidence and strength, but when they were mounted by one of my white belts, they completely panicked. Everyone has to learn patience, starting at white belt. Eventually, by dealing with a superior power, students lose their insecurities and gains patience. This is a benefit to survival training that will last a lifetime.

Of course, I will give the white belt more weapons than just survival, but like the young man who goes to war, my first goal is for him to survive and come back to his family. He doesn't have a lot of skill yet, but if he is smart and focuses on his defense and knowledge, he can survive.

The white belt process teaches patience in situations of having to tap or in holding off the opponent. Eventually, students arrive at a crossroad where I teach this key aspect: how to change the

Helpful Survival Tips

- Always close your elbows. An open elbow is a pathway for armbars, upper body control, and poor posture.

- Always prevent the cross-face control. If your opponent controls the direction of your head, he controls the direction of your entire body.

- Never stay flat. A flat body is an immobile body.

- Don't push. Pushing as a defense anchors you to your opponent and immobilizes your necessary hip movement.

- Use your hips and body pendulum to generate power, not your hands. Your body is a much stronger weapon than your arms alone.

Figure 1.0:
Side Control Survival Positioning

situation to prevent having to tap out.

Needless to say, it is imperative that the white belt learns to tap, tap early, and tap often. To tap simply means, "Okay you got me, let's go again!" Every student should keep in mind that tapping is a positive part of the learning process; therefore, there is no reason to try with all their might to escape in the absence of proper technique.

1-5 SURVIVAL AND THE UPPER BELT

Think back to that white belt that knows some survival. The longer he lasts, the more pressure he puts on the higher rank. This is great for the upper belt, because it forces him to move more and search for the tiniest hole in the white belt's defensive shell. Also, the white belt is going to test the higher rank's accuracy because the senior student will often begin to rush through his movements as his foundation is disrupted by the white belt's survival skills. Usually, this is the point where one should transition into an escape, but the white belt is still likely to remain in the survival position due to his inexperience and lack of transitioning skills. The upper belt will thus get to work his skills in adaptation and transition while being challenged to find new ways to submit the white belt without force or pure strength.

When an upper belt visits the academy, I have a different approach to teaching survival. Schools have various ways of receiving visitors. Sometimes, the instructor takes the biggest and best students and allows them to beat down the visitor to prove their own worth in the academy. I do not believe this is the right approach, and it says nothing about the students' abilities to protect themselves.

In my school, I use the visit of an upper belt to test my students' abilities to survive against somebody who doesn't know about their survival skills. I want to see if they can make the visitor work really hard to find a hole to attack. In addition, I want to see if our special guest has patience and whether he is going to lose his temper or get rough with my white belts. Often enough, the visitor tries to destroy the white belt, especially when he becomes frustrated with the white belt's defense. In this regard, I am truly happy if my white belt can just survive in the face of such an onslaught.

If the visitor becomes too rough with my students, I bring him to my world and show him what it means to survive. Now, he will have to survive against a veteran, and I will discover how his mind works when the tables are turned. Some upper belts make excuses or fake injuries and others accept their relative lack of survival skills. Regardless, the visiting upper belt, gives me the opportunity to watch him both when he is the hunter and the prey. In this way I can analyze his style to see if I want to continue to welcome this guest into the academy. If he shows kindness to the white belts, then I give him the red carpet.

Even when upper belts visit for private lessons, I instruct them in survival. My view is that I cannot change you or give you an entire new game in one private lesson, so I will focus on this most important area of jiu-jitsu. In all honesty, 99 percent of the people who come in seeking these lessons do not know how to survive. If they already understand survival, then I can go further and teach some escapes. Usually, they ask about fancy sweeps, and I tell them that this is the last thing they need. As an instructor, I will not waste my guest's money on these techniques because his defense has got to be tight before he even considers fancy sweeps or the newest attacks. When these private lessons are over the student thanks me for showing him something that he should have learned in the beginning.

1-6 SURVIVAL AND THE AGING PROCESS

For those that scoff at the idea that survival has to be the foundation of jiu-jitsu, look no further than your older students. Gone are the days of superior athleticism and endless endurance, so the emphasis has to be on defense. In this regard, as my students get older I don't tell them that they will be beating younger students, but I state that younger students only using technique are going to have an incredibly difficult time finding space to attack. This is because I teach all my students to seal up their holes. Beating your opponent is about finding where he is exposed. When the younger student faces one of my aging students and finds that there are no holes, he has to get rough to open them. This is a great proof of the technique of the older student and shows why everyone should always strive to seal off holes in

Case Study 1.0:
Helio Gracie - The Ninety-Year Old Warrior

Photo: Saulo's Personal Archive

The last time I trained with Helio Gracie was a truly memorable experience and is to this day the most important class I ever had on jiu-jitsu. What struck me most was how Helio addressed me. He did not hold me in awe for my titles or championships, and what he said more than surprised me. He said, "Son, you're strong, you're tough, you're a world champion, but I don't think you can beat me." At the time, I just looked at him sideways in disbelief. After all, how could a ninety-year-old beat someone who is in his athletic prime? It was at this moment that I realized how he deftly put all the responsibility on me to defeat him. This is the key to Helio; he never says he will beat you, only that you will not beat him.

This is important because he believes he will survive. His survival has nothing to do with perfect timing or strength. Instead, it has everything to do with mastering the defensive aspects of jiu-jitsu. He didn't say he would escape from my position, or that he would do anything else. He said he would survive.

The result of our training only validated that fact. Helio did survive, and I was not able to impose my game on him. Helio proved to me the importance of survivability and the defensive nature of jiu-jitsu. Furthermore, I took from him one of the greatest lessons ever: It is not enough to be able to defeat all of your challengers. To be able to tell any man that he cannot defeat you is to wield true power.

their defense. If you seal off all of them, you can defend against more athletic as well as stronger opponents, and age is no longer a determining factor.

1-7 CLOSING THOUGHTS ON SURVIVAL

Survival is a process that will continue to develop over a lifetime in jiu-jitsu and this is why it is not only the theme of the white belt, but also the theme of jiu-jitsu as a whole. Show me a world champion and time will show you someone who is put here to make him survive.

Judoka Sensei Izumi
practices an Uchimata.

1-0 THE BACK SURVIVAL POSITION

As with any other posture, the goal when defending your back is not only to prevent the opponent from getting you in a position of submission, but also to prevent him from putting you in a more inferior position. Due to the superior leverage and control your opponent has when attacking your back, it is imperative to focus on a preventative posture instead of trying to defend against a submission. The Back Survival Posture is the starting point for all back defense, and it always should be used as a position to return to if something goes wrong in your back survival game plan.

1-1 HAND FIGHTING

Once you achieve the Back Survival Posture, it is important to relax your hands. Not only does this allow you to block the close entry to the choke, but it also allows you to block your opponent's other attacks. In order to maintain his position, your opponent can only attack with one arm at a time. As long as you keep your hands relaxed, you can fend off chokes and arm locks by hand fighting.

With any hand fighting, it is essential that your hands stay close to your body, only meeting your opponent's attack and not chasing it. Chasing his attacks moves your elbows away from your body, opening them up to arm attacks and control.

To establish the Back Survival Posture, I cover the inside collar of my gi with one hand and cross my free hand over it to protect the other side from attack (1).

If he attacks with his right arm, my inside arm will rise slightly to block it. It is important not to reach toward your opponents arm, but instead to simply meet it (2).

Likewise, if he attacks with his left arm, my outside hand will block it without reaching (1).

Once he is done attacking, I always return to my starting Back Survival Posture (2).

1-2 THE SCOOP

Coming up through the jiu-jitsu belts, I always was taught the traditional back defense with bridging escapes and choke defenses. While these moves worked against many of my partners, as the game evolved, I would see guys who had learned to control against them. To progress with these changes, I developed the Scoop. Personally, I think this is the best posture for escaping the Back Control. By shifting your weight down, you eliminate the angle that your opponent needs to attack, and you put him in a situation where he feels he is losing his dominance. What I like even more is that you can do all of this without moving your protective arm, leaving zero openings for your opponent.

Choke Detail

Once my body is in the Scoop position, I have eliminated all of Xande's angles of attack. My hidden elbows prevent Xande from effectively controlling my lower body or attacking my arms. This leaves him feeling disconnected and without control. With crossed arms, I continue to defend against any possible choke or neck control. My extremely lowered base also eliminates the possibility of effective neck attacks. If Xande were to grab my collar, all I would have to do is look upward to negate the angle of the choking technique. At this point, Xande feels exposed and there is a sense that he is losing the position and is no longer in control of my back.

Having established the Back Survival Posture, I decide to get an even better defensive posture by going for the Scoop.

Once my elbows are hidden to prevent control and attacks, I begin sinking my weight downward while opening my base.

Immediately afterward, I slide away from Xande and continue to pull my body toward the mat and away from his upper body. To cement my positioning, I keep my legs bent and away from my body. This prevents him from rocking me to either side and regaining control.

1-3 COMMON MISCONCEPTIONS

Grabbing the Hook:

Some will try to push or pull a hook off them when they have their back taken. Immediately afterward, they try to turn around quickly and face their opponent to escape the Back. Although this strategy may work on less experienced opponents, against a veteran jiu-jitsu practitioner, you are more likely to get choked as your hand leaves your neck and is drawn toward your opponent's hook.

Bridging Posture:

A common escape from the Back is to bridge backward and scoot your hips to the side. However, this can often prove to be quite difficult. The bridging action allows an advanced player to better control you as your upper back meets his upper chest. If your opponent has both underhooks this is even more difficult as bridging does nothing to minimize his control.

Arm Pull Escape:

As in the previous posture, I have mistakenly bridged back into Xande, and I am still completely under the control of his over and under grip. Some try to use this technique to pull their opponent off them by grabbing his arm like a shoulder throw. Although this strategy can sometimes pull your opponent off the Back, it is strength dependant. A wise opponent will simply seize the moment and control with his grip or transition to a choking technique.

Side Posture:

Going to the side while your opponent has neck control can be very dangerous because it increases the leverage of the choke if you go to the wrong side. If you make it to the correct side against a strong or technical opponent, you may be pulled back to the wrong side anyway. In this photo, I have escaped in the wrong direction and Xande has a choke in place.

Ear Block Defense:

A very old-school defense is to block one side of your neck completely by raising your hand to the back of your neck and crossing your free hand to your shoulder (1). Although this does an adequate job of preventing certain collar chokes, it also leaves your body completely open to controls like the over-and-under grip (2) and the Ezequiel choke from the Back (3).

Rigid Neck Defense:

Although grabbing the collars in Rigid Neck Defense may seem like a good idea, actually it is quite hindering. By latching on to your own lapels, you lock yourself to your own gi and simply await the possible control or actions of your opponent.

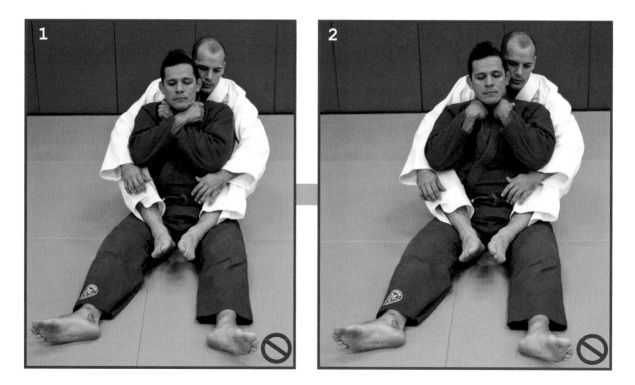

2-0 SURVIVING ALL-FOURS BACK POSITION

For many, being face down on all fours with their back taken is the worst position in which to be because of the heavy pressure and relentless attacks. In an MMA match, there is also the possibility of getting elbowed. Personally, I do not subscribe to this view. Because I use proper leverage, I can remain comfortable as I escape this potentially dangerous position. To do this, I connect my elbows to my body and defend my neck. As before, from this posture all my opponent's options are cut off and he is forced to play from my playbook.

2-1 SOLO ALL-FOURS SURVIVAL

It is easier to understand this technique if I show it first without the hindrance of an opponent on top. In fact anyone new to the technique should first practice this posture without a partner in order to feel the strength of the position. Once you feel comfortable, move on to the following technique and practice it until you feel that you can effectively manage your opponent's attacks.

I begin by completely blocking the inside of my right lapel, as my other hand stays alert in a slightly crossed position. This hand positioning should feel familiar after practicing the Back Survival Posture.	As I bend forward, I insert both my elbows between my knees.	Finally, I touch my forehead down to the mat. Note: You must keep your face down in this position until you have committed to a reversal. Otherwise, you may compromise your base or neck protection.

2-2 ALL-FOURS SURVIVAL DRILL

When you are forced into the All-Fours Posture, you must react to your opponent's superior position and immediately transition into a proper defense. Remember our maxim, "If you think, you are late; if you are late, you use muscle; if you use muscle, you get tired; and if you are tired, you die." With your opponent's weight bearing on you and attacks coming from everywhere, nowhere is this maxim more important! To ensure that you escape the All-Fours every time, drill this starting position to get used to reacting faster and faster.

Xande has my back in the All-Fours Posture. If I do not react quickly, he is sure to capitalize on his positioning.

First off, I bring my right elbow inward and rest it on the inside of Xande's right leg. I use my left arm as a brace to provide working space for the entry of my right elbow.

With my right elbow inserted, I slide my left elbow along the mat until it reaches the inside of Xande's left leg.

At this point, I open my hands and maneuver them to block the collar. Then, I rest the top of my forehead on the mat. With the position established, Xande's weight comes forward as he is forced to compensate for my defensive shell.

2-3 ALL-FOURS DETAIL

Once you are in the All-Fours Survival Posture, your opponent will feel detached and you will have better leverage. Your posture will be stronger and you can better bear the weight of your opponent. In addition, his attacks can easily be nullified as illustrated below.

I establish my All-Fours Survival Posture and my positioning leaves Xande without control of the situation. As a counter, he will attempt to control my body or force a submission.

As Xande tries to underhook my arms, he cannot find the space. To do so, Xande needs to get under my armpits, but I have created a block by locking my elbows to my inner thighs. If Xande tries to grab over my elbows, he cannot find the space because my weight is collapsing over my forearms.

When Xande tries to choke me, he is impeded by a lack of space and my blocking hands. I have completely eliminated the angle to attack. If he continues with the fruitless attack, he will risk reversal as his posture is compromised.

2-4 ROLLING TO BACK SURVIVAL

While you can definitely attain a degree of comfort in the All-Fours Survival Posture, it is not a position in which I would choose to spend my entire time. However, some make the mistake of trying to escape the Back from this position instead of taking their time and transitioning to a stronger escape platform. Just as jiu-jitsu always seeks the path of least resistance, I seek a stronger position of defense in the Back Survival Posture. Once here, I can transition into the Scoop, which is an even better survival posture.

I have attained the All-Fours Survival Posture and defended against Xande's attacks. Now it is time to transition to a better survival posture from which I can mount some escapes.

I raise my left leg, posting it away from my body, and at the same time bring my right shoulder to the mat. I shift my hand position from the right side to the left. Xande's weight shifts toward my right side as he tries to keep the Back position.

Driving off my posted left leg, I push my weight onto Xande's right leg.

Keeping my elbows tight, I pull my body to the left in a swing-like motion. Note: You may be tempted to drive back into your opponent, but this puts you into their game instead of preparing your own posture.

I establish my base and attain the Back Survival Posture.

2-5 COMMON MISCONCEPTIONS

Based Out Too Far:

You may instinctively want to push up off the mat when your opponent is pressuring you on your back. This is an error as it leads to control and possible submissions for your opponent. In the situation below, I have opened myself for double underhook control by Xande and now he is completely dominating my back.

By basing my arms out too far, I allow Xande the option of attacking my neck for a choking technique or over-and-under arm control.

Grabbing the Arm:

Another flawed instinct is to try to pull your opponent over your head in a shoulder-throw attempt. As I bring my arm out to attack Xande, I have ignored the principle of keeping my elbows tight to my body and have given myself to him. At this point, Xande will simply drop his weight downward or roll over his shoulder (as seen below) and go for the choke that is opened up by my shoulder-throw attempt.

Grabbing the Hook:

As stated earlier in the text, if your hands leave your neck defense, the choke is free for the taking. Get used to using the Scoop (1-2). This way, you will use your body to eliminate hooked legs and overcome the instinct to remove the hook with your hand.

When I grab Xande's hook, I open up my neck to his attacks.

Getting Flattened:

Once again, I am in bad posture with my elbows far from my thighs and my head high off the mat. Although I may feel like I have space to work, all I have done is provide Xande the room to flatten me out.

Xande begins flattening me out by slightly opening up his knees and driving his hips forward and downward toward the mat. At this point, I feel the weight of 20 men on my back and I cannot resist this pressure.

Xande continues the pressure until I am completely flattened. His weight feels constant on my lower back and I do not have the strength or leverage to lift him back to the starting position. Now I am in a very difficult position to escape and I likely will be submitted.

All-Fours

3-0 SURVIVING THE MOUNT

The Mount is a marquee position in jiu-jitsu. It is the most dominant and a real proof of technique for the person who has attained it. So when someone takes the Mount, one can assume that person has overcome all defenses and quite possibly is more knowledgeable or skilled in jiu-jitsu. However, that does not mean that the person being mounted cannot survive this position or make his opponent struggle for even the smallest advances.

The Mount Survival Posture is key to Mount survival, and it incorporates the following elements: defensive bumping, side posture, blocking the hips, and flattening the bottom leg. As you get better at using these elements you will see and feel that it leads to predictable outcomes and discomfort for the opponent on top, both of which are key elements to any survival game plan.

3-1 SOLO MOUNT SURVIVAL DRILL

Staying flat while mounted is a huge mistake that must be fixed immediately. The ability to get to your side is crucial when fighting from the bottom of the Mount and the quicker you get to this the better. To do so, I often encourage my students to work on this simple drill to stimulate their muscle memory. Work this and other survival posture drills into your stretching routines and your bottom survival game will improve exponentially.

With my back flat on the mat, I prepare my hands in a defensive position and bend my knees for the coming movement. If I were to be mounted in this position, I would be in trouble because my opponent has the option of attacking either side of my body.

Using my right leg, I slightly push off the mat to elevate my hips and lighten my left leg. I shrimp my hips slightly to the right so my body now faces slightly to the left.

It is important not only to shrimp backward, but to completely collapse my left side to the mat. Once I have established the Mount Defense Posture, I must keep my hands in defensive readiness while I cocoon my body to further cement my base.

3-2 EARLY POSTURE

You should immediately move into Mount Defense Posture when your opponent first takes the Mount. There is a very limited window of opportunity in which you can safely transition into the defensive posture before you feel the pressure of your opponent locking himself into his superior position. As your opponent drives forward into the Mount, he will find himself in an awkward position instead of a dominant one. This is the essence of flowing into the Mount Survival.

When you are drilling these techniques, try to have your opponent step into the Mount from Half Guard, passing the guard, Side Control, and Knee-on-Belly. Work with your partner slowly at first and gradually speed it up to develop your timing and achieve the posture quickly. The faster you can develop your timing, the less weight you will have to bear.

I have successfully achieved my Mount Defense Posture. I am completely on my left side and my forearms are bracing against Xande's right hip. This prevents him from progressing to a higher mount.

From this angle it is easy to see how I have guided Xande to grab my exposed right collar. He is unable to feel comfortable as my posture keeps his hips high off the mat.

Figure 3.2: Defense Detail

Bracing Detail:

This is the proper arm positioning when defending the Mount. I keep my right hand pressing into my opponent's right hip with my forearm serving as a block. My left hand reinforces my right as I stack my hands to increase leverage. I make sure that my left elbow is tucked tight to my body and in front of my opponent's knee to prevent him from pulling himself higher or attacking my arm.

Leg Detail:

In this position, you should always have your bottom leg flat to the mat. This will further disrupt your opponent's base and assist you when the time comes to make your escape. In this example, Xande already feels very uncomfortable because I have my hip elevated and my leg flat which threatens the guard recovery. This will work in my favor as now he is more likely to commit an error as I guide him toward a choke or mount transition.

3-3 NULLIFYING THE CHOKE

Whether you are late in your mount defense or early, chances are your partner will likely grab your collar to attempt a choke or to gain some control. This is because your Mount Survival position has left him with no other options. Positioning yourself on your side with your arms protected, your opponent invariably will make a grab for your exposed collar and try a choke. You can allow this. One hand in the collar is okay, just as long as you do not allow for two or the further progression of your partner's technique. To beat the choke you must follow the Choking Rule, which is simply turning to face your opponent's attacking elbow. If you do this correctly, you will open up the choke and immediately alleviate any pressure. Turning against your opponent's attacking elbow will lead to a rapid, sure-fire choke.

I am flat with Xande in the Mount position. He has his right hand in my right collar and I will be choked or arm-locked if I do not make the proper reaction quickly.

To defend against the collar choke, I have to get to my Mount Defense Posture just as I have shown in the Solo Drill. To do this, I let Xande determine which side I will move to. In this case, his right hand is on top, so following the Choking Rule, I move to face his attacking elbow.

I have completely eliminated the threat of Xande's choke by creating the proper angle. Xande needs me to be flat on my back for the choke, but my bottom collar is too hidden for him to force the position. In addition, my Mount Defense Posture has left him feeling unstable and now he is exposed for my escape.

3-4 ERROR IN CHOKE SURVIVAL

Xande's right hand is attacking with a cross-collar grip and I feel his weight pressing into me because I am still flat on my back. Panicking, I now roll away from his attacking elbow in an attempt to escape the pressure.

I am now aware of my fatal error as I begin to choke myself, but it is too late. Xande finishes the choke by blocking my return path with the cross-collar choke.

3-5 SEATED MOUNT SURVIVAL

One of my favorite things about the Mount Survival is that it leads my opponents to attack my top collar and from there I can initiate a quick and easy escape. However, some experienced practitioners immediately sense danger from my bottom leg and preemptively react to make sure I cannot elbow escape. The result is that they transition to a Seated Mount.

The Seated Mount is a great platform for attacks such as armbars, back chokes, and even taking the Back itself. However, it is possible to survive against the position by utilizing the Seated Mount Survival. The main goal is to prevent submissions and less favorable positions, as well as to provide a platform from which to launch the escape plan.

Xande has mounted me, but I was able to quickly get to the Mount Survival Posture. Xande is feeling uncomfortable and he does not want to lose his advantageous mount. He decides to transition to the Seated Mount.

As Xande begins transitioning to the Seated Mount, I keep my side posture and continue to block his right hip with my elbow and forearm.

Xande has achieved the Seated Mount, but my block is still in place. Now I am blocking him from his right hip to his knee.

Finally, I bring my bottom hand toward my head to protect against any possible collar or neck chokes while my top elbow blocks Xande from attempting an armlock.

3-6 COMMON MISCONCEPTIONS

Straight Arm Push:

For the newer jiu-jitsu player, the Mount is a scary place. I can remember the claustrophobia and fear I had the first few times I was under a heavy mount. To combat this suffocating feeling, you will instinctively push your opponent, thinking that this will alleviate the pressure. But instead of making your life easier, it actually makes it more difficult in four ways. First of all, outstretched arms provide an easy target for armbars. Secondly, with both hands extended, there are no barriers to stop your opponent from transitioning to a tighter high mount. Following this, you are now bearing the weight of your opponent with your arms and you have actually grounded yourself in this position. Finally, your flat posture allows your opponent to choose which side to attack with impunity. This is usually the first instinct that needs to be eliminated for survival.

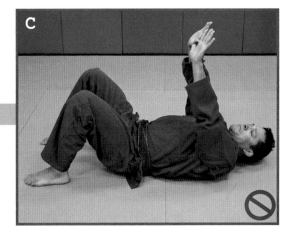

Double Underhook Hug:

Hugging may also seem like a good idea when mounted, but this could not be further from the truth. Although you may feel that your neck is hidden from choke attempts, both your arms are exposed to armlocks and once again your opponent can take a very controlling high mount. In addition, your opponent can apply more pressure on your solar plexus by driving his hips into your diaphragm (B). Obviously, in addition to being dangerous, this is an exhausting position and should be avoided.

THE MOUNT   33

Pushing the Knees:

In an attempt at an elbow escape, a misinformed jiu-jitsu player will attempt to free himself from the Mount by pushing on his opponent's knees. Using both hands to push off like this is both easy to defend and to capitalize against with a submission. To stop me from pushing, my partner has to pull my grips upward off his knees, grab the back of my neck as a counter pressure (B), or attack my completely exposed neck. Remember, if both your hands are away from your neck and your angle of posture cannot block the choke entry, you will be going to sleep soon.

Double-Arm Overwrap:

Whenever I see a student doing this in class, I know he is either trying to stall or to get an unlikely bump escape. Personally, I never endorse these tactics – by latching onto your own lapels in this manner, you essentially lock yourself to your own kimono and await the possible control or actions of your opponent.

4-0 SIDE CONTROL SURVIVAL

The Side Control is a great platform for attacks and positional transitions. Though you do not bear the same amount of pressure as in the Mount, it is equally dangerous when used by a strong, offensive-minded player. To defend this position well, you have to learn the specific defensive hand and body positioning that is the same for all the variations of Side Control as well as the specific goals for the top player. Once you understand what the person on top needs to control you, or to progress his game, you will be better suited to adapt your basic defensive game plan.

When practicing, it is very important to drill each type of Side Control with its specific defense before jumping in and using them all. For instance, your drilling partner should be limited to just one Side Control grip on top while you get comfortable with the defense. Once you get better or more aware, he can then begin to add the variations. This is important because the Side Control variations change the game, and you should not make the learning process more difficult by confusing the defenses before you have learned the basics.

4-1 BLOCKING THE CROSS-FACE

The Cross-Face is definitely a strong position that takes very little experience to use effectively. Because the position has the potential to completely block one side of escapes, every student needs to learn how to overcome it in order to progress in the survival game. From school to school, people learn many different effective escapes from the Side Control. However, if you cannot prevent the Cross-Face, you will be at the mercy of high-level practitioners.

Keeping my outside arm hidden and tight to my body, my inside hand blocks Xande's left hand from trapping my head in the Cross-Face control. Note: My blocking hand operates as a complete hook that envelops his bicep and upper arm completely.

If I do not block Xande's front hand, I will get cross-faced. From here, Xande will drive my neck to the outside and gain control of the direction of the fight. Turning against my neck direction will be incredibly difficult against a tough opponent.

Side Control

4-2 RELEASING THE HAND

As your partner feels your Cross-Face defense, he often will transition to a different Side Control, like the over-the-shoulder grip with the hip-block. Instinctively you may want to follow his arm, but that is the wrong strategy. Doing so will lead to getting your arm crossed over your own face or to a potential armbar. Instead, learn when to release the arm and go for the much safer hip block. More escapes will present themselves this way, and more importantly, you will impede the progress of the submission artist on top of you.

Xande has me in Side Control, but is unable to secure the position due to my Cross-Face block. Frustrated, Xande must change his grips to maintain his position.

I control Xande's bicep until his arm passes above my forehead. Once his hand has passed my forehead, I stop following his arm and place my right hand on his hip in a cupped position (2B).

My left hand maintains its original position throughout, and my right hand stays cupped on Xande's hip acting as an L brace to keep his weight off my body. If he decides to go back to the Cross-Face I will simply return my hand to his bicep as his arm re-crosses my forehead.

4-3 KESA GATAME HAND FIGHTING

Kesa Gatame or the Scarf Hold is a very dangerous position for any grappler, especially when facing a strong wrestler or judoka. Because there is so much pressure coming down on you and your arm is trapped, it is often a nightmare to escape – even for seasoned jiu-jitsu players. Therefore, you have to look at what makes the position so dangerous – the inside arm domination. By dominating the inside arm, the practitioner on top can get better inside weight distribution as well as block all escapes to the inside. To combat this, I have developed my own hand-fighting tricks to frustrate and eventually hide the inside arm from domination. Just as you practice hand fighting on your feet, you always have to be aware of these strategies when you are on the ground as well.

Once again, Xande is frustrated by my Cross-Face prevention and decides to transition into a different form of Side Control.

As Xande transitions into Kesa Gatame, I use his momentum to drive my right elbow to his right hip. My hand stays open as a block against possible chokes or control attempts and my outside arm remains tucked against my body.

Xande decides to go for a modified Kesa Gatame control. As he tries to underhook my outside arm and pull up on my inside arm, I make the mistake of pushing against his left bicep. By opening my right elbow, I allow him to dominate my entire right side.

4-4 REVERSE KESA GATAME

Another transition for the offense-minded top player is to switch his Side Control base to Reverse Kesa Gatame. Instead of facing your head, your opponent is now facing your legs and you cannot see everything he has planned. Once again, the goal is to survive and to do that you have to understand what your partner needs – your inside elbow separated from the protection of your torso. If your partner achieves this, he has your body trapped and can progress the game in his favor. Knowing this, I have implemented the following strategy to block my opponent with my elbows, even if I cannot see everything that he is doing!

I have established a Cross-Face block, and Xande is frustrated.

Xande crosses his left hand over to my left side to initiate the Reverse Kesa Gatame. As Xande swings his hand over, I remove the Cross-Face block, and I dig my right elbow into his side.

Now Xande tries to control my leg and switch his legs while I block his hips with my right forearm.

As Xande switches his hips, I face him slightly. Then I bring my right elbow to the ground to block him from isolating my right arm away from my body. Without this isolation, Xande cannot effectively mount me without fear of escape. My left hand is still tight to my body and underneath Xande to prevent against a possible armlock attack.

4-5 COMMON MISCONCEPTIONS

Cross-Face As Waiting Position:

Just as many stay flat when they are mounted, many allow their partners to cross-face them with an under-the-armpit control. From here, your partner has complete control over you, and as he turns your neck he eliminates one direction of escape. This is very dangerous. If your opponent is strong in this position, he can invoke many submissions as well as transition into more dominant positions. I never let anyone cross-face me.

Inside-Over-the-Shoulder Grip:

Sometimes when your opponent grabs over your shoulder, you may feel you have an opportunity to grab him and roll him forward. However, when you are facing a seasoned opponent, the result is a swift armlock. Even if you are very strong, your opponent only has to sink his weight back a little and post his free hand as he uses his near arm to secure your exposed grip (2). I find these moves to be desperate. As an attacker, I know I have my opponent where I want him when he defends with these tactics.

Outside-Over-the-Shoulder Grip:

Similar to the inside-over-the-shoulder grip, the outside grip is just as dangerous. By focusing on grabbing his opponent's shoulder, the bottom player has missed out on the only real leverage point in this poor position: the head. Again, many try to use this move to bulldoze a reversal and most are unsuccessful. To defend, all my opponent has to do is keep his base low and at worst, open his outside arm to defend against the strong rollover attempt. Once he is done defending, beware – your arm is free for the taking.

Failed Rollover:

Here I use the outside-over-the-shoulder grip to reverse Xande. I start by using a strong bridging motion, using my left leg to push onto my right shoulder, to set up the reversal. I am hoping to get Xande to react to my bridge by pressuring into me.

Immediately, I turn to my left side, hoping to pull Xande over me. Unfortunately, this is easy to anticipate and Xande drops his weight back and pulls up on my outside arm to counter balance.

Outside Hands Clasp:

From the failed outside-over-the-shoulder grip, many will try to stall the match out by bringing their free inside hand up under the armpit to clasp it with their outside hand in a hug across the back. While this may leave you with a momentary feeling that you have escaped an armlock on your outside arm, you really have opened up your entire right side to attack by your opponent. More than likely, he will cross-face you and dominate your inside arm. Once you are here, you are open to a myriad of same-side armlocks, chokes, and position changes.

Worried about my left hand, I desperately grab Xande across his back with my right hand. My hope is to stall out the match.

Instead of waiting with me, Xande puts me in a tight cross-face and dominates my right arm by driving his left knee toward my head. Now I am in a very bad position. Even if I let my hands unclasp, my arm will be stuck and Xande can start attacking me from this control.

Outside Underhook:

The outside underhook is a more advanced misconception that also needs to be discussed. If you break this move down it makes sense. The idea is to underhook your opponent's far arm with the intention of sliding out from under his body. However, when you start this position without blocking the Cross-Face, it is very difficult. As I go for the position, my opponent keeps his hips ready and transitions into a possible arm attack.

I establish an underhook in an attempt to push Xande away from me and escape.

Reading my intentions, Xande rolls his base toward my head and transitions into an over-the-shoulder grip. From here, my arm is exposed for a possible Kimura lock or armbar.

Side Control

Outside Underhook to Choke:

As a continuation of the previous posture, it is important to realize that your opponent has a lot of options. Because my inside arm is on his hip instead of blocking the Cross-Face, I have given my opponent the perfect opportunity to choke me as my outside arm goes for the underhook. I will get choked if I do not protect my neck.

With Xande in good positioning, I decide to go for an underhook to create room for an escape. I have forgotten to block the Cross-Face, but I choose to go for the escape anyway.

Instead of adjusting toward my head for an armlock, Xande slightly rolls to his right to pressure my underhook. Feeling that both my arms are away from my neck, Xande brings his arm across my neck for the choke.

Now it is too late for me. Xande drops his elbow and finishes the choke while my defending arm is useless under his pressure.

5-0 KNEE-ON-BELLY SURVIVAL

The Knee-on-Belly position is an old-school, pain position. I really enjoy this position because you can make your opponent feel you and he often will give up the submission just to have you take your knee off his midsection. I remember these feelings from when I was learning to survive the Knee-on-Belly position, and I devised my defense in a way that both prevents submissions and relieves the pressure of the weight.

You must remember that your opponent has base, weight, and gravity on his side, while you have movement and your tight defense. As in defending against the Mount, it is crucial that you disrupt your opponent's ability to bring his weight to bear on you in this position, and once again you need to learn body movement and positioning to do this.

5-1 SOLO KNEE-ON-BELLY PREVENTION

As with the other solo postures, use this as a guideline for how high to stretch your leg. For those who tire easily, consider doing leg lifts and forward stretches with a partner to gain the endurance and basic flexibility to use this position effectively at the highest level.

Prevention Mind-Set–In Focus

On a regular basis my students ask me, "Saulo, how do you have the confidence to survive in these positions against great grapplers and why do people get better and better positions on me?" My answer is simple. I have the confidence and correct mind-set because I have prepared for this position and tested it against the best in the world. For the average student, it may seem difficult to gain this confidence, especially when your opponents are blowing through your Side Control defense into the Knee-on-Belly, but it is more than possible when you have developed the correct mind-set.

It is important to realize that all of the defenses in my Solo Knee-on-Belly Prevention posture, as well as all my survival postures, are dynamic. By dynamic I mean that these positions should not be used with rigidity and strength, but with an adaptive mind-set. Once you decide to use your jiu-jitsu on the bottom without resorting to strength, you will find that you gain confidence as your partner has to use more and more strength to surpass you. To help with your mental development try this drill: every time you feel your opponent having to muscle through your defense, take this as a mental victory that your jiu-jitsu holes are getting smaller. Soon enough, as your confidence catches up to your awareness of body positioning and technique, your classmates will be unable to pass easily from Side Control to the Knee-on-Belly.

5-2 STRAIGHT-LEGGED PREVENTION

Often enough, the best way to deal with the Knee-on-Belly is to prevent it from ever happening. This is why I use the Straight-Legged Prevention while I am under the Side Control position. Different from the traditional posture of crossing the leg, I can gain a much greater sensitivity to my opponent by lifting my leg up against his body. I can feel his movements and changes better as my leg acts like a gauge of his intentions. Also, as a tool, I can use this perfectly with my Cross-Face defense to close off the gap, even if my opponent tries to force the position. As you will see, the more my opponent tries to get the position, the deeper my defense penetrates.

Xande has me in Side Control, but I was able to get to my Side Control Survival posture and block his Cross-Face attempt.

Sensing that Xande wants to transition to the Knee-on-Belly, I kick my right leg straight up and drive my right knee into his hip.

If Xande decides to commit to the Knee-on-Belly transition, he will feel my knee blocking him as it sneaks in between his hip and thigh. As Xande tries harder for the position, he will actually assist me in my prevention.

5-3 IMPORTANCE OF PREVENTION

If you fail to achieve your Side Control Survival Posture and/or to utilize the Straight-Legged Prevention, it is a sure bet that your opponent will transition to the Knee-on-Belly. Simply trying to cross your inside leg over your outside (like I am attempting to do in 2 below) is not enough. Without controlling the Cross-Face with your inside elbow driving inward and the Straight-Legged defense presenting constant pressure, your opponent will have plenty of space to progress to the Knee-on-Belly.

5-4 RUNNING SURVIVAL POSTURE

The Running Survival Posture is one of my favorite postures because it uses such great leverage and represents the evolution of the Knee-on-Belly Survival and escape. Instead of fighting into my opponent and turning inward to escape, as taught traditionally, I roll away from him, tricking him into thinking he can take my back. When he takes the bait, he discovers he cannot take my back or get the submission, and frustration ensues.

This move shows the evolution of jiu-jitsu because it utilizes two principles very well: adaptation and technique over strength. Many people know the traditional defenses to Knee-on-Belly, and they are prepared for them. Therefore, I had to discover a way to adapt to this. By using the Running Survival Posture and going away from your opponent, you also go against popular jiu-jitsu dogma that says you should never show your opponent your back. However, by doing so, you eliminate the fight of turning inward and struggling against better positioning. You will find that it is much easier to turn away from your opponent using this posture, and as long as you follow my guidelines below and protect yourself, you will have plenty of escape opportunities.

In this position, I am late and Xande has already attained the Knee-on-Belly. I keep my outside arm tucked inside as usual and my right hand high with the elbow hidden to prevent against submissions.

Even with my protection, Xande's position is too strong. I need to alter it to better manage Xande's weight and to control the survival. To do so, I begin a slight bridge and roll to my left.

3

I block Xande's knee by bringing my top elbow over and then under his knee. I also make sure that my top elbow is closed so that he cannot regain control of my upper body.

4

Now on my side, I can better support Xande's weight than when he was pressing his knee into my abdomen. I continue to transition to my survival posture by lifting my top leg and bringing it over my bottom leg in a scissoring move.

5

I continue to scissor my top leg toward my head while my bottom leg remains in base.

6

I finalize my position by sealing the gap between my top quadriceps and my top forearm. This will prevent Xande from getting arm and upper body control. My top hand still protects my neck and my bottom elbow provides base and mobility by staying in a tucked position.

5-5 EXPOSED ROLL

It is extremely important to close off all your holes as you attempt to roll away from your opponent toward the Running Survival Posture. If you remember to seal your forearm to your quadriceps, protect your neck, and use your top leg to create a barrier, you'll be fine. If you forget any one of these important elements, your opponent can transition to the Back or initiate a submission.

1

I have decided to initiate the roll toward the Running Survival Posture, but already I have made the mistake of keeping my top elbow open.

2

As I get to my side, I have failed to block Xande from grabbing my collar and now he is in an over-and-under control.

3

Knowing that if I return to my back I will choke myself, I continue to roll.

4

I make one final mistake by leaving my top leg behind me. Seeing this, Xande quickly begins stepping over to block my hip and take my back.

5

Escaping this position will be very difficult. Xande has complete control of both my upper and lower body. He has the choke sunk in with my head on the perfect side to finish me.

5-6 COMMON MISCONCEPTIONS

Stiff Arms:

As with every other defense, it is never acceptable to use the stiff-arm defense while in a disadvantageous position. By doing so while under my opponent's Knee-on-Belly, I essentially lock myself to him, severely limiting my options. Also, my opponent can easily counter this push with his posture and balance. Needless to say, my arms and neck are now exposed to multiple submissions.

With Xande dominating the Knee-on-Belly position, I aggressively try to push him off with both arms.

Reacting to my strength coming at him, Xande postures back and uses the opportunity to get a controlling cross-collar grip. Note: By slightly altering his positioning, Xande has completely shut down my defensive attempt.

Open Knee Push:

The Knee-on-Belly position can produce an incredible amount of pressure and the crushing sensation is often overwhelming. As a reaction to this, some instinctively try to push off what they feel is the cause of so much of their torment – the knee. As the opponent stays in position, they push even harder, and the result is often the opening of the elbow. In doing this, the practitioner on the bottom has given the top player everything he needs to control the arm and go for a spinning armbar, straight armlock, or Kimura.

Feeling Xande's crushing pressure, I mistakenly try to push his knee off my body to get some reprieve.

I just fell for the oldest trick in the book. Xande simply reaches inward with his near hand and traps my opened arm at the triceps.

Close Push and Grab:

Sometimes, during a match, your opponent's posting leg will come close enough to your body for you to grab it. Don't. Often enough, the bottom player will reach under and grab the belt while the outside hand tries to straight-arm the top fighter backward. Although it seems like this push-and-pull action would be effective, it once again opens up your body as your elbows gain too much distance from your core. I have seen far too many triangles and armlocks as a result of people trying this position.

Here, I am trying to push Xande backward toward his dead angle (See Escapes, Figure 7.2).

Meanwhile, I am pulling him downward with my inside arm. However, this leaves me open and exposed for the submission.

The Blue Belt's Secret Weapon: ESCAPES

"First learn to become invincible, then wait for your enemy's moment of vulnerability."

—Sun Tzu

2-1 WHAT DOES IT MEAN TO ESCAPE?

When I talk about escapes, I am referring to the ability to transition out of an inferior position or an attack. In jiu-jitsu, there are four basic positions of survival: the Mount, Back, Side Control, and Knee on Belly. These are also the positions you must be capable of escaping because if you remain in them, they lead to bigger problems.

Though the ability to escape positions is vital in jiu-jitsu, the time will come when you need to escape relentless submission attacks as well. This is why I also instruct submission escapes with an emphasis on the mechanics of the technique. This way, you can adapt one escape to many. You do not need to know how to escape a hundred different armbar variations, but you must understand how escaping the armbar works.

Escapes and survival are the foundations to an attacking jiu-jitsu game. If you know your opponent cannot keep you in an inferior position or finish the fight, you will be more confident attacking him. This works not only as a confidence builder for you because you attack repeatedly without regard for your opponent's defense, but also as a demoralizer for your opponent because he must face someone he cannot hold who attacks him continuously.

2-2 SURVIVAL LEADS TO THE ESCAPE

The escape always stems from your ability to survive. You must first survive the bad position or basic submission before you can escape from it. To escape, you must use your opponent's strength against him. Everything your opponent will do to attack you is based on how you take him out of his comfort zone. This is the basic premise of survival, which is the stepping-stone to escaping. Here, you will develop timing and a game plan to escape.

2-3 TIMING AND ESCAPING

Escapes are based on timing. One of the goals of surviving is to put your opponent into an awkward posture. From here, he will become predictable, heightening the chances that you will escape as he responds exactly the way you want. Do not wait for the timing. Make it.

With every technique, there is also a correct moment to execute the move perfectly so it will require very little of your strength. This is the moment of perfect timing. For instance, if you have a proper Mount Survival Posture, your opponent only has so many options. When he responds by trying to muscle the wrong choke, you are ready to off-balance him and reverse the position. However, if you have not drilled the technique, you will be late in your attempt. Tardiness leads to the overuse of strength. Never rely only on strength.

2-4 TIMELINES OF ESCAPES

The longer you survive, the more time you have to plan your escape strategy. If you have to escape right away, it is less likely that you will do so efficiently. That's why tournaments are not a good measure of how good someone has become. Instead of being slow, using more feeling and thought, competitors are rough and react with more strength. Escaping is all about patience. So do not worry about whether you can escape hard or fast; just make sure you can escape once. Once is all you need to turn the tide of any match.

2-5 OVERCOMING THE STALLER

Over and over, I hear students complaining that they cannot escape when someone is holding them in a stalling position. Here's what I tell them, "If you keep yourself in a horrible relationship, are you the victim or partially at fault?" Likewise, it is your fault if your opponent is able to hold you because you should have the weapons to set yourself free.

Don't make excuses that you are too weak or too small either. Remember, jiu-jitsu was developed by a 130-pound man, not a giant. If it were a matter of strength alone, he never would have been able to escape. So, if you let yourself be held, it is your fault; this is something that you have to deal with and learn from. If someone dedicates himself to holding you, you must not lock yourself to him. Of course, people who stall out the game are frustrating to face, and sometimes what is frustrating can become dangerous. This is why you must step back and realize the kind of person with whom you are dealing. You have to

Helpful Escape Tips

- Always begin an escape by first securing the survival posture. This will ensure time and positioning to set up your escape.

- Add limits to your drills when training escapes. An upper belt should not focus on blocking a lower belt's escape when drilling, but rather focus on submissions or transitions.

- Never rely only on strength to escape a position. Learn the technique and commit it to your body memory in order to develop perfect timing and movement.

Photo: Catarina Monnier

Gabriela Bermudez opens up the game for her partner while providing herself with escape practice.

be open-minded with a strong mental preparation to prevent yourself from becoming emotional.

To deal with a staller, recognize what he is before you face him. This is one of the principles of strategy. If you don't recognize him, you may fail. Sun Tzu's *The Art of War* teaches that you must know who you face and be aware at all times. Once you can do this, you will avoid situations where your opponent can inhibit your movement.

2-6 ESCAPES AND THE BELTS

Personally, I think the white and blue belt stages of development are the perfect time to learn how to escape. Students in these stages are still too inexperienced for complicated attack sequences, combinations, and perfect weight distribution, but they do find themselves in poor positions quite often. This is why it is so important for white and blue belts to drill at this level.

High-ranking purple, brown, or black belts, prove my theory when they come to my academy and I take the Mount and tell them to escape. Most thrash around and struggle until exhausted. Then, I always hear the same thing, "I don't remember the last time someone mounted me!" I reply, "I know, because no one ever pushed you to that level of defense, so you never had a chance to absorb it." Higher belts always should have strong defense, which is why I start my students training their escapes early.

2-7 TRAINING ESCAPES

Often enough, a student becomes frustrated when he cannot escape a particular position or submission. This is where drilling escapes is useful. If you are surprised with a submission, be sure to reproduce the attack in which you were caught several times so that your body instantly recognizes when it happens again. Your body has to feel it, and feeling comes from repetition.

Keep in mind that jiu-jitsu takes time; it is a long path. As I already stated, the white and blue belts need to drill often, but they also must drill effectively. Getting comfortable with body movements will take a lot of practice and a great way to do so is to place limitations on what you can do to control a certain reaction.

I cannot have a top student take the Mount and expect a white or blue belt to escape. This is because the school's blue, purple, and brown belts all know the same techniques. With everyone sharing the same knowledge, the upper belts can stifle the progression of new white and blue belts!

You may ask, "How can a brown belt take advantage of training with a white belt?" The brown belt benefits by fine-tuning his timing and sharpening his submissions.

How can a white belt progress? By feeling how a good student can put him in danger and then working the escape. That's the only way for him to train escapes as a white belt.

Just be careful to remember that when practicing escapes, the top person cannot frustrate his opponent by holding him. The top person should always attack so that both students can progress.

6-0 ESCAPING THE BACK

Once the Back Survival position is achieved, it is paramount to impose your game and escape the position. Though the Survival Posture will buy some time and eliminate much of the threat of submission, it is still a dangerous position to remain in. Therefore, I developed the following move to escape the back. It is a movement based on timing and the knowledge that my opponent only has one real goal: to maintain his position. Because the Survival Posture is so strong, I can easily predict my opponent's movements and lead him directly toward allowing me this escape.

Beginning in the Back Survival position, I keep my elbows tight to my body with my hands blocking the possible choke while my hips scoop low to the mat. At this point, Xande already feels vulnerable for the escape.

I chamber my right leg, bringing my right knee tight to Xande's right leg. At the same time, I drive my right elbow to the inside of Xande's right knee.

In one purposeful motion, I kick my right leg straight down, removing Xande's right hook. Immediately, I bring my right elbow to the ground; this will prevent Xande from regaining his hook.

4

To advance my positioning, I re-chamber my right leg and I close the gap between my right thigh and elbow. It will be next to impossible for Xande to regain control without an incredible feat of strength.

5

Keeping my defensive posture, I extend my left leg and I hip escape toward the right. In doing so, I have driven Xande to my side and he no longer has the angle to transition to my back.

6

I swiftly turn over with my right arm and leg to transition to the top position.

7

Keeping my posture low, I stabilize the top position by hugging Xande's left leg. Note how I drive my head into Xande's centerline to prevent his mobility and possible escape.

6-1 COMMON MISTAKE

Upon first glance, this escape simply looks like a fast transition from the back to the knees, but the secret is really in the hip escape and elbow blocks. Without either, your opponent is sure to regain some control over you in either an over-and-under grip or by following you up to your knees. Review these errors and note the importance of creating the proper angle to escape as well as the necessary elbow tightness to prevent control.

I kicked out Xande's right hook and I am ready to escape the back.

Although I correctly rechambered my right leg to block the hook, I have not closed my right elbow to my right thigh adequately. Xande is likely to use this space to get under my right armpit and recoup the back control.

Feeling uneasy with my defensive positioning, I explode into Xande's left leg as I try to escape to the top. Unfortunately, by doing so without a preparatory hip escape, I have committed a fatal error.

Xande easily follows me to my side and continues to hold the Back position.

6-2 BODY LOCK ESCAPE

The Body Lock is a formidable control that for some seems an impossible position to escape. Although many use this control in MMA and gi-less matches, it is becoming just as commonplace in gi tournaments. Personally, I do not attack with the Body Lock because I feel the control locks me onto my opponent's back too much. I prefer to use the mobile hooks instead. However, many people do use it, so it is important to understand how to escape this potentially devastating position. In addition, it is important to note that I do not change my escape style or movement for this different control. Instead, I make small adaptations to what I already do to ensure that I can fit this escape into my repertoire.

Xande has me in the Body Lock. To defend this, it is important that I immediately start driving forward while keeping my elbow tight to my body.

I continue pushing forward until my elbows lock over the top of Xande's lower left leg.

Next, I collapse my weight directly to my right side. I should be falling at a ninety-degree angle. I always fall toward my opponent's locked foot. I have just locked Xande's right side to the mat using my weight and now I have the time to work on my escape.

Immediately, I find the crook of Xande's right knee with my right elbow and slide my elbow toward the mat. This pressure, in conjunction with a slight hip escape to the right, pops open the Body Lock triangle.

I step my right foot over Xande's right leg, making sure to keep my hips pressing into Xande's bottom leg and hip. This locks Xande in the bottom position.

6-3 ESCAPING DOUBLE-UNDERHOOK CONTROL

The Double-Underhook Control is an upper body control that students should drill alongside their standard back escape drill. The motion is similar to that of the Body Lock escape, and it is key that all my students use functional body movements like these to escape inferior positions. The theory behind this movement is simple: kill your partner's bottom leg using your weight and he will not have the mobility to stop your escape. If you fail to do so, you have a fight on your hands.

I have chosen the wrong escape posture and Xande has taken the Double-Underhook Control.

As in the previous series, I bend forward to prevent Xande from pulling me backward.

Following this, I collapse my body directly to my right side and I drive my weight onto Xande's right leg. Note: You can choose either side based on personal preference.

Utilizing a slight hip escape to the right, I smash my hip into Xande's right knee and effortlessly open his right hook.

This large step to the right serves three purposes: it creates base, opens my hips for escape, and prevents Xande from regaining his hook.

I escape my left leg by circling my foot over Xande's left foot.

With a solid hip escape, I completely free my legs from Xande's and I force him onto his back.

I drive Xande's legs toward his left side and I take side control with hip-to-hip pressure.

6-4 ESCAPING ALL-FOURS DRILL

The drill for escaping All-Fours puts all of the previous techniques together: All-Fours Survival Posture, All-Fours Survival Roll, the Back Survival Posture, and finally, the Back Escape. Because this movement encompasses so many survival and escape positions, drill it often and with precision.

1

I'm in the All-Fours position with Xande pressuring me from above.

2

This is not a good position to be in, so I initiate the All-Fours Survival Roll.

3

As I land face up, I make sure that I am in the Back Survival Position. Once I establish this, I can begin my escape once again.

4

I kick out Xande's right hook while driving my right elbow to the mat.

Immediately, I bring my right knee up toward my body meeting my right elbow to the thigh.

With a large hip escape to the right, I change the angle so that Xande cannot follow me to the top.

In a fast and calculated move, I step over Xande's left leg with my right to transition to the top.

I cement my positioning by hugging Xande's left leg and keeping my forehead pressing into his centerline.

7-0 SOLO MOUNT ELBOW ESCAPE DRILL

The Mount is a daunting position to escape. Often when sparring or in competition, a jiu-jitsu player becomes mounted because he is exhausted, or his opponent is more experienced and advanced. In any case, he has the full pressure of his opponent on top of him, and this is not the best place to practice his escaping movements. To acquire the proper escape technique and engrain it into muscle memory with perfect mechanics, practice this without an opponent. Once accomplished, it is much easier to execute the perfect motion against a mounted opponent.

I start in the Mount Survival Position with my posture aligned on my right side. My hands are creating a frame and my left leg is flat to the mat.

In one powerful motion, I bridge onto my left shoulder. My left hip must be elevated off the mat.

Immediately, I follow up the bridge with a strong hip escape to my right. As I do this, I bring my left knee tight toward my body. Now I am in a strong escaping position.

7-1 MOUNT ELBOW ESCAPE

In most jiu-jitsu schools across the globe, the Upa, or bridge escape, is taught as the first primary escape from the Mount. However, in my school, I teach a variation of the elbow escape. I do not focus as much on the Upa because it is very hard to use in high-level competition. That is not to say that it doesn't work. What I am proposing is that the elbow escape is more efficient, especially this version of it. In the following technique, you create the timing. When you get to the Survival Posture, your opponent will more than likely attack your collar to make up for his imbalance. This is the right time to go for the escape. Remember, create your own timing!

Though Xande has me mounted with his right hand in my collar, I am able to safely attain the Mount Defense Survival Position.

I bridge off my left shoulder to elevate Xande's and my hips. This opens a gap between Xande's body and the mat.

With a large hip escape to my right, I am able to sneak my left leg inside of Xande's right.

Using my framed arms on Xande's hips, I create space to free my left knee.

Next, I use my newly freed leg as a hook to elevate Xande's right leg.

Once Xande is elevated, I have the necessary space to free my right leg. I end the escape in the Butterfly Guard.

THE MOUNT ✳ 61

7-2 SEATED MOUNT ESCAPE

As you begin to master the elbow escape, your opponent's common reaction is to transition into the Seated Mount. The Seated Mount is a wonderful position that nullifies the elbow escape to a certain degree. However, never give up on your positioning or stop believing in your jiu-jitsu. From the Seated Mount, you change the angle and continue from the elbow escape to the Seated Mount escape. Learn to chain your defensive actions and escapes together with your opponent's actions and your bottom game will feel unstoppable.

Once again, I find myself in the Mount Survival position with Xande cross gripping my right lapel.

Xande has faced me before and he knows that I have a good elbow escape; he decides to transition to the Seated Mount to keep his favorable position. Xande slides his left leg toward my head while blocking my left hip with his right foot.

I transition to the Seated Mount Survival position by blocking the choke with my left hand and pushing on Xande's hip and right knee with my right arm. My left elbow and leg provide a base for the position.

With one focused drive, I push into Xande's right knee, collapsing his base. As this occurs, I sit straight up at a ninety-degree angle.

Without delay, I fall directly to my right. If I continue forward, Xande may take my back.

Keeping my weight centered to prevent sweeps and back attacks, I square my legs and I achieve base in Xande's Closed Guard.

Figure 7.2: Dead Angle Detail

The dead angle is the key to this technique. By focusing on your opponent's weakest link to his defense – his knee – you are forcing him into what is called the dead angle. The dead angle is always the angle where the opponent is without base. Whenever you try for any sweep or reversal, try to remember the dead angle and feel where the opponent can potentially save himself with an arm or a leg. By always attacking toward the dead angle, you will find yourself achieving reversals and sweeps at a much higher frequency.

8-0 SOLO SIDE CONTROL DRILLS

The following drills are the two most important drills to master when it comes to escaping the Side Control. If you only watch the movement and try to mimic it in sparring, you will never have the muscle memory to execute the techniques with the speed and timing they require. Therefore, it is vital that you practice these solo drills often to absorb these movements into your muscle memory.

GUARD RECOVERY:

Use this drill to master the basics of guard recovery dynamics. Always begin the drill with proper Side Control Survival Posture and be sure to practice both sides equally.

I begin the drill by going to the Side Control Survival Posture. I make sure I have my inside leg elevated to "defend" against the Knee-on-Belly and Mount. My left arm is flat to my body and my right arm is acting as a cross-face block.

Utilizing my left leg, I push off the mat and bridge onto my right shoulder. This bridge is different from a normal bridge because I lengthen my body and thrust my hips into my opponent as I bridge onto my shoulder. My body is almost entirely on its side. This exaggerated, long bridge creates the space I need to move my hips.

Following my bridge, I hip escape immediately into the space I have just created.

I bring my right elbow to my knee and start to pull my head away from my imaginary partner.

I continue to pull my head back until I am perpendicular to my starting position.

TO ALL-FOURS:

The All-Fours drill is excellent for developing a quick transition time to your knees. This is an important drill that easily can be integrated into the Guard Recovery drill. Once you are familiar with this motion, try to sporadically go from Guard Recovery to All-Fours.

I go through the previous sequence until I arrive at the hip-escaped position.

I bridge off my right shoulder using my left leg as a post. At the same time, I scissor my right leg under my body. Note: the key to this transition is to tuck your right elbow close to your body. By doing so, you allow yourself the mobility to transition from your shoulder to the All-Fours. If it is not tucked, you will get stuck in this position.

I sprawl my right leg back and begin posting on my left hand as I free my right shoulder.

I walk my legs close to my body so that my knees are tucked under my torso. This is called the Elevator position and it is a great leverage point for leg takedowns.

Side Control

8-1 SIDE CONTROL TO GUARD RECOVERY

The Side Control, also known as 100 Kilos, is a gateway position in jiu-jitsu. It is referred to as a gateway because it is the launching point for so many superior positions and submissions. Therefore, you must escape the Side Control before the situation becomes dire. One of the most effective escape routes is to recover guard. Recovering guard does two things: it brings you back into a neutral position and it has the effect of demoralizing your opponent who must now pass your guard all over again.

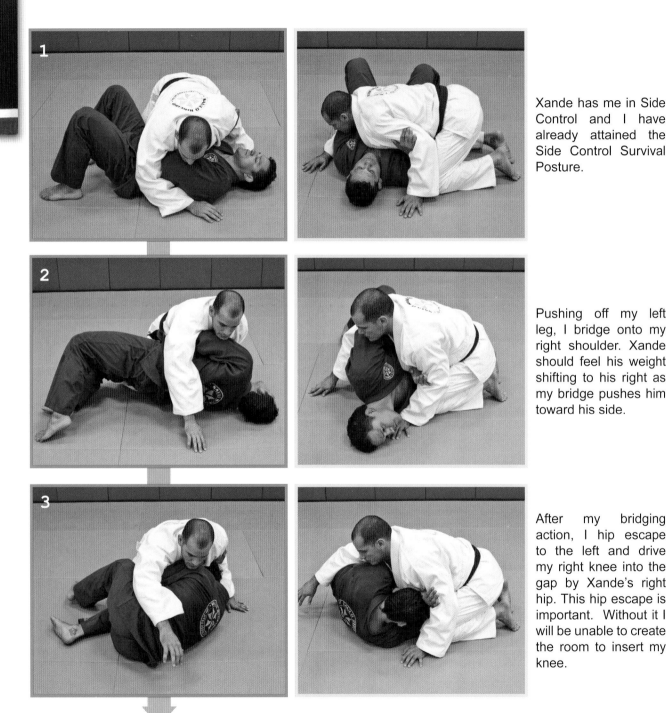

Xande has me in Side Control and I have already attained the Side Control Survival Posture.

Pushing off my left leg, I bridge onto my right shoulder. Xande should feel his weight shifting to his right as my bridge pushes him toward his side.

After my bridging action, I hip escape to the left and drive my right knee into the gap by Xande's right hip. This hip escape is important. Without it I will be unable to create the room to insert my knee.

Figure 8.1: Trapping Misconception

Some try to trap their opponent's near leg after they have finished their bridge, but in my opinion, this is a bad strategy. First, it locks you to your opponent's game and it greatly inhibits your mobility. Movement and spatial awareness are both key for bottom players, and I don't like techniques that restrict the bottom game. Secondly, by locking your opponent's leg, you have allowed your hips to be far too close to his. This greatly impedes your ability to use the defensive bridge and can also lead to a stagnated game.

As my right knee starts penetrating Xande's defense, I begin swinging my head away from him. This will properly align us both and allow me to recover the Full Guard. My arm brace will facilitate this action as it prevents Xande from controlling me during the escape.

I consolidate my position and have regained the Open Guard.

Figure 8.2: Bridging Detail

Because I do not use the trapping technique, my legs are completely free to bridge and create a better angle to recover guard. Aside from this, the bridge also lets me feel in contact with my opponent without having the undesirable effect of being locked to him. This is an important aspect when making space and finding holes, so use the bridge often and always work to create some space!

| I am recovering the guard, but I am running out of space for my knee to penetrate. | Instead of locking Xande's right leg, I opt for a secondary bridge to create more space. | Now I have the free space to continue pushing my right knee to the outside. | I recover the Open Guard. |

8-2 SIDE CONTROL ESCAPE TO THE KNEES

I do not tell my students to learn either the Guard Recovery or the Escape to the Knees position. Instead, I tell them they must know both. There will be times when a savvy opponent will not let you recover guard and you will need the ability to get to your knees. Getting to your knees also offers options like wrestling-style switches, guard recovery, and takedowns. This is a strong series of techniques, and when combined with the Guard Recovery, they offer a very well-rounded escape game.

HIP ESCAPE:

All side control escapes are predicated on your opponent's positioning, pressure, and balance. In this situation, my opponent is strongly resisting the escape to guard and is insisting on keeping his legs away from mine to prevent the recovery. This is the perfect time to go to the knees and initiate a takedown of your own. If your opponent is pulling away from one escape, he is running toward the other!

Xande has me in Side Control, but I have already bridged onto my right side.	I can feel that Xande is fighting very hard to prevent me from recovering guard, so I decide to go to my knees. I punch my head to the inside of Xande's left arm and I scissor my right leg under me in a hip-escape motion.	I grab with both my arms behind Xande's knees and I suck my knees under me into the Elevator position. At this point, I am in a great position to attack Xande with a takedown.

BRIDGING:

Oftentimes, an opponent will preemptively stop the guard recovery by blocking your hip and legs with an arm. Although he may feel secure, thinking that he is blocking your hip-escape movement, he may not realize that the block does little to prevent your bridging action. By bridging into your opponent, you will create the space to transition to your knees and initiate your own counters.

Once again I am in the Side Control starting on my side. This time, Xande is blocking my right hip with his right arm (1).

Instead of hip escaping with the leg scissor to go to my knees, I have to bridge into Xande to make the space (2).

Now that I have the space I can easily scissor my legs and go to my knees (3).

I end in the Elevator position, ready to take Xande down (4).

8-3 SIDE CONTROL RUNNING ESCAPE

This is one of my favorite and most effective escapes. Not only does it feel effortless to get to your side and stay secure, it also provides a very smooth transition to the guard. Drill this move often and be sure to unleash it on your opponent anytime he blocks an entire side of your body from the Side Control position. Remember, your opponent will try to attack your back, so be prepared with a strong Running Escape Survival and you will assuredly get the escape.

Xande has me in Side Control and he is completely blocking my right side with his cross face and hip block. I cannot turn into him to escape.

First off, I have to free my right hand. To do so, I push off of Xande's left shoulder with my right hand to make the space to escape my arm.

Once this space is opened, I shoot my arm through as I continue to push on Xande's shoulder. As I escape my arm, I begin rotating my body to the left side.

Now that my arm is free, I close off my side to Xande by stepping my right knee up to my right forearm. By keeping my elbow tight, Xande no longer has any control over my upper body. This is the Running Escape Posture.

By pushing off my toes and bridging onto my left shoulder, I have freed my hips for the coming escape.

In one sweeping motion, I pendulum my right leg in a horizontal arc. This pendulum, or rocking-chair motion is key to this type of guard recovery.

My foot has passed Xande's torso, and we are now square to each other.

I clamp my feet down and I prepare to use the Open Guard.

8-4 ESCAPE FROM KESA GATAME

Many judo players and wrestlers are monsters on the mat when it comes to using the Kesa Gatame, or Scarf Hold, position. I have seen people struggle or get submitted from under this pin countless times, and this should not happen. Escaping the Kesa Gatame actually is quite easy once you understand what your opponent needs. Pinning you with Kesa Gatame requires control of your near arm and armpit while remaining heavy on top. To nullify the Scarf Hold, remember to hide your near side elbow close to your body and use it as a hip block. Use the bridge to push your opponent's weight farther away from you. Once you do this, you will always have ample space to recover guard with the techniques previously shown.

Xande has attained a modified Kesa Gatame position. Although his hips are pressing into me, I am able to transition into the Kesa Gatame Survival Posture.

Typical of many of my escapes, I begin by bridging into Xande to create space for my hip escape.

Following the bridge, I commit to my hip escape. This opens a huge space under Xande's right armpit.

Penetrating with my right knee, I shoot my leg into the open gap between Xande's right arm and torso. My arm frame ensures that Xande does not advance his position.

I circle my head away from Xande and recover the Open Guard.

8-5 ESCAPE FROM REVERSE KESA GATAME

Although the Reverse Kesa Gatame may feel different or more threatening than the standard Scarf Hold, it is really quite disarming. However, one extra problem is the uncertainty of this position. When your opponent has you pinned here, he has some very strong options, such as taking the Mount or going for the Kimura armlock, but you are more or less blind to what is being planned as he is facing away from you. Do not let that faze you. Be aware of mount attempts and do not overexpose your arms to armlocks. In addition, be careful not to let your opponent manipulate your legs for wrestling-style leg-ride techniques. By working your bridge with blocking elbows, many of your opponent's options will evaporate before they even materialize.

Xande has the Side Control and is looking for the Mount. However, I have moved to the Reverse Kesa Gatame Survival Posture and I am ready to initiate my escape.

With my right elbow tucked in front of Xande's hip, I bridge into him to make space. Note that it is crucial that my elbow remains tucked in front of Xande's hip. If Xande gets past my elbow, my bridge will be fruitless.

Following my bridge, I hip escape hard to my left. My right elbow will act as a frame and actually will help me get more distance out of my hip escape.

I slide my right knee into the newly opened space between Xande's left flank and the mat.

I continue pushing my right knee through and arrive in the Open Guard. From here, I am in a good position to mount my own attacks.

8-6 ESCAPE AGAINST WRESTLER'S PIN

Sometimes opponents are so tough, strong, and aggressive that they can force you out of a good survival position on tenacity alone. I would not say that this is good jiu-jitsu, but it is something to be prepared for. When an opponent gets through the Side Control Survival and secures the far-side arm with the cross-face, do not fret–react! You cannot hang around in this control with your arm exposed to attack, but you can use your arm to drive your opponent off axis. The following escape is very effective, and it follows one of the oldest jiu-jitsu maxims, "Where the head goes, the body follows."

Xande has me in Side Control and he has my left arm underhooked in a wrestler's pin position. If I do not act quickly, my left arm, as well as my neck, will be vulnerable to attack.

In one calculated motion, I bridge hard into Xande, pushing his face away from me with my left arm. This takes Xande off axis as his body follows the path of his face which creates a moment of opportunity for me.

Capitalizing on Xande's moment of imbalance, I hip escape and bring my right knee toward his right hip.

I pull my head away from Xande and I continue to drive my knee upward toward open air.

Finally, I recover the Open Guard position.

Knee-On-Belly

9-0 KNEE ON BELLY RUNNING ESCAPE

I have learned many Knee-on-Belly escapes, and the Running Escape is the best. Once you master this technique, you will avoid all the chokes, armlocks, and pressure that make this position so dangerous. Once again, knowing what your opponent needs in this position guides your escape. Your opponent wants you to escape toward him because the Knee-on-Belly Position works best when the person on the bottom pushes into the person on top. Even if the person on top does not manage to finish the submission, often he can transition back into Side Control easily. This is not a fair trade, and that is why I use the Running Escape. It allows you to turn away from your opponent while staying safe from submissions. You must turn away from your opponent, not into him.

Xande has me in the Knee-on-Belly Position and he is dominating my entire right side with his grips. It is impossible to turn into him and the pressure is tremendous. I regain my composure by feeling out my Knee on Belly Survival Posture.

If I escape toward Xande, I am sure to get choked, so I initiate a turn to my outside. It is important that I keep my right arm inside of Xande's left arm; otherwise, I will trap myself.

Once my right arm is clear of Xande's knee, I tighten the space by stepping my right leg up to close the gap between my arm and thigh. I am in the Running Escape Posture.

I do not want to stay here forever, so I begin my escape. I do so by rolling onto my left shoulder and pushing off the mat with my toes.

Next, I pendulum my right foot in a low-level, horizontal arc. This will carry my body toward the proper escape path.

I finish the pendulum motion square to Xande, and I am ready to initiate my Open Guard game.

10-0 ARMBAR ESCAPE MOVEMENT DRILL

Most people learn to do the Stacking Armbar Defense as their first armbar escape. While this escape makes use of many of the same stacking principles, it goes beyond the Stacking Armbar Defense technique by creating the proper angle to beat the armbar. Therefore, it is important to slowly practice the drill movements to get used to the nuances of the angle change. Once you are comfortable here, you will always be able change the angle when your opponent attacks your arm, and your defensive skills will shoot through the roof.

1

Xande has me in an armbar from the guard. I am grabbing my own hand and I lift my right knee off the ground. I am in a semi-stack, but I am not pressing forward with all my weight.

2

Instead of driving my weight toward Xande's head in a typical stack, I start moving my weight toward my free arm and in the direction of Xande's feet.

3

As I continue, you can see how Xande's feet are getting closer and closer to the ground.

4

At this point, I have pinned Xande's feet together and negated any chance of him getting the armbar. I pull my left arm out and add more pressure on his left leg.

5

Bringing my base to rest on top of Xande's legs, now I am ready to pass the guard.

Figure 10.0: Illustration of Weight

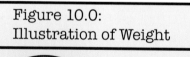

Xande's legs are upright and in good position to pressure an armbar.

Xande's legs are smashed together and he does not have the angle to finish the attack.

10-1 COMMON MISCONCEPTIONS

Standing Up:

When faced with an opponent with a strong armbar attack, some practitioners try to stand up and either force their way out of the submission or transition into a stack defense. Standing this way is a bad strategy and will often lead to a swift armbar and a sore elbow.

Xande has caught my right arm in an armbar. I grab my right hand to let off some pressure.

I decide to stand and force my way out of the submission.

Standing without posture is always a bad move and Xande capitalizes on my mistake with a strong armbar attack.

Stacking:

Stacking defenses work. The principle of weight distribution as a defense is essential, but I find this particular defense far riskier than changing the angle with the stack.

Again, Xande has caught my right arm in an armbar. I begin stacking forward to alleviate the pressure.

As I creep forward, Xande secures my left leg with an underhook and starts to swing me off balance.

Xande simply guides my weight toward the direction I have been stacking, and I feel myself getting swept.

To make matters worse, Xande is now in a perfect position to finish a match-ending armbar.

10-2 ARMBAR ESCAPE TO GUARD PASS

You may have noticed that by changing the angle of the armbar, you have created the opportunity to pass the guard. This momentum must be seized! The following is a simple and highly effective guard pass that should be done immediately after defending the armbar. Do not wait for your opponent to recover guard and attack again! Pass the guard while you have control.

Xande has my right arm in an armbar and I am grabbing my own hand to release the pressure.

I move directly to my left and change the angle by forcing Xande's legs together.

At the same time, I release my free left hand, cross-face Xande with it, and sprawl my weight onto my toes.

With my left leg, I take a big step over Xande's legs. I keep my hips low so that Xande does not have the space to escape.

Finally, I step my right leg over his legs and I establish the Side Control.

10-3 ARMBAR ESCAPE TO GUARD PASS 2

This is the second guard pass option off the armbar defense. I like this one especially without the gi. By going toward the back side of your opponent, you open him up to not only the Side Control, but also back attacks, chokes, and head and arm attacks. This move should be mastered alongside the previous technique to develop mobility. This way, you always will pass the guard and defend his guard recovery directly from escaping the armbar.

Once again, Xande has my right arm secured in an armbar. My right knee is off the mat to assist in the stacking motion.

By stacking to my left, I drive Xande's legs together. The armbar is no longer my main concern.

I have pulled my left arm free and am now adding more downward pressure on Xande's top leg.

Reaching my right arm across Xande's body, I secure the cross-face as I drive my hips on top of his left thigh.

Now I can pull my previously threatened arm out and grab Xande's back. I walk around the side and either take Xande's back or Side Control.

10-4 ARMBAR ESCAPE FROM BOTTOM

Escaping the armbar when you are on your back can be a pretty brutal position. You have your partner pushing on your triceps, your face is getting smashed, and your biceps feels like it is being detached from the bone. To beat this submission, you should once again pay attention to what your opponent needs to finish it. When your opponent breaks your armbar grip, he has to do so by pulling on the forearm as a lever, not the elbow. Finishing the armbar has nothing to do with pulling the elbow back and everything to do with pulling the forearm. This is very important to keep in mind because with this knowledge you can escape the armbar.

Xande has just caught my right arm and is fighting to secure the armbar. I clasp my hands together to buy myself a little time.

Knowing that Xande needs to armbar my forearm, I turn slightly to my left and feed him my elbow. This way he cannot force the armbar by turning my forearm.

Next, I lift my head and right shoulder to release Xande's left leg from my face. This also has the desirable effect of making Xande less able to jeep his position.

Feeling secure with my deep elbow defense, I release my left hand and push upward on Xande's left ankle.

5

As I further elevate Xande's left leg, I secure it in a figure-four grip with my previously endangered arm.

6

I step my legs slightly to the left and now I have the necessary angle to push myself on top of Xande.

7

Continuing to push on Xande's left leg, I transition to the top.

8

I have arrived in the Armbar Defense Posture. I straighten my right hand to make it easier for the coming escape.

9

I easily slide my arm directly back and escape the armbar.

11-0 TRIANGLE ESCAPE TO PASS

The triangle is one of the deadliest and most common submissions in the jiu-jitsu arsenal. To choke someone with a triangle, one must break the posture, create an angle for the top leg to cross the shoulders/neck, and close both sides of the carotid arteries using the leg and the opponent's arm. Because I know this is the goal of the choker, I focus on an escape that does not give my opponent the angle, choking arm, or posture he needs to complete the submission. When I add in my signature pressure, I get a very high percentage guard pass as well.

Xande has me in a triangle attack position and my posture is in the process of breaking down.

In one motion, I swing my body to the left and bring my right knee up to block Xande's left hip. I further secure the hip by locking my right elbow to my right knee. Now, my positioning is perpendicular to Xande.

Continuing my escape, I drive my posture to my right and toward the mat. This creates a stacking action against Xande and awkwardly twists his legs.

To release his lock, I sprawl my right leg into Xande's left hip and thigh. It is impossible for Xande to withstand the leverage of this technique.

Pulling my previously trapped right arm free, I comfortably transition into the Side Control position.

11-1 COMMON MISCONCEPTIONS

Grabbing the Knee:

By grabbing toward your opponent's knee, you are forgetting one important principle; the legs are stronger than the arms. Usually, this type of defense results in the complete breakdown of posture as the guard player uses his leg power to vacuum in the defender.

Pulling Away:

This time I have panicked and decided to frantically pull away. Unfortunately for me, Xande can secure my arm and finish the triangle as I flail backward. I actually assist him in creating a better angle of attack because I am trying to escape without posture.

Stacking:

Although stacking directly forward seems like it can stall out a triangle, this tactic will not work against an opponent with long legs or an experienced triangle expert. You will only buy him the time to create the angle slowly for an even tighter triangle.

Wrong Turn:

The bully pass is often a tactic used by bigger guys to escape the triangle by trying to pass under the leg. However, the problem with this strategy is that it tightens the choke as you turn the corner to escape. This is a risky move and I advise against it.

12-0 CLASSIC GUILLOTINE ESCAPE

The classic guillotine choke is a great submission due to its simplicity. Most beginners and intermediate students love this submission; therefore, get used to its defense. An integral part of the way I defend against this submission, as well as others, is to turn my hips. Master this technique when you are passing and escaping and you will always manage to put your partner in an uncomfortable situation.

Xande has me in the classic guillotine. Both my arms are free.

To release the pressure of the choke, I grab Xande's choking forearm with my left hand and secure it to my chest. At the same time, I bring my chin down and grab Xande's gi over his left shoulder with my right arm. In doing so, I avoid the immediate threat of the choke.

Coming up onto my toes, I drive my right shoulder into Xande's throat.

In one fluid motion, I step my left leg backward over my right. Meanwhile, I pull Xande's choking arm toward the sky in a circular motion.

The twisting of Xande's spine forces his guard open and I immediately step my right leg over his left.

I free my right leg and secure Xande's side.

In this case, Xande is able to resume control of my head, so I use the blade of my right forearm and pressure the choke across my Xande's trachea.

The pressure is unbearable and Xande's only option is to release the headlock and defend the choke. I finish in Side Control.

12-1 ARM-IN GUILLOTINE ESCAPE

As students get better, they are less likely to leave their necks exposed for the classic guillotine. This is where the arm-in guillotine becomes a threat. Many high-level jiu-jitsu players, like Renzo Gracie, have become masters of this submission. Although tricky to escape, this submission can also be a difficult one to finish. Your opponent needs to make a space in which to push your head, so make sure he is flat. If you use your trapped arm as a hip block, you can escape this dangerous submission with the same ease as the classic version.

Xande has caught me in the guillotine with my right arm trapped.

I release the choking pressure by grasping Xande's right forearm with my left hand. I must pull the choke away from my neck while I sink my chin downward.

With my right arm, I clamp down on Xande's left thigh. At the same time, I drive my weight forward and then to the right. Xande should feel his guard twisting open.

4

As Xande's legs are forced open from the pressure, I step my left leg backward over Xande's left leg.

5

Following with my right leg, I pass Xande's legs and pull my head free from the headlock.

6

I consolidate the Side Control position.

13-0 SOLO FOOTLOCK ESCAPE DRILL

The purpose of this drill is to acquaint you with the turning defense for the foot lock. As with all drills, it is crucial that you practice this on both sides before practicing with your partner.

I begin flat on my back with my right foot elevated in a mock foot lock.

Using my grounded left foot, I execute a small hip escape to my left as I turn my toes to the right. This simulates the foot lock escaping action.

As my right foot falls to the ground, I rise to a ready Open Guard position.

13-1 FOOTLOCK ESCAPE FROM GUARD

As your guard develops and gets harder to pass, some students will opt to forego the pass and go directly to the straight ankle lock submission. Be wary of this tactic and prepare yourself by practicing this escape. The goal of this escape is to change the angle so that when your opponent falls back for the lock, he is left empty handed. Escapes like this are always more effective because they do not rely on gripping and holding, but rather on proper body mechanics and movement.

Instead of passing my guard, Xande grabs onto my right foot and attempts a straight ankle lock.

Before he can fall back, I bridge off my left shoulder and hip escape slightly to my right.

As I land from my bumping action, I point my left foot to the left.

Xande falls back in an attempt to finish the submission.

When Xande lands, my foot easily comes free due to my foot turnout.

I chamber my right leg toward my body and now I am ready to pass the guard.

14-0 KIMURA ESCAPE FROM HALF GUARD

The Kimura armlock or Ude Garame is a highly effective and versatile submission from the Half Guard. It gets its name from the great Japanese judoka, Masahiko Kimura, who used the technique against Helio Gracie during their famous match. Watch out if your opponent manages to get the lock. He needs your posture to be low and your trapped arm free from your body. Once this happens, it is almost always a sure-fire submission or reversal. Therefore, beat the lock with an upright posture and a locked arm. Once you are comfortable here, you can even utilize a submission of your own, either to end the fight or free your arm.

Xande is attacking me with the Kimura armlock from his Half Guard. I grab my belt to delay the submission.

I posture upward to bring Xande to his side. Now Xande does not have a favorable position to finish the submission.

I reach down and grasp my own arm. This entangles Xande's arm into an armlock of my own. As I pull to the left, Xande has to release the submission or become a victim of his own attack.

14-1 KIMURA ESCAPE TO ARMBAR POSTURE

Sometimes an opponent is so strong that he will not release his grip on the Kimura, even if his shoulder is being cranked out of socket. Instead of hurting him by insisting on the previous technique, I transition to this variation. In this technique, you will be introduced to the proper leverage of the brace and the principle of using body movement to counter your opponent's attacks.

Again, Xande is attempting a Kimura armlock from his Half Guard. I secure my belt with my left hand to prevent the finishing hold.

Driving my weight to my left, I force Xande onto his right side. My right hand is on his hip and acting as a brace.

Bracing with my right hand, I pull my knee skyward. This creates the perfect angle to free my right foot.

Once my right leg is out of the Half Guard, I step around Xande's head with my left leg.

My left shin lands under Xande's left armpit and my right leg clamps down on Xande's head. The former Kimura lock is now a perfect setup for the armbar!

Figure 14.1: Bracing Detail

Notice that my right arm is bracing against Xande's hip in this picture. The term brace is important because I am not using this arm to push or pull, but only to keep Xande in this position and to assist with my posture.

By pulling my entire body, I can easily escape my right knee. If I only push with my right arm, it is a fight of arm strength against leg strength. My block prevents Xande from being pulled off the ground by my upward momentum. This is the importance of bracing.

Perfecting the Purple Belt: THE GUARD

> "Even if a hundred ton boulder should fall, I would be safe! No need to try to stop it, just move out of the way. You do not have a problem if you do not try to take it on yourself. Most people suffer because they try to take upon themselves things which they do not need to."
>
> —Koichi Tohei

3-1 THE PURPOSE OF THE GUARD

The guard is your safety net when everything goes wrong. This is your point of return, and every jiu-jitsu player must become acquainted with using this highly technical position. It is safe because it combines the elements of surviving, escaping, and submissions within one unique area. Unlike other aspects of jiu-jitsu, all of these elements are present at the same time every time you play the guard.

Survival within the guard means making it difficult for your opponent to punch or submit you. This is possible because you have the power of your legs to keep a space between your opponent and you. Controlling the distance is the key to survival in the guard.

Hip movement is vital to good guard work. If you cannot use movement in your guard, then you don't really have a guard; every time you go to use it, your opponent will pass it immediately. Thwarting your opponent's passing attempts with angle and positioning depends on your ability to move your hips!

To attack from the guard means submissions and sweeps. Strategically, you must have attacks in your repertoire. This keeps your opponent off guard and constantly on edge as he defends multiple submission attempts, clearing the way for the final submission or reversal.

3-2 PREVENTION & PRESSING THE ACTION

The ability to put your opponent in a disadvantageous position is imperative to good guard movement. You do this by creating a different angle, therefore putting him in a place where he is not ready to progress to the pass or some other technique. When he does react, you can read his intentions easily because you are controlling the situation. Creating an angle puts you in control. Whenever you play with the guard, always play on your side. If you are in front of him, you give your opponent two sides to pass. When you play guard on your side, however, you know his only possible route. He is going to have to move to try to adapt. Angle equals discomfort for your opponent.

When you play with the guard, it is important

to see it as a position where you are losing. This forces you to press the action. Because you already have gravity against you, why would you let your opponent initiate the action? This is not acceptable. Therefore, if your opponent is about to open your guard, open it first and create the proper angle. Now he has to play your game.

3-3 CONTROLLING THE SPACE WITHOUT PUSHING

You have to control the space between your opponent and you without pushing excessively. Every time you push with your hands, you anchor yourself to the ground. If you move your body instead, it creates completely different angles. As an exercise, start with your back flat on the mat and support your partner's weight with stiff arms. Now, when you try to escape your hips, you will find that you can barely move because your body is grounded by your arms supporting his weight.

Photo: Catarina Monnier

Gabrielle Bermudez demonstrates controlling the space without pushing her opponent to a group of students.

How much hip movement can you have when you are extended like a tripod? Hardly any. You're stuck.

3-4 OPEN BEFORE CLOSED

Whenever I teach the guard, I emphasize the Open Guard over the Closed Guard. This is because the Closed Guard gives you the sensation that you are safe. So insecure people usually maintain the Closed Guard at all costs, thinking, "Why take the risk of being passed?" Well, life is about taking risks. You have to jump for higher goals rather than just staying safe. While you feel this false sense of security, you are not progressing.

Although the Closed Guard is certainly effective, it gives you a limited world in which to work, while the Open Guard expands your horizons. You can do whatever you want in the Open Guard, but you expose yourself at the same time. This is why you need to acclimate yourself to the Open Guard game. It is a risk, but the journey is worthwhile. It is best to conquer the unknown first than to stay in the Closed Guard wondering what you will do once you open your legs.

3-5 COMFORT IN THE GUARD

As you get used to the many different guards in this section, you should begin to single out positions where your body feels naturally comfortable, depending on your flexibility, athleticism, and body type. The important factor is that you develop a fluid game where you can safely navigate between different guards, survivals, escapes, and submissions from one comfortable position. In addition, everyone should know at least one go-to guard.

For me, the Sit-Up Guard with the hand in the collar is a very comfortable position. If I'm here, I can be here fighting you, or I can be at the beach, watching a movie, or listening to a conversation. This is my natural position, and I am relaxed here, so it should be a natural position in my jiu-jitsu, too. If you are using the guard and are anxiety ridden, you are not enjoying the art of the guard. An effective guard is based on comfort.

Your guard must be dynamic. Take my Sit-Up

Case Study 3.0:
Rafael Lovato Jr. - Effective Use of the Guard

Photo: Rafael Lovato, Jr. archive

When I look at the guard of Rafael Lovato Jr., I see a great position that was developed through disciplined training. The thing that people do not understand about Rafael is that he went through hell to develop all of his skills. His guard is a great example of a high-level defensive guard. That his guard is incredibly difficult to pass lends further credence to his skills of survival and escape. I have seen him in many matches against the world's best, and in most situations, his opponent made zero progress passing his guard. When it comes to killing, Rafael also does his fair share from the guard, but he does so with comfort. Watching Rafael play the guard is akin to watching someone play football or surf Pipeline. He is comfortable out there and his opponents suffer because of it.

Guard, for instance. I have everything from here: Closed Guard, X-Guard, Butterfly, Foot on the Hip, and every other guard I can think of. Plus, I still have sweeps, control, escapes, submissions, and survival. It is such a simple guard and it leads to everything. That is the beauty of simple jiu-jitsu. This is what you have to find for yourself.

In my guard, I just ask my opponent, "What do you want?" I am in a completely safe place, and I give him the option to choose. The ball is in his court, or at least he thinks so. I have seen it all and I know how effective the relaxed guard is. With comfort comes confidence.

3-6 LEARN TO PLAY EVERY GUARD

I love to play every guard, especially when I'm bored and there are no competitions going on. Because my goal is not focused on competition anymore, on something I have to sharpen, I can maximize my time enjoying the intricacies of the guard game. And sometimes, this is when I pick up on new things because I'm no longer sticking with the tournament plan.

Sometimes I even tell my students, "Today you are going to be Pe de Pano, you are going to be Shaolin, and you are going to be Marcelo Garcia – play like that." It's a chance to do something different. That difference is creates growth in

your jiu-jitsu. All the guards have their usefulness. If I play too much Butterfly Guard, I'm going to get tired, and it is destined to get boring. So, I will play Spider Guard and Half Guard and do a lot of different things that will take me toward the same goal: growth in my jiu-jitsu.

3-7 GUARD TRAINING METHODS

The best guard training method is to limit what the student can do from the guard. The first thing I teach my guys is that if you cannot move your hips, your legs have no power. If you cannot move your hips, you cannot create angles. And if you push, you block your hips. What most people do is push, push, push. To counter this tendency, I limit what body parts you can use.

When you train with both hands in your belt, you will feel your ability to flow between the Turtle and Guard Recovery develop. You will do rolls, side-to-side movement, and fluid motions without pushing. You cannot push with your hands in your belt and I think your hands deceive you in jiu-jitsu. People get very dependant on pushing and gripping.

If the student is a white belt, it is easier to break his instinct to push. My white belts will never

Introduction

have this problem because I have them train for so long with their hands in their belts. They use this method so much, that when they get their hands back they will use them for attacking. That's what the hands are there for – attacking.

3-8 GUARD AND THE PURPLE BELT

As with every other position, you will learn the guard at the white belt level. However, it is not until purple belt that you will really feel the guard falling into place. At purple belt, you should see your guard developing into a game full of defense, sweeps, reversals, favorite positions, and combinations. This is not to say that your guard will be ineffective at the white and blue belt levels, only that in those earlier levels you will have more important things on which to focus your development.

The goal for the purple belt is to dive into the guard only when his survival skills and escape skills are at a solid level. Then, he will have the confidence to attempt whatever he wants without having to suffer for his attempts. Once again, build your guard on top of a strong foundation.

Helpful Guard Tips

- Controlling the space – It is imperative that you keep your opponent in a range where you are in control of the action. This means controlling his hips to prevent his forward pressure, pulling to prevent his escape, and breaking his posture for submissions and attacks.

- To disrupt passing attempts, always create an angle that forces the pass to one side.

- Never allow your opponent to pass in front of your knees. Your knees are your legs' final barriers in keeping the guard.

- Utilize good hip movement. Your ability to seamlessly transition your hips from side to side is the basis of proper guard mechanics.

A. CLOSED GUARD AGAINST KNEELING OPPONENT

The Closed Guard against a kneeling opponent is the guard that uses a close range for attack and defense. Due to proximity and leg control, there are ample opportunities to apply chokes or arm locks, and to break the opponent's posture by controlling the head or arms. The goal is to keep the position without allowing the opponent an opportunity to stand while attacking relentlessly. However, I do have some additional advice, do not develop a lopsidedly strong closed guard to open guard game.

Though this position is a great weapon to have, it can also be debilitating to overall guard improvement. This is because the position can be so strong that students often forego necessary open guard development. No one person's closed guard is unbreakable, and eventually all must develop an open guard system for attack and defense or else be passed easily. Keep this in mind and develop a closed guard that serves a weapon, not a crutch.

15-O CLOSED GUARD ARM WRAP

Breaking your opponent's posture is one of the most important tenets of the Closed Guard game. Keeping his posture broken is the key to submissions and positional domination. The arm wrap is a control that teaches some of the most important aspects of the Closed Guard. In this series, you will learn a simple and effective way to break your opponent down and keep him trapped in a threatening position. The keys to this position are using body weight to bring your opponent with you, creating angle for attack, and then positioning your legs so that your opponent cannot sit back. These concepts are always the same in jiu-jitsu, so use this basic move as a tool for improving your body mechanics.

I hold Xande in my Closed Guard. My right hand is cross-gripping his right collar while my left hand grips his right arm behind the elbow. With this control, I completely dominate Xande's right side.

I break Xande's posture down by using a slight pull toward me and to the left. He stops his forward momentum by putting both hands on the mat.

3

With a strong pull of my right grip, I heft my body toward Xande and wrap my left arm over his right, close to the armpit. My right hand penetrates toward my chest as my elbow clamps down to control the arm.

4

I fall back to my right side, creating an angle. Now I can start thinking offensively.

5

I still do not have the proper angle to make Xande uncomfortable, so I drop my left leg to the mat and hip escape to my left while my right arm blocks his left elbow. Using the space created by my right arm block, I put my right foot on Xande's hip and penetrate my knee to the inside of his left arm.

6

Once my right knee crosses the plane of Xande's left shoulder, I place my left foot on his right hip and pressure my knees together. This locks him in the Arm Wrap position and opens up multiple submission opportunities.

Figure 15.0: Blocking Detail

The blocking action of the right arm is crucial. I do not want my opponent to reach over my right arm and control my elbow. If he does, it is likely he will initiate a pass of his own or regain some control. To combat this, I use the same philosophy as the cross-face block. To do this, I make a hook with my right forearm and hand, and let it loosely follow my opponent's elbow. I do not force my opponent's arm downward; this is a battle of strength. Instead, I redirect his actions so that his arm is going away from me. In most cases he will bring his arm back naturally to avoid exposing himself.

15-1 SOLO ARM WRAP CHOKE TO STRAIGHT ARMLOCK

When a student first goes for the straight armlock, often he loses the position as he try his hardest to crank down on his opponent's elbow. This is usually because he is not straightening his body at the proper angle. I cannot repeat this enough: jiu-jitsu is about the movement of your entire body and not just the squeezing of your arm muscles! Practice this movement a few times to get used to perfect positioning for the straight armlock attack, and then move on to the following technique with your partner.

Imagining that my partner is in my Arm Wrap guard, I use my right arm as the Arm Wrap control while my left hand crosses into the choking position.

Moving slightly to my left side, I bring my left elbow toward the mat to simulate cross-choking action.

Pushing my right knee downward, I move my body to the left and bring my head straight back. This simulates the body posture for the straight armlock.

15-2 ARM WRAP CHOKE TO STRAIGHT ARMLOCK

Complementary moves are two or more moves that, when combined in a chain, allow you to go between one and the other. The choke and straight armlock from the arm wrap position are complementary moves. However, these moves are also very special in that they actually can be applied at the same time to completely overwhelm your adversary. The following is a great sequence that showcases the attacking power of this incredible position.

Xande is in my Closed Guard and he has both arms on my chest to prevent my mobility. I cross-grip his left sleeve with my left hand and sneak my right hand behind his left elbow.

With a firm pull of my left hand, I bring Xande's posture forward and create the space to dive my right arm inside of Xande's left.

3

I continue to pull Xande's arm until my left arm wraps my head. My right arm drives skyward until my right shoulder is clear of Xande's left arm.

4

My left arm maintains control over Xande's left arm until I have completed the Arm Wrap with my right arm. This time, I feed my right hand to Xande's right lapel.

5

Placing my right foot on the ground, I hip escape to my right to create the proper attacking angle. With Xande's left arm secure, I release my left hand grip.

6

In one overwhelming action, I place my right foot on Xande's hip as my left hand grabs his left collar for a cross-collar choke.

7

To finish the attack, I clasp my right knee onto my right elbow, creating tremendous pressure on Xande's left elbow. As I pull my head away, I also drop my left elbow to ensure the choke. Depending on how my opponent struggles to defend, I will finish either submission with ease.

15-3 CLOSED GUARD OVERWRAP

When I am in the academy, I love to play a snake-like and smothering game. The overwrap is a position that is perfect for this gameplan. With the overwrap attack, I can break the posture effectively and then trap my partner's head and upper body against my chest. Once more, my body weight, legs, and angle of attack do the work for me. The result: a claustrophobic body lock that will trap even your best opponents.

Xande is in my Closed Guard. He is pushing both hands into my chest to keep posture and to prevent me from sitting up.

To break Xande's posture, I begin circling my right hand over Xande's left arm and then I drive my hand into the space between his left elbow and torso.

Once my right hand has penetrated behind Xande's left elbow, I can sit up and bring my right arm high behind Xande's neck. Reaching with my left arm over Xande's right shoulder, I meet both my hands behind my brother's neck.

As my right hand secures my left wrist, I fall back to the mat, bringing Xande's body with me.

5

Once again, I need to create the proper angle to attack, so I step my right foot to the mat and hip escape to the right.

6

I stabilize the position by placing both my feet on Xande's hips and squeezing my knees together.

15-4 OVERWRAP TO BACK

The overwrap grip is a great starting point to take someone's back. I have seen Rickson Gracie use this move millions of times and I am always impressed with how he continually refines and successfully uses movements like this. Practice this movement to improve your overall grappling coordination. You cannot simply shuck your partner's arm off your neck. Instead, your limbs and body have to be in harmony with each other. Total body coordination is the key!

1

I have Xande in the Overwrap Guard. I place my left foot between his hips in preparation for taking the Back.

2

Xande's left arm is preventing me from taking his back. To move it, I shuck my shoulder toward his elbow as I look away from his arm. This creates an angle for his arm to slide out. To counterbalance this action, I extend my right leg to create drive on my shoulder shuck.

3

Now that I have passed Xande's arm, I release my top arm and place my right foot on the mat. I maintain control of Xande's body by grabbing his right shoulder blade with my left hand while my head and upper body put pressure on his left shoulder.

4

Pushing off my right foot, I hip escape slightly to the right and then I sit-up onto Xande's back. My right arm controls Xande's right hip to prevent him from rolling away to escape.

5

Further escaping my hip, I drive my left knee to the outside as I bring my hips onto Xande's. From here, I am in a great position to take the Back or finish with a submission.

Figure 15.4: Escaping Hip Details

1 **2** **3**

I have seen many students and top-level players get stuck when trying to free their hips from under their opponents. Usually, this is because a student tries to pull his body up using his right arm on the hip (1). Instead, use your right arm as a block to prevent your opponent from rolling and then slightly hip escape. Your opponent will feel the sensation that he is falling into you and he should consolidate his base (2). This is the timing to escape your bottom (left) knee from under your opponent (3). The secret is in your bottom knee – once you have it turned to the outside, your hips are free to transition to the top.

15-5 SCISSOR / KNEE SHIELD

As you get better, your opponents will start defending the previous moves by posting their hands on your chest and fighting hard to prevent you from breaking their postures. Take advantage of your opponent's defensive mindset by sliding in the Knee Shield and Scissor to disrupt his gameplan. This is a great guard in which to initiate sweeps and submissions and it is usually there for the taking when you face stalling tactics and overly defensive opponents.

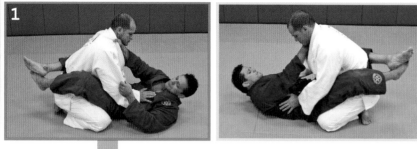

I have Xande in my Closed Guard with my right hand cross-gripping his right collar and my left hand grabbing his right elbow. Xande's hands are pushing into my chest to prevent me from sitting up.

Placing both feet on the mat, I keep my legs tight to inhibit Xande's mobility.

Using my right foot, I hip escape to the right. At the same time, my left leg straightens and falls into the Scissor Sweep position.

As my right knee penetrates inside Xande's left arm, I place my right foot on his hip to maintain proper distance. My right shin will now serve as shield, or block, against Xande's weight.

Figure 15.5: Knee Angle Detail

It is important always to keep your knee pointed upward when using the Scissor/Knee Shield Guard. Never let your knees come together, even for a second (1). If you commit this error, a knowledgeable opponent easily can smash your legs together with his weight and continue with a guard pass (2). This can be a difficult scenario from which to escape, and the best strategy is prevention by keeping your knees angled away from each other.

15-6 CLASSIC ARMBAR

The classic armbar is one of the most effective submissions from the Closed Guard. Although there are unlimited variations of this attack, the following technique remains one of the most basic and technical attacks out there. At the heart of it, the armbar works because your hips act as a fulcrum and your hands pull on the end of the lever, your opponent's wrist, to apply force against his weak elbow joint. The aspects of sliding your head toward your opponent's body, using the foot on the hip as an axis, and the principle of the heavy leg all make this one of the strongest guard attacks. Like all moves, this should be practiced until it is engrained in your muscle memory. I recommend watching footage of Roger Gracie and Xande Ribeiro to see this basic move used at the highest levels of jiu-jitsu.

Xande is in my Closed Guard.

My right hand cross-grips Xande's right arm just above the elbow as my free hand locks his forearm. This creates a viselike grip on Xande's right arm. Meanwhile, I place my left foot on Xande's right hip.

Pushing off Xande's hip with my left foot, I slide my back on the mat until my head is near his left knee. As I create this angle, my right leg assists by sliding high into Xande's left armpit and then forcibly swinging downward at the heel. This pendulum motion of my heel, in conjunction with my primary change of angle, pushes Xande's posture to his right.

Only when Xande's posture is disrupted to his right do I swing my left leg over his face. I finish the classic armbar by squeezing my knees together, pushing downward with my legs, and pulling down with both hands at the end of the lever – Xande's right wrist.

15-7 ARMBAR TO CROSS CHOKE DRILL

The next drill is a perfect tool to build a great double attack for your Closed Guard. The best thing about the cross choke and armbar is that both can be set up with the same hand and body positioning. Therefore, you should get used to flowing between them to keep your opponent off guard. For instance, if your opponent defends the armbar, you can attack with the cross choke. If he focuses on defending the cross choke, you switch back to the armbar. Master this drill and you will always find safety by transitioning between the two submissions.

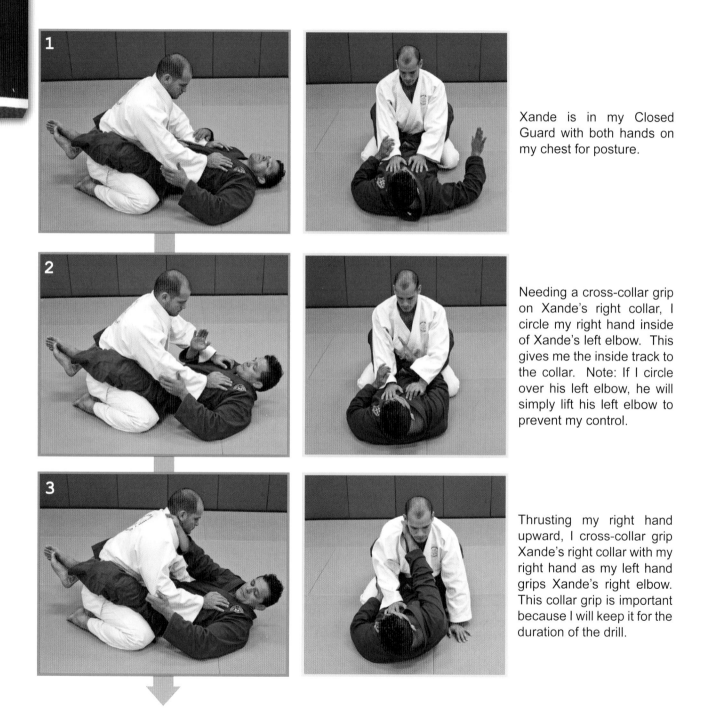

Xande is in my Closed Guard with both hands on my chest for posture.

Needing a cross-collar grip on Xande's right collar, I circle my right hand inside of Xande's left elbow. This gives me the inside track to the collar. Note: If I circle over his left elbow, he will simply lift his left elbow to prevent my control.

Thrusting my right hand upward, I cross-collar grip Xande's right collar with my right hand as my left hand grips Xande's right elbow. This collar grip is important because I will keep it for the duration of the drill.

I place my left foot on Xande's hip, squeezing my knee toward his torso for control.

Pushing with my foot on his hip, I slide my upper back on the mat until my head is close to Xande's left knee. Meanwhile, my right foot swings to the center of his back. Note: My foot on his hip also lifts my hips to ensure that I have body contact under Xande's armpits.

In one motion, I swing my left leg over Xande's head as my left hand controls his right wrist. I finish the submission by pushing my legs downward while my hips thrust into his elbow. This creates the leverage that forces Xande's arm upward. My left arm grabs at his wrist and applies opposing pressure to get the tap.

When Xande pressures into me to defend the arm-bar, I do not fight against his weight. Instead, I swing my left foot back to his hip and pull him using his forward momentum. Immediately, I grab his left shoulder with the blade of my left arm close to his right carotid artery. Closing my left elbow, I sink in a very tight cross choke.

Closed Guard

15-8 BRABO CHOKE

The Brabo choke is an ingenious submission that was created by my friend, Leo Vieira. It capitalizes on the defense of a knowledgeable opponent and makes him pay! To develop this choke, practice all of your chokes. The more threatening your choking submissions are, the harder your opponent will try to resist them. This resistance is the key in timing the Brabo choke and success depends on it. The best part of this move is that your first submission attempt does not have to be a feint; if your partner does not defend – choke him. If he does defend, then the Brabo choke is a highly effective plan B.

I have Xande in my Closed Guard and already I am attacking with the cross-collar grip.

As I attempt the cross choke with my left hand, Xande quickly defends by grabbing my left wrist to prevent the hold.

While Xande wrestles with my left hand, I place my right foot on his hip and pressure his left arm inward with my leg. This temporarily traps his arm in this position.

Quickly, I reach over the top of Xande's left arm with my left hand and grab behind his lower tricep. Using my arm and leg in unison, I pressure his left arm to his right.

I continue pulling until Xande's left elbow is straight and passes his centerline. At this point, I can remove my right foot from his hip and place it on his back.

With Xande's posture broken and my right leg now creating pressure on his back, I release my left hand and grasp Xande behind his head. To finish the Brabo Choke, I pull with my right hand while my left hand pulls his head.

Figure 15.8: Deep Collar Detail

Getting the deep collar is an art in itself. Often during a training session, your partner's collar will move out of alignment and it becomes very difficult to grab the collar without slack. Get used to using one grip to open up the collar, even lightly whipping it to loosen up the tension. Then feed the collar to your penetrating hand. This process of feeding the collar to your free hand will result in a threatening collar grip that can be used from almost everywhere.

I have opened up Xande's right collar with my left hand.

Without letting go of my left hand, I feed Xande's right lapel to my right hand. If it is still difficult to find slack, I can pull further with my left hand to open a route for my gripping hand.

15-9 CLASSIC TRIANGLE CHOKE

Just like the armbar, there are countless options for getting the triangle choke, and this one is my favorite. The triangle choke is one of the major submissions in jiu-jitsu and it is remarkable for its efficient use of force. By trapping your opponent's head and arm between your legs and applying inward pressure, you are applying the power of a large muscle group, your legs, against a relatively small one, his neck. In this set-up for the triangle choke, I swing my hips to expose my opponent's neck to attack. The foot on his hip is a great place from which to attack.

Xande is in my Closed Guard and is feeling threatened by my cross-collar grip and sleeve control.

I place my left foot on his hip and my right foot on the mat.

Extending my left leg, I hip escape far to my right. As I do this, I swing my right leg outward. Xande is feeling exposed and imbalanced.

Thrusting my right foot skyward, I circle my leg over Xande's left arm, only stopping when my knee makes contact with his neck and shoulder.

Pushing off his right hip, I bring my head slightly to the right to create a proper angle. The lock and choke are most effective with the right angle. My right calf slides behind his neck.

Locking my left knee over my right ankle, I am ready to finish the triangle choke. To submit Xande, I simply squeeze my knees together while keeping downward pressure with my right leg.

Figure 15.9: Angle Detail

Note that as I hip escape away from him and swing my leg to the outside, Xande is left very exposed. If he attempts to hold on to my right leg, I will continue the momentum of my leg swing until his grip breaks. This is a great posture for the bottom player. Aside from the triangle, the armbar, and many other submissions, are also readily available.

15-10 SOLO HIP BUMP SWEEP

The following is a great drill to master the mechanics of the Hip Bump Sweep. When you practice this move, think of the beginning as the twisting of a coil. The bump is the unleashing of all the tension built from that twisted coil. This is the essence of the Hip Bump Sweep and it is a great way to visualize the power you can generate from this technique.

I begin the Hip Bump Sweep Drill by sitting upright on the mat with my left hand posted behind me and my right arm crossing my centerline.

Pushing off my left foot and my posted left arm, I drive my hips directly to my left to simulate the initial sweep.

Stepping over with my right foot, I attain the top position.

15-11 HIP BUMP SWEEP

The Hip Bump Sweep is often one of the first sweeps learned in jiu-jitsu. This is because it is also one of the most effective. However, some begin this move by reaching over the opponent's shoulder. While this certainly is not wrong, I believe it is more efficient to attack toward the elbow. Turning your body to the side is easier than reaching upward, and this has the added benefit of putting more coil into your hips. As you get used to this technique, you will notice that all this tension results in a fast, powerful reversal.

Xande is in my Closed Guard with his hands posted on my chest. His weight is shifted backward and the timing is perfect for the Hip Bump Sweep.

As I sit-up to my left side, my left hand posts on the mat behind me while my right hand cross-grips Xande's right sleeve. My right elbow then clamps down on his elbow for control.

Pushing off with my left foot and arm, I drive my hips directly to my left to sweep Xande off balance.

Xande falls directly to his back and I land in control of the Mount position.

Figure 15.11: Hip Detail

The perfect time to use your hip thrust is when your opponent is already off balance to his side. Your low arm positioning and posted arm will disrupt his base (1). Then, use your hip bump to seal your opponent's fate (2).

15-12 FLOWER SWEEP

This sweep is so important that I make sure all my students know how to use it. Beyond sweeping, this move is rich with principles that appear elsewhere in jiu-jitsu. "Lightening the foot" is one such principle (See Figure 15.12). Through the use of this sweep, you will learn to drive your opponent's weight to one side to lighten his load on the other. By learning to control your opponent's base, you will be able to play with his balance and control him like a puppeteer. Although this principle pops up in some of the moves you have already seen, like the classic armbar from the guard, it is much more apparent here. As an exercise, practice this technique and then work through this book, noting every move that uses this key principle.

Once again, Xande is in my guard and I have cross-collar and sleeve control.

I place my left foot on the mat, making sure that it is blocking Xande's right leg from posting. Always block the same side as the controlled arm.

As I slightly swing my hips to the left to create a better angle, I grip Xande's left pant leg at the ankle.

In one motion, I swing my right leg toward Xande's head and then downward as I pull Xande's left leg toward my head. This pushing of my legs drives Xande to the right and lightens his leg for my pulling action. The pull of my right hand opens his base for the sweep.

Fully committed to the sweep, I pull Xande's left leg high off the ground as my momentum drives him to his right shoulder.

Xande's inertia pulls me to the top Mount position.

Figure 15.12: Lightening the Foot

It is vital to use your push and pull in a concentrated effort. I cannot hope to lift Xande's left foot unless I have driven his body weight off it. This is why I use the power of my legs to drive Xande's weight away from his left foot. Once there, he can do nothing to stop me from pulling his leg to the roof. Like all jiu-jitsu, this is effective due to proper angle and leverage.

B. CLOSED GUARD AGAINST STANDING OPPONENT

The Closed Guard against a standing opponent is the guard that teaches how to disrupt your opponent's balance and move your body for reversals. Though there are some submissions available from here, it is more likely that you will reverse your opponent by compromising his balance. Because your opponent is standing, there is a greater range from which to attack. You must treat a standing opponent differently than a kneeling one. Incorporate the following techniques into your game to build an indestructible Closed Guard!

16-0 FRUSTRATING STANDING BASE

When your opponent stands to open your guard, your first thought always has to be to disrupt his balance. Standing up while someone has his legs wrapped around you is a precarious operation and you should make sure your opponent feels that. The following technique outlines my strategy for using the legs to continually pull your opponent back to the ground. The standing position can be powerful for the passer, so get used to breaking this posture before he can initialize his pass.

Xande is standing in my guard with hands posted on my chest. If I do not act, he could potentially open up my legs and impose his game.

I climb my legs higher on Xande's lower back and then pull them toward my head to break his posture.

I prevent Xande from getting his posture back by grabbing his head and arm for control.

Xande realizes that the position is lost and returns to his knees. I am in a great position now to initiate some attacks of my own.

16-1 HIP PUSH SWEEP

Sometimes your opponent will still manage to stand in your Closed Guard and pursue the guard opening. In such a case it is important to dictate the pace by opening your guard before he can force it open. If he manages to be the one who opens it, he likely will be in a position to control your legs and hips. This will assist him in his potential pass. Luckily, the Hip Push Sweep is a great way to beat this. The time to initiate this sweep is when your opponent is posturing back to break open your guard. As he is going back, release your legs and amplify his backward momentum by pushing his hips. Remember, jiu-jitsu is about giving way to force, and this is the perfect move to see this philosophy in action.

Xande is posturing up in my Closed Guard and is about to open my legs.

However, Xande has committed the error of keeping his legs on the same line. I grab behind both his ankles and open my legs. As my lower back falls to the mat, I shift my hips slightly to the left and place my right foot on Xande's left hip.

Pushing off with my right foot, I sweep Xande backward. He cannot regain his composure because I have both his ankles blocked.

Xande falls to his back and I transition my weight onto my right elbow. I will keep my right foot on his hip until I am ready to move to the top position.

Using the Technical Lift, I finish the sweep by moving into Xande's guard. Xande cannot rush into me because I maintain control over both his ankles.

Figure 16:1 Technical Lift

The Technical Lift is a method for transitioning from lying on your back to standing on your feet. You must learn this movement, as it will be useful anytime you have your back to the mat.

With Xande swept to his back, I am ready to move to my knees.

By pressuring on my right elbow and posting on my left leg, I can lighten my right foot and begin swinging it under my body.

Once my right foot has circled behind me, I can now sit-up into Xande's guard.

16-2 CLASSIC UNDERHOOK SWEEP

Eventually, your opponent will become wise to the previous move and defend it by posturing forward to counterbalance your pushing action. This is the perfect time to go for the Classic Underhook Sweep. The important detail is not to push your hips into your opponent's. Instead, you need to drive your hip into his knee. The knee is much weaker than the hip and your opponent will lose stability much sooner with this method.

Xande is standing in my Closed Guard with both hands pressing into my chest. By keeping his posture very low, he has made the previous sweep very difficult.

As I underhook Xande's left leg with my right arm, I shift my body toward the trapped limb.

I push my hip into Xande's left knee, easily sweeping him toward his rear left.

Xande lands on his back with me in front of him. Worrying about a possible escape, I decide to stabilize the position.

5

My legs are trapped. I free them by turning toward Xande's left leg and creating an angle to take the Mount. If I try to go directly forward, my own body will impede my progress and he likely will escape.

6

I finish my reversal in the Mount position.

16-3 ROLLOUT AGAINST UNDERHOOK DEFENSE

Just like the previous move, you need a contingency plan for when a move fails. This is the backup plan when your opponent defends the Classic Underhook Sweep. Often, your opponent will stagger his legs and pressure his front knee inward to block your hip. At this point, all the strength in the world will not push your opponent's knee outward. Once again, the answer is to give way to your opponent's strength and roll away from his pressure. In doing so, you will set up this fantastic sweep that is sure to catch him off guard. Once you have this move in your repertoire, integrate it with the previous two techniques to develop a complete sweeping game against the standing guard pass.

1

Xande is defending my Underhook Sweep attempt by posturing forward with his left knee. If I wait too long, Xande will break open my legs and pass the guard.

I open my legs before Xande can take control.

Without delay, I roll over my right shoulder toward Xande's rear left. For my hips to clear Xande's knee, I must push off the mat while swinging my left leg around the front of him.

Landing on all fours, I retain control of Xande's left leg.

As I raise my head off the mat, I drive my body into Xande's shin while I pull at the heel. This creates a hyperextension of his knee and forces him to fall backward.

I finish the sweep by sitting all the way back. Because I glue his leg to my body, the sweep follows the direction of my movement.

16-4 COMMON MISCONCEPTIONS

No Control:

Here I have waited too long and Xande manages to open my legs. At this point, it is too late for me. I did not control any part of Xande's body and now he is in complete control of the pass.

Bulldozing Forward:

If I just try to grab and pull to sweep with the underhook it will not work. The secret is in moving your body next to his leg and sweeping toward his knee. If you only try to bulldoze the sweep, a good practitioner should be able to maintain his posture.

Stalling:

I cannot stall when my opponent stands in my guard. If I stay square to Xande without controlling him, it is likely he will pass with ease. This is a working position and it is a dangerous area in which to rest.

17-0 GUARD PASS DEFENSE

If you cannot escape the guard pass, you do not have a guard. This goes back to the basics of what it means to use the guard. Even if you are a sweep and submission master, your skills will not matter if you cannot prevent your guard from being passed. There is a preventative aspect to jiu-jitsu always. Master these principles and you will have unlimited time to attack submissions and sweeps.

A. UNDER-THE-LEG PASS DEFENSE

Under-the-leg passes are usually the first passes taught in jiu-jitsu classes. These moves always involve the swimming of one or both of your opponent's arms underneath your legs and then lifting one or both to his shoulder. What makes these passes effective is the stacking pressure created by your opponent's body weight as it drives your legs into your body. With this in mind, you cannot let your opponent control your legs. Use your leg circling motion from the Spider Guard drill to esgrima or circle your feet to the inside. If you are late and your opponent gains control of your legs, use the following two techniques to safely escape these passes.

17-1 SINGLE UNDER-THE-LEG PASS DEFENSE

Seeing as this is one of the first guard passes taught in jiu-jitsu, it should also be one of the first pass defenses learned. From white to black belt, you will face many opponents who favor this simple yet effective pass. Some have years of experience with it and these people are masters of sucking away your space. Therefore, you must develop this defense to the highest level. The key details are blocking your opponent's penetrating shoulder with your hand and making space to liberate your knee. Once you can effectively escape your knee downward, guard recovery and submissions are there for the taking.

I have successfully circled my left arm under Xande's right leg and my right arm is pressing his left leg down, threatening the pass.

As an initial block, Xande puts his right hand on my left hip and his left hand on my shoulder. He straightens his arms without locking his elbows. This prevents me from easily reaching his side and buys him some time.

Placing his left foot on the mat, Xande then hip escapes to the left.

Now Xande has the necessary space to turn his right knee toward my body and drop it to the mat.

Xande continues to slide his right knee down until it clears my upper body. He then puts his foot on my hip to reconstitute the guard.

Using his right foot on my hip, Xande brings his left foot toward my right hip, and he aligns himself in the guard position.

17-2 DOUBLE UNDER-THE-LEGS DEFENSE TO SWEEP

The double under-the-legs maneuver is another pass that you will defend against frequently. Like the previous technique, you cannot let your opponent pull your hips onto his chest. Once there, it will be much more difficult to escape as he stacks your legs into you. Get comfortable defending this pass before this happens! The following is a great example of an early defense and sweep against this dangerous pass.

This time I have the double underhooks and I want to use a stacking pass on Xande.

As a first line of defense, Xande drops both his feet to the mat. Xande keeps his legs heavy to combat my instinct to overpower them.

Next Xande sits up, posts his right hand on the mat for base, and cinches down on my belt with his left hand. His posting arm will prevent me from driving him onto his back.

Xande executes a sit-out maneuver by switching from his right hip to his left and driving his left elbow to the mat. At the same time, he reaches down and grabs my left pant leg with his right hand. His sit-out action, combined with pulling on my belt, catches me by surprise and sends me face-first to the mat.

Continuing his momentum, Xande drives forward while lifting my left leg to get the reversal.

I land on my back and Xande takes the Side Control Position.

B. OVER-THE-LEGS PASS DEFENSE

Passes that go over the top of the legs are just as formidable as their under-the-leg counterparts. Once again, mobility is the key and you must develop an instinctive hip escape to combat all the variations. The goal of the over-the-leg passer is always to control your legs and hips with downward pressure and then move his body to your side. The theory for defending against this is always the same. Use hip movements to create angle or to escape the control, and straighten your body to realign yourself with your opponent. If you are both on the same line, he cannot pass your guard. Once here, establish your angle and prevent the pass with early movement and angle changes.

17-3 LEG-SQUEEZE DEFENSE

If your opponent manages to hug both your legs, he has a very strong pass at his disposal. Don't fret. Look at his control and see what he lacks. Obviously, both his arms are busy controlling your legs, so he cannot release his grip easily to control your upper body. If he does, recover the guard. Use this to your advantage. In the following move, be sure to pay special attention to how Xande drives my head away from him and then turns his body to break my grip. The first motion taxes my grip to the limit and the second breaks it easily.

Xande has his knees locked together and I am in a great position to pass the guard.

As an initial defense, Xande sits up on the same side of my head and posts his right arm for base. He then reaches under my head with his left hand and grabs the cross-collar grip.

To escape my grip on his legs, Xande straight-arms my body away from him while turning face down and away from me. This gives him the space necessary to free his knees.

Xande finishes the defense by turning back into me and establishing the Open Guard.

17-4 FAILED LEG-SQUEEZE DEFENSE

In principle, you are driving your opponent's head away with your collar grip, but it is less efficient to do the same with a push. One reason is that often you will have to use both hands to get the necessary drive into your opponent's head. This inhibits your ability to escape your body onto your hip, and the result is just a sore neck and wasted strength. In addition, because the legs are trapped, there is no available knee or leg to impede the pass.

Once again, I have Xande's knees squeezed together and I am attempting to pass (1).

Instead of grabbing my collar, Xande opts to push my head away from him with both hands (2).

I capitalize on Xande's error by grabbing his left collar with my right hand. He is still hoping to push my head away (3).

By turning my head in the direction of the push, I easily escape this nuisance and pull myself up to his Side Control (4).

17-5 OVER-AND-UNDER SMASH DEFENSE

The Over-and-Under Smash Pass may seem like an under-the-leg pass, and the truth is that it can be. However, in this variation, the pass is used as a hip block and not a stack. Once the block is achieved, the goal of the passer is to walk his legs over the bottom leg and establish Side Control. Although this pass can feel daunting to defend against, continue with your gameplan of escaping the hips and focusing on your opponent's weakest link. In this case, focus your attention toward your opponent's exposed, underhooking arm and transition into a clean, crucifix-style position.

I have Xande flattened out and I am in a good position to pass with the Over-and-Under guard pass. Xande braces his right hand on my left shoulder to inhibit the pass.

To make space, Xande places both feet on the mat.

Next, he hip escapes backward and to his left to gain some space for the reversal.

With space between our hips, Xande comfortably sits up and grabs the back of my belt with his left hand. While coming up, Xande traps my right arm with his left leg in a scissor hold.

Xande slides his right knee out and finishes his transition to the top. My right arm is still trapped and I am at risk for multiple arm attacks and chokes.

17-6 FAILED OVER-AND-UNDER SMASH DEFENSE

Once again, Xande goes for the wrong option and tries simply to push my head to the inside. If you insist on using this style of defense, you must remember two things: always push your opponent's head toward his body and keep your outside leg high to prevent the pass. If you fail to do so, your opponent will always have an easy guard pass.

This time, Xande tries to defend the Over-and-Under Pass by pushing my face toward the inside.

Xande has committed a pivotal mistake and I easily step over his leg as he continues his push. By pushing my face inside, Xande has actually helped my body move in the direction of the pass.

I anchor the Side Control position.

17-7 SAME-SIDE KNEE BLOCK

This is one my favorite and one of the most simple guard passes, and the defense to it is just as basic. The goal of the passer is to drive his outside knee to the mat while keeping hip-to-hip pressure. To do so, the passer ideally needs you, the person on the bottom, to be flat on your back. This is the first goal of the defender: always keep an angle and never let your opponent flatten you. The second goal is to use your top knee and shin as a wedge to keep distance between your opponent and you. Thirdly, learn to use this wedge as an axis to pivot your head away from your opponent's to realign the guard. These three defensive measures are fundamental, so learn to use them now and look for them in other later techniques.

Xande is using the basic Open Guard and I am trying to pass on my feet.

Trying to get an advantage, I drop my left shin on Xande's right thigh and pressure into him for a pass attempt. He immediately places his left knee in front of me to block my path.

3

As I try to drive my weight onto him, Xande places his left hand on my left shoulder to further frustrate my advance.

4

Pushing off with his left shin, Xande pivots his body away from me and successfully nullifies my angle of attack.

5

With proper distancing, Xande escapes his right leg and re-establishes the Open Guard.

17-8 FAILED SAME-SIDE KNEE BLOCK

Remember, your top knee is a block against your opponent's weight. To effectively carry his weight, your knee should be pointed at least forty-five degrees away from your other leg. If your knees get too close to each other, your opponent will be able to drive your knees together with his body weight and nullify your defense.

Again, I try to pass with my Same-Side Knee Pass and Xande initially defends with his left knee block.

This time, Xande mistakenly grabs my right collar with his left hand, thinking he can use it to push me away.

Capitalizing on Xande's error, I underhook his exposed left arm with my right and collapse my weight onto his left leg. From here, I am in a great position to pass the guard.

17-9 KNEE-SLIDE BLOCK

The Knee-Slide Pass, or Knee Up the Middle, is one of the most powerful passing techniques in jiu-jitsu. Though it can be quite uncomfortable for you as a guard player, it is pertinent that you strengthen your resolve and focus on your defensive tactics. As with the defensive aspects of the last technique, once again, these movements will come in handy. Remember, it is the movement that is critical, not the technique. A million techniques are worthless without good movement.

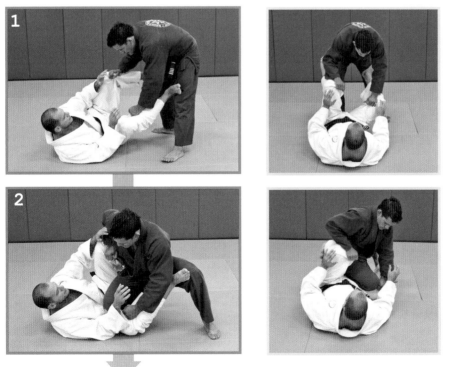

Once more, I am in Xande's Open Guard trying for a pass. I am gripping both his knees for control.

Pushing down on Xande's right leg, I drop my right knee on top of his thigh to initiate the Knee-Slide Pass.

3

Xande's first line of defense is to block my forward momentum by placing his left shin between his body and me.

4

Similarly to the last defense, Xande pushes me away with his left hand on my left shoulder.

5

Pushing off his knee, Xande pivots his body away from me.

6

Fearing that I am about to miss the pass, I try to stand up and run around the left side of Xande's body.

7

Xande simply rides my movement with his left hook and faces me to regain the Open Guard Position.

17-10 EARLY TORREANDO GRIP BREAK

The Torreando Pass, or Bull Fighter, is a common and highly effective method for passing the Open Guard. Its success is built on the fighter's ability to keep a distance from his opponent, lock the guard player's legs to the ground, and step to the side to complete the pass. The best way to counter this pass is with an early defense. Whenever your opponent pins your legs to the ground, always use this momentum to sit-up and grab the cross-collar in a Butterfly Position. The rule of this position is that you always have to break one of your opponent's grips, preferably the grip on your bottom leg. This will prevent your opponent from lifting your legs and forcing a second pass.

| I am in Xande's Open Guard, but I am gripping both his knees in an attempt at a Torreando Pass. | As I push Xande's knees to the ground for the pass, Xande sits into me and cross grips my collar with his right hand. He posts with his left hand to prevent me from pushing him onto his back. | Xande needs to break one of my grips on his pant legs, so he hip escapes back while stiff-arming me with his collar grip. My hand pops right off of his leg, and I lose control of the pass. |

17-11 COLLAR DRAG OFF TORREANDO DEFENSE

Once you have committed to the early defense, your opponent often will think his control on one leg is enough and will continue his original pass. As he walks toward your collar-gripping hand, launch your counterattack. The collar drag technique is a powerful move that will catch even the best jiu-jitsu players off guard. Integrate this into your Torreando defense, and your defensive game will become much more threatening.

Xande has managed to defend my Torreando Pass early and already he has broken my control of his left pant leg.

As I try to walk around to Xande's right side to pass the guard, he springs the trap.

Xande pulls down on my collar in the direction of my movement and switches his hips to face me. This sends me facedown– fast.

Continuing with his momentum, Xande turns into me and grabs my leg as I shoot past him.

Using his collar and leg grips, Xande rolls me over to complete the sweep.

17-12 ANKLE PICK OFF TORREANDO DEFENSE

Similar to western boxing, combinations are the key to success in jiu-jitsu. You cannot always expect your first option to work, especially against a strong, athletic, or knowledgeable opponent. This is where the ankle pick comes in handy. As you defend the Torreando Pass and attempt the collar drag, your opponent may choose to lower his base and resist the forward pull. This feeds right into the action-reaction paradigm of jiu-jitsu. As your opponent resists backward, pursue him in that direction for the easy sweep.

Xande has successfully defended my Torreando attempt and now is initiating his game.

Fearing that he will try the collar drag, I step my right leg back as I base toward my rear.

Rapidly, Xande rushes into me, pushing my posture back with his collar grip. At the same time, he grabs behind my right ankle with his left hand.

Then, Xande posts his left foot behind him for base.

And pushes off his left toes. At the same time, he drives with his right arm and pulls my foot off the ground with his left.

Xande maintains his control as he finishes the sweep.

17-13 LATE TORREANDO BLOCK

Sometimes, even the best guard players are late to defend the pass. In the case of the Torreando, a fast passer often can get the jump on you and instantaneously move to your side. Do not give up and accept the pass. Stiff-arm the passer's shoulder to halt his progress and regain your composure. Then, go back to your hip escape and straightening game to realign the guard.

Xande has me in his Open Guard and I am in control of his knees.

In an attempt at the Torreando Pass, I drive Xande's knees to the ground. This time, he is late to sit-up with the early defense.

3

I step around Xande's legs, passing to his right side. He manages to block my effort by straight-arming my left shoulder with his left hand.

4

As Xande holds my body in place, he hip escapes to his left to make space.

5

Next, he slides his right leg in front of my legs as he brings our bodies back in line with each other.

6

Xande finishes by squaring his hips and recovering the Open Guard.

17-14 TWO-HANDED TORREANDO BLOCK

Although the previous move works on most occasions, there are still times when your opponent will fight for his life to continue with this pass. Most of these passers will try to collapse their hips onto you to smash their way to Side Control. You cannot allow this to happen. Utilize your inside hand to support your opponent's hips while continuing with your shoulder brace. Do not relax here, but hip escape quickly and recover the guard. This movement makes a great drill and should be practiced equally from both sides.

Again, I have driven Xande's legs to the ground and he is late to defend the Torreando Pass.

Xande tries the same defense as before by placing his left hand on my left shoulder.

This time, I defend by collapsing my weight onto my shoulder to break through his defense. Xande counters by placing his right arm on my hip to alleviate the pressure.

Immediately, Xande hip escapes to his left to make space.

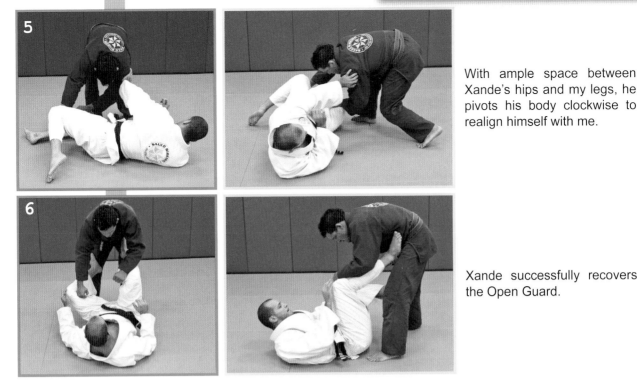

With ample space between Xande's hips and my legs, he pivots his body clockwise to realign himself with me.

Xande successfully recovers the Open Guard.

17-15 STRAIGHT ARMLOCK

The last time I trained with Rickson Gracie, this was one of the submissions he used on me, as well as everyone else. The beauty of this technique is in its simplicity. As the opponent tries to rush over your guard, you simply pivot your hips, control the arm, and get the tap. This is the magnificence of Rickson's game; tapping your opponent using only what he has given you combined with fluid body movement.

Xande is frustrating me with his feet-on-the-hips style of Open Guard, so I try to smash through his guard by pushing his right leg down while I hug his body with my right arm. Xande counters by controlling my right arm at the elbow.

Sensing my overexposure, Xande squeezes his knees together at my shoulder and traps my right arm.

As I try to pull my arm back, Xande pressures his legs downward on my elbow, catching the Rickson-style straight armlock.

17-16 OMOPLATA OFF STRAIGHT ARMLOCK

This is a move that combines well with the previous straight armlock and is one that I have seen my brother and Rafael Lovato Jr. use many times. As your opponent tries to pull away from the previous armbar, you let him go, taking the Omoplata as it presents itself. There is no fight in this technique, only the continuation of the movement that began with the guard pass and armbar attack.

To defend Xande's feet-on-the-hips guard, I try pushing his right leg down while I hug his body with my right arm. This time, I try to keep my weight centered to prevent myself from being armlocked.

With Xande's left knee crossing the plane of my back, he can push my face away from himself to make space. I cannot pass over to the side because his left knee is blocking me.

As Xande continues to push my head away from him, he uses his right foot on my hip to elevate his hips and climb his left knee high up my back. At this point, my arm is completely trapped.

Xande easily passes his left leg in front of my head into the omoplata position.

Grabbing my right wrist with his left hand, Xande escapes his right leg. Xande's legs are driving down heavily to keep me facedown on the mat.

Xande sits up while hip escaping slightly to his right. This further breaks down my posture and ensures a very controlled finish.

He finishes the submission by hugging my left hip to prevent my roll and sitting up slowly to apply the shoulder lock. Note: This move should be applied slowly and with control to prevent damage to your opponent's shoulder.

18-0 BUTTERFLY GUARD

The Butterfly Guard is the perfect guard for sweeps, especially when facing an opponent on his knees. Often called the "Hooks Guard", the Butterfly Guard is better described as a sitting guard position that uses a combination of leverage, momentum, and coordination to master.

This guard is a perfect fit for people with shorter legs, smaller stature, and a lack of flexibility. It works especially on heavier opponents because you have the capacity to off-balance them. This is because you can change the sides as you work the Butterfly Guard and redirect the game. The Butterfly Guard is a very offensive guard in terms of reversals, but not as aggressive in terms of submissions.

18-1 CONTROL AND DISTANCE

Controlling distance, movement, and your opponent's body are vital in the Butterfly Guard. Therefore, get comfortable with changing the range of this guard by moving in and out of attacking distance. As you learn more and more attacks, you will find that you can attack from either distance as you seamlessly flow between the two. Generally, the outside posture (1) is great for attacking submissions while the inside posture (3) is perfect for controlling the body with sweeps.

Xande has me in his Butterfly Guard. His right hand is grabbing a cross-collar grip while his right foot is between my legs serving as a hook. He has achieved the perfect angle by hip escaping slightly to his right and shifting his body off axis from mine.

To assist his base, Xande posts his left hand behind him. This will ensure that Xande is mobile enough to keep me in his guard if I start moving.

Circling his right arm under my left armpit, Xande makes a deep underhook, finishing with the belt grip for control. He further stabilizes his position by placing his head under mine – this prevents me from controlling him and placing him on his back.

18-2 CONTROL AND MOVEMENT

The best way to control the movement phase of the Butterfly Guard is to keep a slight angle. In doing so, you will free one of your arms to be posted on the mat behind you. This gives you the added benefit of mobility and base. If your opponent moves from side to side, you can follow easily by pushing your hips off the mat as you turn to face him. If your opponent tries to push you on your back, your posted arm will serve as a preventative brace to support your upright posture.

Xande has perfect inside posture and is controlling the Butterfly Guard.

I quickly move to the right to disrupt Xande's control.

Posting his left arm back slightly, Xande simply shifts his right leg to keep it between my legs.

Trying to expose Xande to the pass, I rapidly change directions to the left.

Once again, Xande rides my movement and uses his posting hand to pivot his hips in front of me.

18-3 SOLO BUTTERFLY SWEEP

Although the Butterfly Sweep looks like a simple rocking-chair motion, there is more to it than that. As you fall to your side, it is important to slide your bottom foot back and post it on the mat. Focus on this important detail. Once you have your foot posted, you can generate a great push off the mat. This amplifies your hooking sweep as it drives through even the toughest defense.

Xande is in a mock Butterfly Guard position.

In a continuous motion, Xande rocks his body to the left as he slides his left foot under his right knee.

Once Xande has fallen completely to his side, he pushes off the mat with his left foot while his right hook swings upward. In addition, Xande lifts his right elbow to simulate an off-balancing action.

18-4 CLASSIC BUTTERFLY SWEEP

The Classic Butterfly Sweep can only work when all the aspects of control, timing, balancing, and leverage are in harmony. For such a simple looking technique, this is actually quite technical and it will take some time and attention to master. This move has to be initiated from the proper angle. Doing so will create a perfect "hole" into which you drive your opponent. As with the solo drill, focus on the smaller movements, like using your body weight to pull your opponent to the mat, driving his posting hand inward along with your bottom foot, and driving off the mat with your posted foot.

Xande has me in the proper Butterfly Guard position to begin some attacks.

Once he is sure of his control, Xande grabs my right arm with his left.

Sweeping me toward my right arm, Xande drops his weight directly to his left and tucks my right hand to the inside while he slides his left knee under his right. At this point, I am completely off balance.

Pushing off his left foot, Xande raises his right hook in an arching circle to send me onto my side.

Unable to maintain my balance, I am swept onto my back.

Xande pulls his right leg under my armpit and consolidates the Side Control position.

18-5 FAILED BUTTERFLY SWEEP

One of the problems with staying square with both underhooks is that it makes it very difficult to accomplish the Classic Butterfly Sweep. As you swing your body from side to side, often you will feel that your opponent can base his hips low to the ground to minimize the sweeping effect. This results in your being flattened out in a disadvantageous position.

Xande has his hips square to me and is using the double underhooks to attempt sweeps.

Xande swings to his right and tries to take me off balance. Because he does not have a proper angle of attack, I easily follow him and keep my base close to the ground.

Xande sits up again to try the other side.

This time, Xande falls to his left and I counter by driving my body slightly toward his left hip. From here, I blanket my weight over Xande's right hip. I will not allow him to sit back up.

Using my right arm, I wheel Xande's body flat in front of me. This is a great position for me to nullify the power of his hooks and to pursue a guard pass of my own.

Figure 18.5: Inadequate Posture

Even if Xande manages to keep his head lower than mine and obtains the double underhook control (1), I can still survive his sweep attempt (2). This is because there is no empty space for me to be swept into. When Xande has the proper angle, he creates a huge space for my body to collapse into as he drives me to the mat. You have to make your opponent feel that he is being driven off balance, and he simply does not feel that when you play square with him.

18-6 WING SWEEP

Although the Butterfly Guard with the collar-grip control is often seen as a submission-oriented position, there are times when sweeps are possible. This is one such occasion. Often, when you are fighting in this position, your opponent will try to hug your top leg and initiate a pass. It is important not to lose your composure. Instead, control his hugging action and attack with the beautiful Wing Sweep. This is a highly effective counterattack that should be in everybody's Butterfly repertoire.

This time I am in Xande's Butterfly Guard and I am keeping my distance to avoid being underhooked or controlled. Xande uses his right hand in a cross-collar grip.

Feeling that Xande has exposed his right leg, I begin to wrap it with my left arm in pursuit of a guard pass.

Having perfectly read my intentions, Xande grabs my left sleeve with his left hand.

The collar grip is no longer necessary, so Xande releases the grip and grabs the center of my belt with his right hand.

Xande scoots his body toward me to get his hips closer.

Falling back while pulling on the belt grip, Xande brings my body onto his.

At the same time, Xande pulls with his sleeve-gripping left hand while he pushes his left hook skyward. I am unexpectedly thrown to my left.

Xande follows me to the top and obtains the Side Control position.

BUTTERFLY GUARD   ✳   151

18-7 STRAIGHT ARMLOCK DRILL

The straight armlock is the easiest armlock to get from the Butterfly Guard. However, it does take practice to develop the speed and precision required to finish this technique. Often enough, a strong, aggressive opponent will power out of the submission if it is not attacked perfectly. Therefore, drill this technique on both sides until you are confident in your ability to trap the arm, hip escape, and submit your opponent in one continuous motion. Be sure to use your body for the submission in a similar fashion as the straight armlock from the Closed Guard.

I face Xande in the basic Butterfly Guard. Xande holds my knees to prepare a pass.

Without delay, I circle my right arm under Xande's left until my hand reaches under his armpit.

As my right hand grips Xande's lat muscle, my left hand reaches over to control his left shoulder and upper arm.

I grip my hands together and lift my right elbow upward. This action pushes Xande's left arm onto my shoulder. I lock my head onto Xande's wrist for control.

Falling back to my left side, I place my right foot on Xande's hips and use my knee to push his body downward. Note the distance between Xande's elbow and the mat – this is the space I will drive his elbow into.

I finish the submission by driving Xande's elbow downward with my grip and knee while my head keeps Xande's arm straightened.

18-8 CLASSIC CROSS-CHOKE

The classic cross-choke is one of the most basic and also one of the most advanced techniques in jiu-jitsu. In other words, the technique is simple, but to implement it successfully takes great skill. This is why I use Helio Gracie's version of the technique. The Butterfly is probably the greatest guard from which to cross-choke because you can disrupt your opponent's base while he tries to defend your grips. The beauty of Helio's version is that you bring your hips underneath your opponent's and attack the choke while he is reconstituting his base.

I have Xande in my Butterfly Guard and I am cross-gripping his right collar with my right hand.

In one motion, I scoot into him and fall to my back. As I fall, I lift Xande with my right hook while pulling him toward my head with my collar grip.

I release the tension in my hook and Xande falls back into the guard position.

As he settles, I sit-up into him and pull Xande's head into my chest. Pulling with my elbows, I choke him with the classic cross-choke.

18-9 PALM UP-PALM DOWN CHOKE

The Palm Up-Palm Down version of the cross-choke is equally as effective as the last technique, and some would say even easier to get. However, if I try the same setup as before, I will be unable to finish properly. This is why I use this feint. By tricking my opponent into thinking that he will pass my guard, I can easily get the deep cross-collar choke. Do not worry about getting your guard passed, your choke and leg positioning should be enough to distract your opponent and prevent his escape.

Once again, I have Xande in my Butterfly Guard and already I have cross gripped his right collar with my right hand.

Falling back and to my left side, I let Xande drop his weight on my knees.

While Xande focuses on my legs, I grip his left shoulder next to his collar. My right palm is facing upward and my left palm is facing down. The choke is already very tight at this point.

Xande panics and tries to pull back, releasing the pressure on my legs.

I escape my right foot to Xande's outside and use it as a hook. This removes the barrier between him and me, and I can easily pull him back into the choking position for the tap.

19-0 SPIDER GUARD

The Spider Guard is a useful modern guard that employs double arm control over the guard passer. This is the guard where if you really want to hold somebody, you can. Passing this guard is also very dangerous because movement often leads to dangerous sweeps and submissions; this can be quite frustrating for the passer. Learn this guard and get used to the idea of "riding" your opponent's movements and guiding him like a puppet master.

When you use this guard be careful when trying to adapt your grips. Adapting collar grips to grips that break posture is not so hard to do without the gi, but grabbing both arms and holding on to play a true spider game is very difficult when there is nothing to grab on to. The grips are just too easy to break. This is a gi grappling guard that is difficult to apply in the context of MMA or submission wrestling. It can be a winning guard, but in the long term it can be detrimental to your development because it forces you to focus too much on the gi.

19-1 CONTROL AND MOVEMENT

When establishing the Spider Guard, it is critical to have complete control over your opponent every step of the way. Never attempt to transition to both spider hooks at the same time; you will lose control and your opponent will pass. Instead, develop a methodical circular leg movement to remove your opponent's grips one by one. Once your Spider Guard is in place, acquaint yourself with using alternating leg pushes and pulls to offset your opponent's balance and to set up your own attacks.

Xande has me in his Open Guard. Both his feet are on my hips and he is gripping both my sleeves. As with any Open Guard, Xande's hips are elevated off the mat for mobility.

To insert his left foot on my bicep, Xande circles his foot inside in a counterclockwise rotation. Xande keeps his right leg on my hip until he has control over my right biceps.

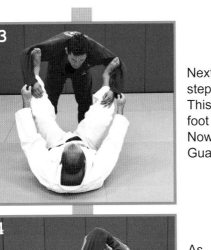

Next, Xande repeats this step with his right leg. This time, he circles his foot in a clockwise arc. Now, he is in the Spider Guard position.

As I move to my left, Xande bends his right leg and straightens his left. With my right arm rotating up and forward and my left leg pulling down, I am pushed off balance.

I realign myself square to Xande to recompose my balance.

This time I move to my right to test Xande's position.

Anchoring his feet to my biceps, Xande simply holds on and rides my arms until we are face to face again.

Figure 19.1: Hook Rotation

To emphasize the hook rotation, I stand in Xande's Open Guard and grab both his pant legs at the knees.

Keeping his right foot pressed into my hip, Xande releases his left leg and begins circling it counter-clockwise.

At the end of the revolution, he puts his left foot on my biceps near the crook of my elbow.

Xande drives my right elbow upward and to the right to take control. As he does this, he releases his right foot on my hip and begins circling it clockwise to the inside.

He continues his circle until his foot makes contact with my left bicep.

Xande extends his right leg and assumes control of the Spider Guard.

19-2 FAILED CONTROL AND MOVEMENT

If your opponent tries to circle his hands above your shins or below your calves, watch out – he is trying to break your grip! You can combat this with side-to-side hip movement, circling your feet, and push/pull leg extensions. If you do not react, you will find yourself in the following situations. Remember, when you are in the Spider Guard, you must move!

FAILURE TO STRAIGHTEN LEGS OR CREATE ANGLE:

Xande has me in the Spider Guard.

Quickly, I drop my hips as I angle my elbows to the mat. Xande fails to counter by straightening his leg or creating angle. His heels begin to slip off my biceps.

Once my elbows circle underneath Xande's heels, I drive my body forward. This stacks him and clears the way for my guard pass.

FAILURE TO MAINTAIN BICEPS PRESSURE:

Again, Xande has me in the Spider Guard.

Using my grips on his knees, I drive Xande's knees together. For a second time, he has failed to create proper pressure on my biceps and his inability to break my knee grip is proving costly.

I push Xande's feet to the ground. Immediately, I should pass with the Torreando while he continues to grip my sleeves.

19-3 SWEEP OFF A PASS

Most jiu-jitsu players like to keep their distance from the Spider Guard and pass it on their feet. This is a great tactic, and it is often very effective. However, the following technique is a great classic Spider Guard sweep that works best when your opponent is dedicated to the pass. By letting your opponent pass your guard, you actually trap him in your spider web. Once he realizes what has happened, it is too late, and he gets swept.

Xande has me in the Spider Guard and I am looking to pass.

As Xande drops his right leg to the mat, I step past his leg to pass the guard. He maintains his left spider grip and hook as he grabs my left pant leg.

Next, Xande bends his left knee, and I seize the moment to collapse my weight into him.

4

I land on top, but Xande drives my body off balance by straightening his left leg to the outside.

5

This action drives me onto my right shoulder and lightens my left leg. Xande uses this momentum to lift my left leg to assist the sweep.

6

Xande follows the sweep and ends on top.

20-0 CROSS-GRIP GUARD

The Cross-Grip Guard is another modern guard that owes its existence to the evolution of jiu-jitsu. Many great competitors such as Marcio "Pe de Pano" Cruz, Roberto "Roleta" Maghalaes, and Robson Moura have had great success with this guard position. Cross-gripping his sleeve while gripping his same side leg completely dominates one side of your opponent, while your feet frustrate his balance and posture. This is a great guard, especially for taller people, because it opens so many sweeps, Omoplatas, and triangle chokes.

20-1 POSTURE

Although some people just cross-grip the sleeve and grab the same side foot, I do not think this is enough. From experience, I know that my opponent will be pushing down on my legs as he tries to impose his game. Therefore, I utilize my feet as a hook and biceps control. This establishes a much stronger posture from which I can easily manipulate my opponent's balance.

Xande has me in his Open Guard and controls both my sleeves while pressing his feet into my hips.

Next, Xande releases his grip on my right arm and grabs a two-on-one grip on my left sleeve.

With a hip escape to his left, Xande pivots his head closer to my body and grips my left leg with his right hand.

Feeling that I still have control of his right knee, Xande circles his left foot counterclockwise until his foot rests on my biceps. Once there, he uses his foot to frustrate my movement.

Xande stabilizes the position by swinging his right foot inside of my right leg, hooking his foot behind my knee.

20-2 FAILED POSTURE

I cannot overemphasize the importance of involving your feet as a hook and biceps control. Aside from their obvious control, the actual positioning of your feet keeps you at an angle that makes passing very difficult. The following is an example of what happens when you fail to properly use your feet and create angle.

Xande has the cross-grip, but he has failed to hip escape, control my biceps with his left foot, and hook my knee with his right.

With nothing in the way to stop me, I cut my left knee to the inside as I push Xande's right leg downward.

I press my left knee forward to leave Xande in a very defensive position.

20-3 CLASSIC TRIPOD SWEEP

The Cross-Grip Guard is a great platform for sweeps and the Classic Tripod Sweep is one of my favorites. In this move, your body acts as a tripod as you grip your opponent's ankle with one arm, hook the leg with your bottom foot, and push on his hips with your top foot. The result is an effortless sweep that trips your partner backward. As you drill this technique, focus on the push-and-pull aspect of the move as you drive your legs in opposite directions.

Xande has me in a modified Cross-Grip Guard position with his right foot pushing into my hip.

He then transitions to the Tripod position by circling his left hook clockwise until it locks behind my right knee.

Without missing a beat, Xande pushes hard with his foot on my hip while blocking me with his right-hand grip. As he does this he lifts his left hook to topple me backward.

Xande transitions into the top as I land flat on my back. He removes his right foot from my hip as he moves to his knees.

Still controlling my right leg, Xande also drops his right knee on top of my thigh to pressure my guard.

20-4 CROSS-GRIP BACKROLL SWEEP

Knowing that the Tripod Sweep is a viable threat, many sparring partners will keep closer to you to prevent the maneuver. This is the perfect time to attack with the Backroll Sweep. Because this move works in the opposite direction of the Tripod, it serves as a great complementary technique. As you feel your opponent pushing back into you, pull him right into this move. Timing is critical, so get used to going between this and the previous technique until your body recognizes when to pull for the Backroll or push for the Tripod.

Xande has the Cross-Grip Guard and I am struggling under his control.

With a pull of his left-hand grip, Xande drives my body forward and on top of him. He uses his right knee to keep my weight off him.

Next, Xande backrolls to send me flying to my back.

Continuing the backroll, Xande rides the momentum until he lands in the top Half Guard position.

21-0 DE LA RIVA

The De La Riva or Outside Hook is the brainchild of jiu-jitsu expert, Ricardo De La Riva. Although the move originated many years ago, De la Riva is credited for popularizing the position around 1981 and developing many of its sweeps and submissions. This can be a very offensive guard as it leads to triangle chokes, submissions, and sweeps. In addition, guard passers often dread this position for its ability to manipulate the balance of the standing guard passer.

21-1 STARTING POSITION

The De La Riva Guard is known for its outside hook, but the ability to control your opponent's heel and push his hips with your free leg is just as important. The following drill should help you understand the splitting action of the De La Riva. As you hold one of your partner's legs in place, you force him into the splits by forcing his other leg back. This off-balancing is integral to this guard position.

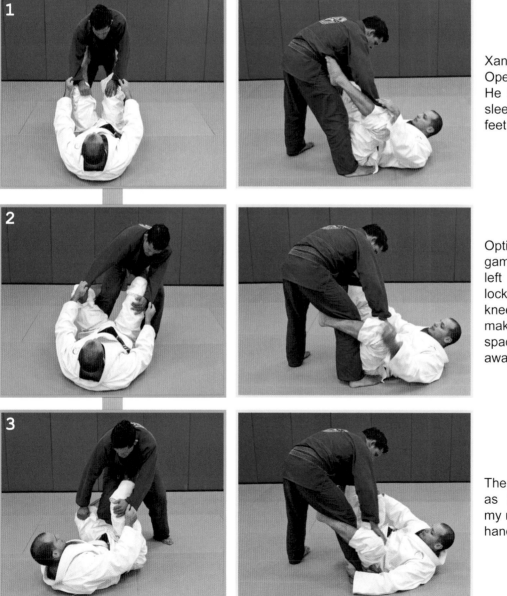

Xande has me in the Open Guard position. He is controlling both my sleeves while pressing his feet into my hips.

Opting to change the game, Xande circles his left foot outside until he locks it behind my right knee. His right leg helps make the appropriate space by pushing my hips away from him.

The position is cemented as Xande grabs behind my right ankle with his left hand.

21-2 POSTURE BLOCKED

As you control your opponent, you cannot let him square up to you and forcefully remove your hook. Always use your free foot to push off on his hips and frustrate his base.

Xande is attempting to put me in his De La Riva Guard, but forgot to push my hips away from him.

Because he is not in control of my hips, I simply push down on his left knee while turning my right knee outward to remove the De La Riva hook.

21-3 ROLLOVER SWEEP

This is a great go-to move from the De La Riva Guard. I love this technique because you do not have to release your control as you attack. All you must do is shift your body and extend your foot on the hip as you pull on your opponent's sleeve. The splitting motion of your feet, when combined with the inward drive of his arm, easily topples your opponent over his shoulder for the sweep. Remember, always attack with what you have before needlessly modifying your technique.

Xande has me in his De La Riva Guard.

2

Xande initiates the Roll Over Sweep by moving his right foot from my hip to my lower left thigh.

3

In a combined effort, Xande pushes on my left thigh while he pulls my left arm toward his body. This sends me off balance and I have to break my fall using my right hand.

4

Continuing the pulling and pushing motion, Xande drives me onto my left shoulder.

5

Xande follows me to the top position to complete the sweep.

Figure 21.3: Hook Release

Notice that as Xande sweeps me, he maintains his initial position until I have been completely rolled onto my shoulder (1). Once he can no longer push my thigh or pull my grip any farther, he releases his right leg and prepares to transition to the top (2). Only when Xande recovers his right leg under him will he have the leverage to finish sweeping me onto my back.

21-4 DE LA RIVA TO TOMOE-NAGE SWEEP

As with every sweep, I like to use its opposite side in case my opponent resists. The Tomoe-Nage is a wonderful complement to the Roll Over Sweep. As your opponent drives into you in hopes of resisting the Roll Over, he walks right into the Tomoe-Nage. To be effective with this sweep, get used to bringing your hips underneath your opponent's while lifting upward with both your hook and foot on the hip. While in the academy, be sure to control your partner's body with your arms and legs to ensure that he does not fall too hard on the landing.

Xande has me in his De La Riva Guard, this time choosing to control both my sleeves.

Using his right leg, Xande pushes into my hip to force my reaction. I take the bait by resisting his pushing motion. Now he has the perfect opportunity to launch his sweep.

Feeding off my forward momentum, Xande scoots toward me to get his hips underneath mine. As he does this, he pulls on my sleeves and bends his knees to support my incoming weight.

De La Riva Guard

Xande continues to pull me as he brings his knees toward his belly and then pushes his right foot and left hook upward. At this point, I feel light and my forward momentum carries me into the sweep.

I land flat on my back as Xande uses the momentum to backroll to the top.

Finishing in the Mount, Xande is in an excellent position to attack with a submission.

22-0 SIT-UP GUARD

The Sit-Up Guard is a continuation of the De La Riva position. Often as you force your opponent backward (or he steps this way on his own volition), you follow him into the Sit-Up Guard. This sit-up action, similar to the Early Torreando Defense, should be second nature by now. Although submissions are unlikely, this is a great position for sweeps and takedowns.

22-1 POSTURE DRILL

The transition between the De La Riva Guard and the Sit-Up Guard is an important one to master. The following drill is a great warm-up for open guard practice and should be followed both forward and in reverse to illustrate the connection between these two guards. A key element to the Sit-Up Guard is not to be lazy. As you sit into your partner, there is often a tendency to hug his leg and release your control of his sleeve as you drop your foot off his leg. This is a mistake. Without driving your opponent back with your foot and controlling his arm, he can easily pressure into you and pass the guard. Drill this move until you can comfortably control the Sit-Up position.

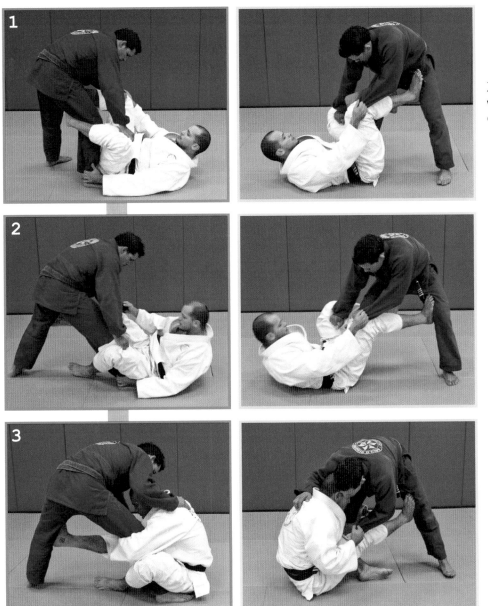

Xande is controlling me within his De La Riva Guard.

Xande decides to transition to the Sit-Up Guard. He drops his right foot toward my lower thigh/knee and pushes my left leg away from him.

As I step back with my left foot, Xande sits up into me and hugs my right leg with his left arm. His left leg encircles my right foot, trapping my leg in place. To keep control of me, he maintains his sleeve grip and pushing pressure on my thigh.

22-2 SIT-UP GUARD TO CLASSIC SWEEP

Similar to the De La Riva Roll-Over Sweep, the Classic Sweep follows the same philosophy and gets the same result. Once again, this is my go-to move from Sit-Up Guard as it leads to so many other favorable outcomes. If your opponent is proving difficult, you can always transition to single leg attacks and the following sweep to continue your sweeping bombardment.

Xande has me in the Sit-Up Guard and is in total control of me from the bottom.

Driving off his left leg, Xande propels his body to the right. This drives me forward and I place my right arm on the mat to prevent the sweep.

At this point, Xande pulls on my right sleeve to drive my left shoulder to the mat. Meanwhile, Xande has sucked his right leg back under him and he is ready to finish the sweep.

With a continuous pull on the sleeve grip, Xande sweeps me onto my back and takes the Side Control position.

22-3 REVERSE ROLL SWEEP

If your opponent reaches up with his free hand and tries to disrupt your posture, seize the opportunity and sweep him with his exposed arm. Instead of fighting and struggling to get the Classic Sweep, you completely change the angle with this surprising sweep. Remember, jiu-jitsu gives way to strength, and it should never meet it head on. This technique is a great example of giving way to force in order to achieve your objective.

Once again, Xande is controlling me from the Sit-Up Guard.

As Xande tries to initiate the Classic Sweep, I grab his left shoulder to try to push him off balance.

Instead of forcing the previous sweep, Xande gives way to my force and grabs my exposed right arm with his right arm.

Without waiting, Xande pivots to his left, falling to my backside.

Xande lands under my rear. Both my feet are in front of me and my base is compromised. This causes me to start falling backward.

Rolling to his right side, Xande assists my falling motion to get the sweep.

Xande finishes the sweep by rolling into the top Half Guard position.

22-4 FAILED REVERSE ROLL SWEEP

When doing the Reverse Roll Sweep, you have to commit to sliding all the way underneath your opponent's hips. If you stop half way, your opponent will easily pass your guard and change the game. Commit to your movements and trust in your jiu-jitsu.

Xande is gripping my right sleeve and attempting the Reverse Roll Sweep.

Unfortunately for my brother, he has not committed to bringing his body completely underneath mine, and he is trying to pull my arm for the sweep.

Without Xande's body underneath me, I easily sit down and begin working on a Half Guard pass.

23-0 REVERSE DE LA RIVA GUARD

The Reverse De la Riva Guard is one of the latest guards to evolve in jiu-jitsu. This preventative guard is a result of people learning how to break the De la Riva hook to impose their games. By transitioning to the Reverse De la Riva, guard players now have even more opportunity to continue with their sweeping attacks, or perhaps return to the De La Riva Guard.

This guard can be really frustrating and the great thing about frustrating guards is that they make it easier to break your opponent. This all comes back to having no mind and building an automatic reaction.

23-1 POSITIONING

The De la Riva Guard is a great starting point to transition to the Reverse De la Riva. Get comfortable with moving between the two guards just as you would between the Sit-Up Guard and the De la Riva. A good way to look at it is the Sit-Up Guard is the forward/backward transition of the De la Riva, and the Reverse De la Riva is the side-to-side transition. As you attain this position, it is okay to drop your previously hooked leg on top of your opponent's foot as long as you control his ankle. In addition, it is crucial that you keep your top knee angled upward to prevent yourself from becoming controlled.

Xande has me in the De la Riva Guard. This time, I am controlling both his knees.

As I turn my right foot to the outside to release Xande's left hook, I push his left leg toward the mat. Xande counters this by grabbing the cross-collar grip with his right hand.

Then Xande stabilizes the Reverse De La Riva Guard by hooking his right foot behind my upper-right thigh.

23-2 REVERSE DE LA RIVA DRILL

The Reverse De la Riva is a great guard to inhibit your partner's movement, and this drill can help you realize the potential of the position. Starting in your Reverse De la Riva Guard, ask your partner to turn away to free his foot. You should be able to hold onto him using your hook, bottom leg, and heel grip. This also simulates very realistic responses from surprised opponents. As your partner returns to the starting position, pull him toward you with your legs, abdominals, and grip to enter into sweeping range.

Xande begins in the Reverse De La Riva Guard.

As I turn around and attempt to pull my leg free, Xande has to use his hook and ankle-trap position to control my escape attempt.

When I turn back into him, Xande grabs my left lapel with his right hand.

Xande sucks his knees and feet toward his face while tugging with his right wrist to pull me forward. My base is now compromised with his hips underneath mine.

23-3 FAILED POSITIONING

Notice that in the following position, Xande has pulled me toward him, but he has not kept his top leg pointing upward. As I move into him, I simply push his knee down and control the position. With his hips restricted, it is likely that I will pass the guard.

I am in Xande's Reverse De La Riva Guard and I am pushing downward on his right knee.

Xande has failed to keep his right knee in an upright position. This allows me to push his knees together and sets up an easy guard pass.

23-4 KNEE PUSH SWEEP

The Knee Push Sweep is probably the sweep that I have been using the most lately. This move incorporates a lot of leverage and I really love sweeps that focus your energy onto your opponent's weakest link. Similar to the Underhook Sweep against the standing guard pass, you push your opponent's knee to the outside to dissolve his balance. The knee can only bend so far while standing, and the result is an easy sweep. Notice that the key is in how you pull your opponent toward you. Do not cross grip your opponent to pull him to you. Instead, grab the same side lapel to bring his entire body forward. Once there, execute this easy sweep.

Xande has me in the Reverse De La Riva Guard. He has his right hand on my left lapel for pulling power.

By pulling with his legs and lapel grip, Xande manages to bring his hips underneath mine.

Next, he releases his lapel grip and underhooks my left leg by the knee.

While holding my right leg in place, Xande extends his legs and drives my right knee to the outside. This unbalances my weight to the right and lightens my left leg for the easy pickup.

Unable to keep my balance, I fall to my back.

Xande finishes the sweep as he postures into my Open Guard.

The Half Guard is currently one of the most utilized and debated guard positions. There are those that see it as an attacking position while others see it only as halfway to being passed. My view is that the way I use the Half Guard depends on how my opponent is moving on top. If he is blocking my sweeps and stalling, then I am likely to recover guard. However, if he is engaging with me, I usually like to sweep and take the top.

The Half Guard is a great guard for people who are neither flexible nor athletic. It is not a purely offensive guard. The best kind of guard is one that combines submission attempts with escapes, survival, and sweeps. This is where you really want to be. The Half Guard does not have many high-percentage submissions, and it is mostly for reversing or sometimes stalling. However, it is a guard that is necessary, and I believe you need every type of guard position to cover all possible situations.

24-1 REGAINING GUARD OR CONTROL

When you first begin to use the Half Guard, it is likely that it is because your opponent has forced you into this position as he tries to pass your guard. This is not the time to practice a sweep you may have seen. As a first step to developing your Half Guard game, become comfortable with recovering the full guard. Although this may seem conservative, it will pay off with huge dividends as you later experiment with sweeps and submissions. This move is important and it always should be used as your lifeline back to the full guard.

I have Xande in the Half Guard, but he has managed to underhook my left arm.

To setup my recovery, I step back my left leg, chambering it close to my rear.

3

In unison, I bridge off my left leg as my left arm punches to the right. This forces Xande's head away from me and gives me space to escape.

4

Immediately, I hip escape to my left.

5

Utilizing the space from my bridge and hip escape, I place my left shin in front of Xande's abdomen.

6

Pushing off with my shin, I swing my head back so both our bodies are on the same line. I stabilize the position by sliding my left knee upward to block Xande's pressure.

24-2 IMPROPER CONTROL

Following are some common fallacies and misconceptions regarding Half Guard control. Study these movements to ensure that you are 100 percent comfortable with the reasoning behind the perfect body positioning.

Trapped Arm:

Here, I have allowed Xande to flatten me and get the underhook on my left arm. I am making no efforts to escape, and Xande will inevitably tighten his control and escape. In addition, my left arm is exposed to potential armlocks.

Whizzer:

Although I have the cross-face block and my left arm is underhooking Xande's right arm, he has my right arm whizzered, and I am at risk for arm attacks and chokes.

Reaching for the Legs:

This time, I have a good underhook on Xande's right arm, but I am reaching too far to underhook his left leg.

I am too exposed and Xande easily sets in a cross-face control. He does not worry about my leg grab because I cannot get under his legs when they are close to each other and driving away from me.

Xande has established his position, and I decide to close my Half Guard. Unfortunately for me, this locks me into his game and does nothing to assist my escape.

24-3 DEEP CONTROL

The Deep Half Guard is my go-to position for attacking sweeps from the Half Guard because it offers me so many opportunities. By sliding completely underneath my opponent, he cannot back his hips away from me and his cross-face becomes all but useless. In addition, I can offset his balance to either side with impunity. The key to getting this position is in how you release your opponent's weight forward as you slide your weight underneath.

I have Xande in my Half Guard, and I am using my left shin and hand to keep distance between our bodies.

Releasing Xande's weight off of my shin, I turn inside as his weight carries him over me.

I continue to turn into him until our bodies are perpendicular.

With control of Xande's belt with my right hand, I establish the Deep Half Guard. He is off balance with my hips directly underneath his.

24-4 GETTING EVEN DEEPER

Sometimes, you get to the Deep Half Guard, but your opponent still manages to escape his hips back. At this point, your goal is to get your hips underneath your opponent's with the least possible effort. To accomplish this, use the pendulum swing. By straightening your legs from the inside to the outside in a wide arc, your hips will automatically transition underneath your opponent's. This is proper body mechanics at its finest.

Beginning in the Deep Half Guard, I need to get under my opponent instead of facing him.

First, I initiate a strong pendulum motion by straightening my legs to the right.

I follow this by swinging my legs to the left. As I reach center swing, my hips slide directly underneath Xande's.

Terminating my swing to my left, I find myself in a very deep Half Guard position.

I hug Xande's right leg to finish the position. A sweep from here is almost inevitable.

24-5 BACKDOOR TO BACK

Once you have achieved the Deep Half Guard, you must always get the sweep. In my opinion, this is the best sweep from this situation. To be successful here, establish a hook to lift your opponent's trapped leg and move it away from you. Be careful not to forget about your body movement. You must use your shoulder to drive your opponent's weight forward as you move his leg. This opens up plenty of space for you to come to your knees and take the Back.

I begin with Xande in my Deep Half Guard.

To initiate the sweep, I hook my right leg underneath Xande's right ankle. My high knee and arms will prevent Xande from pulling his leg back.

Using my right hook, I push Xande's leg toward my left. As I do this, I begin scissoring my left leg back.

Coming to my knees, I drive Xande forward by pushing him with my shoulder pressure.

I escape my head and maintain control over Xande's right leg.

Knowing that he can no longer scramble away from me, Xande drops his weight and I finish the sweep on top of the Turtle position.

Figure 24.5: Hook and Shoulder Detail

As I push Xande's right leg away from me, it is vital that I bump him forward with my shoulder. This gives me the space I need to come up to my knees and finish the sweep. If I miss this critical piece, Xande will turn to his right and pass my guard as I move his foot away from me.

24-6 BOTTOM ARMLOCK - KIMURA

Although many like to teach the Kimura lock from the Closed Guard, I actually think it is better to teach it from the Half Guard. From the Half Guard, I can really lock my opponent into the submission as I take my time to erode his defense. The key to this position is twofold: keep your legs locked to prevent the spinning armbar counter and drive your body to the inside until you are perpendicular to your opponent. Once perpendicular, you will easily beat your opponent's defense by rotating toward his head and levering the power of your body against his defensive grip.

Xande is in my Half Guard and I am controlling his right wrist with my left hand.

Reaching over his right elbow with my right hand, I clasp my left wrist in a figure-four lock.

Next, I penetrate my body deeper until my body is perpendicular to Xande's. As I do this, Xande defends the Kimura attack by grabbing inside his right thigh.

I continue to inch to my left until I cannot progress any farther. Then I shift my entire body to the right to break Xande's defensive grip. The submission comes on very fast and Xande has no other alternative but to tap.

24-7 INCORRECT KIMURA

I have seen this mistake over and over. One person gets the figure-four hold and he immediately tries to muscle the submission from this sideways position. Have patience with this submission! It is not a race, so get the proper positioning before trying the attack and you will avoid the following situation.

I have achieved the figure-four lock on Xande's right elbow and I am trying to attack the Half Guard Kimura.

Instead of shifting my body to the left to make the proper angle, I turn immediately to my right to wrench the submission. From here, Xande can defend easily and eventually escape or counter with his own submission.

The Brown Belt's Mission:
PASSING THE GUARD

"It is a power stronger than will. Could a stone escape from the powers of gravity? Impossible."
—Isidore Ducasse Lautreamont

4.0 THE PRINCIPLE OF PASSING THE GUARD

Passing the guard is never a fair match because it is always two against one. It is me and the gravity of the world against you – the guard player. How can this be a fair match? I have all the elements of passing, plus my friend gravity against your sole body. So, I must take advantage of this.

I will never battle you one against one; this is the course of struggling and desperation. Instead, the first thing I do is make sure you cannot lock me with any kind of game and that I can consistently put my weight into you, with help from my friend gravity. This is the theory. If you cannot hold me with a sneaky game and I am able to drive my weight toward your body, I will be able to pass your guard. It is that simple.

4.1 THE BUILDING BLOCKS OF PASSING

Like everything in this book, I see passing as survival, escaping, and killing. This is no different from any other aspect in jiu-jitsu. I am not interested in acquiring and teaching a million

positions, but only those core areas that translate to a million positions.

Survival in guard-passing is the ability to prevent submissions and sweeps with posture and proper angle. Once you can survive in the guard, you can kill it. This is important for high-level passing. If you are constantly defending submissions, you are not passing. You are drowning. Learn posture and angle to eliminate your opponent's threat.

Escaping the guard depends on your ability to escape submissions and sweeps to get back to survival. In the guard, there is one benefit. You always have gravity on your side. Use your weight and angle to increase the effectiveness of your escapes and turn the cards on your opponent's attack.

By now you may think killing refers only to submissions, but it is actually the ability to pass with complete control as well. This is domination.

4.2 PREVENTATIVE ASPECT OF PASSING

When it comes to passing my opponent's best guards, my goal always is to prevent him from ever getting where he wants to be. If I let him go too far, I will be in for a fight and I do not

Case Study 4.0:
Saulo Ribeiro - Choosing Your Strategy

Photo: Catarina Monnier

Although I love to play the guard in the academy, in the tournament I do not have the time to wait for my opponent's reaction because I want to impose my game to win. So, it isn't about me being comfortable, relaxing, and playing. It is about being sharp, getting to the point fast, and shutting down my opponent. That is what competition is all about. It has nothing to do with the beauty of the art. It only has to do with winning the game that I am playing.

Since I was a white belt in judo, growing up in Manaus, I loved the top game. When I started doing jiu-jitsu, I began developing my guard until it was at a high level. However, my true nature is to be on top, and that is where I will always feel the most comfortable. So, when I compete, my strategy is to stay on top. This comes naturally because of my comfort and natural tournament aggression.

Look at your nature and feel where you want to be when you compete. Then, develop a strategy that maximizes your game and sets you up for victory.

want this. My jiu-jitsu is based on anticipation. I don't have to solve a problem if I can prevent it from materializing.

Furthermore, it is unlikely that all the different types of games are present at any one academy or in every competition you will fight. You cannot expect to beat each type of game, especially if you do not encounter each type regularly. So, the smartest way to prepare for these games is prevention. My jiu-jitsu is preventative. Some say, "What happens if he holds here and holds there and does this and pulls that?" I say, "If you let it go that far, you're in trouble – you're in his game." You deserve to tap and he deserves to get the kill. You let it go all the way over the edge. That's when you tap.

Learn to get into your position with control and understand all the different aspects of blocking your opponent's game and you will rarely have to deal with it. As with everything, control is essential.

4.3 PRE-EMPTIVE ASPECT TO PASSING

As you develop your passing game, it is vital to focus on the preemptive aspect of passing. This means you should be the one dictating the pace, opening the guard, and controlling him afterward. Doing this ensures your control of the game and sets up what you want to do next. Failure to do so results in stagnation as you struggle to deal with your opponent's guard game and fight to regain control. Seize your opportunity and be the one to dominate the opening, control, and pass from the beginning.

4.4 GUARD PASS TRAINING

Similar to guard training, there must be limits on guard-pass training to assist the passer in his skill acquisition. You are never going to be able to expand your skills if your opponent can do everything. If you try to pass without limitations, you will be defending yourself against sweeps and submissions, instead of focusing on that which you are trying to better.

A good drill is to have your opponent play certain guards that trouble you while trying to pass with all options. As you progress, let him apply more and more of his attacks until he is using his entire arsenal to stop your progression. This is how to gauge when your guard-passing skills are improving.

4.5 PASSING AND THE BROWN BELT

Passing the guard becomes a pivotal part of the brown belt's game and must be understood before reaching the black belt. The brown belt needs to develop his awareness, balance, and sensitivity so that he can adapt his passing principles to many types of opponents and guard games. Once again, the brown belt can do so because he has developed the building blocks of his survival, escapes, and particularly his guard, to a high level.

The brown belt is the guard-passing belt because a student needs the experience and knowledge of guard games in order to become an efficient passer. Just as soldiers become field commanders, guard players often make great passers because they know what it takes to control the guard; therefore, they understand how to deconstruct the position as well.

A. PASSING THE CLOSED GUARD FROM THE KNEES

The Closed Guard from the knees is a dangerous place to be. To learn how to defend the Position, first look at the goals of the guard player. The primary goal for the guard player is to break the posture. By breaking someone down within the guard, it becomes much easier to control, submit, and sweep him. The second goal is to attack with submissions and sweeps, even if the guard passer is postured.

As a guard passer, be concerned with keeping your posture and base, defending your neck, protecting your arms, and controlling your opponent's hips and posture. Always fight to establish a strong posture where your neck and arms are safely protected. If you don't, your opponent can easily initiate arm attacks and sweeps. Do not allow your opponent to sit-up into you or pull you into a broken-down Position. Defend your neck! Protect your arms. Your arms are exposed in front of you when passing the guard, so keep them occupied by controlling your opponent's posture and hips while you prepare your escape. Always be wary of your opponent's hip movement. Get used to moving with him as he escapes and moves, meanwhile stifling his range of motion with your legs and arms.

As a general rule for passing on the knees, always work your technique and be willing to reset. Anytime your opponent gets close to an attack, you should always address the attack and reset back to the beginning. The goal is to pass, not to submit!

25-0 BLOCKING THE COLLAR GRIP

Once you have set yourself in posture, it is very important not to give anything back to your opponent. I never like to go backward in my jiu-jitsu, and that is why I like to prevent my opponents from getting a favorable grip once I am in posture. The following strategy is great for preventing the collar grip with simple adjustments and posture. Stick to simple movements like these and remember not to go backward!

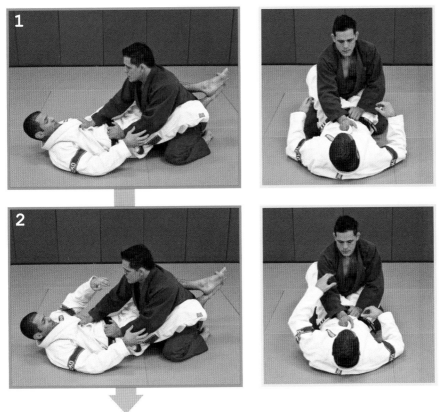

I am in Paulo's Closed Guard. My arms are staggered in front of me for posture and Paulo has been unable to gain control.

Paulo reaches over my right hand with his left to grab my collar.

As Paulo's hand approaches my collar, I deflect it away by driving my right elbow upward. At the same time, I angle my body and head to the left to keep myself at a safe distance.

Noticing my elbow is up, Paulo tries to sneak his left elbow underneath my arm and attack the collar.

Paulo has just made a tactical mistake. I turn my body back into him and drop my right elbow to trap his arm.

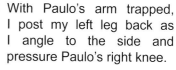

With Paulo's arm trapped, I post my left leg back as I angle to the side and pressure Paulo's right knee.

Driving my weight back and to the side, I create a wedging pressure that pops open Paulo's guard. From here, I can begin working the guard pass.

25-1 DEFEATING THE CROSS-COLLAR GRIP

Sometimes, your opponent manages to get the cross-collar grip anyway. The first step to beating this hold is not to panic. The second step is to understand the dynamics of the position. The goal of the cross-collar grip is twofold: to pull your posture downward or to set up the submission, preferably the cross choke. Knowing this, your goals are not to let your opponent break your posture and to use the proper angle to defeat the threat of submission. Using angle is a lot easier than complicated defenses and escapes. Therefore, it should be your first line of defense always.

When practicing this drill, master it to both sides. It will feel more native to one side, but you have to seek an ambidextrous defense because you never know what side your opponent will attack. In addition, always turn away from the grip and never toward it. If you make a mistake, it's lights out for you!

I begin the drill inside Paulo's Closed Guard. Both my arms are in front of me and I have yet to posture to my side.

Paulo reaches up with his left hand and grabs the cross-collar grip.

By turning to my right side, I unravel the strength of Paulo's position. My left hand becomes my posting arm as I move my right hand to the knee. I lift my right leg for base.

While pressing slightly on Paulo's left knee, I move my weight back and to the left to wedge open Paulo's guard.

I return to the Closed Guard and now Paulo grips my other side with his right hand.

Once more, I turn my body away from the grip, eliminating any threat of a potential collar choke. My right arm now posts on Paulo's midsection while my left hand braces against his knee. I post my left leg back for leverage and balance.

Paulo is unable to keep his legs locked as I move my body back and to the right.

25-2 OVERHOOK GUARD ESCAPE

The Overhook Guard is a very simple and highly effective way for your opponent to control you. To beat this guard, you should think about what it means to control it. First and foremost, your opponent's overhook and leg pressure keep your posture low. This leads to an increase in standard submission attacks, like cross chokes and straight armlocks. Secondly, this guard works best on the action-reaction principle. For example, if you pull your posture back, you open yourself to the straight armlock. Likewise, if you push or pull your arm another way, you may open yourself up to the omoplata or cross choke. Therefore, the secret to escaping this guard is blocking your opponent's attacking arm while using proper alignment to escape. Take your time with this defense and do not fall into the overwrap trap!

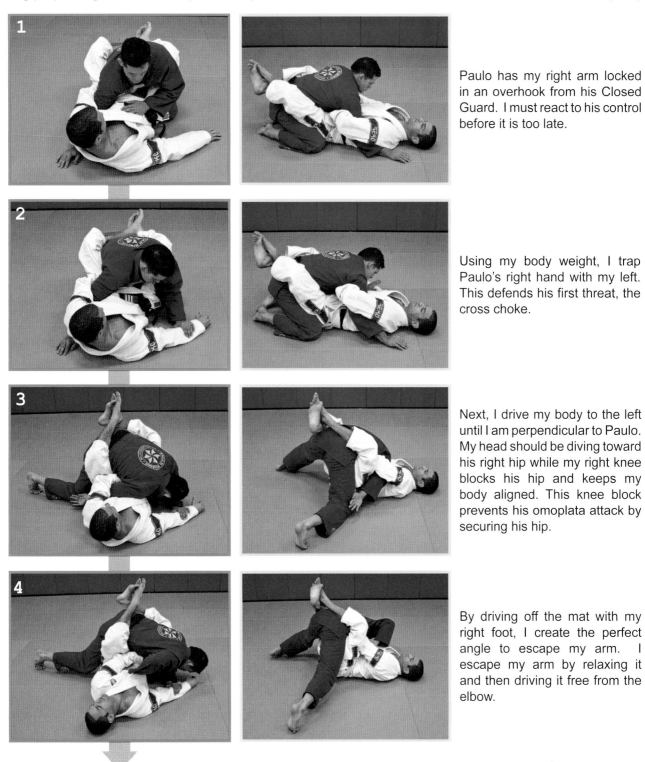

Paulo has my right arm locked in an overhook from his Closed Guard. I must react to his control before it is too late.

Using my body weight, I trap Paulo's right hand with my left. This defends his first threat, the cross choke.

Next, I drive my body to the left until I am perpendicular to Paulo. My head should be diving toward his right hip while my right knee blocks his hip and keeps my body aligned. This knee block prevents his omoplata attack by securing his hip.

By driving off the mat with my right foot, I create the perfect angle to escape my arm. I escape my arm by relaxing it and then driving it free from the elbow.

I continue to block Paulo's hip as I slide my right elbow toward his left hip.

Paulo's overhook has been thwarted and now I can focus on posturing out of his guard.

25-3 ESCAPING OVER-THE-SHOULDER BELT GRIP

The over-the-shoulder belt grip can be one of the most paralyzing situations for a guard passer. Your opponent has complete control of your posture and can transition easily to a triangle choke if you posture back or make a mistake. To beat this guard, focus on freeing your shoulder by turning away from the grip. Once you escape your shoulder, the belt grip becomes meaningless.

Paulo has successfully broken my posture as he controls me from his Closed Guard. He has his right arm in an over-the-shoulder belt grip to keep me tight. I must escape this position and regain my composure. My first line of defense is to keep both my hands on his chest to prevent a possible attack.

Next, I step my right foot to the left while keeping my hips low for base.

To nullify the escape, I pivot my body to the right as I lift myself with my left arm. I continue my turn until my left shoulder is free.

To break open Paulo's legs, I shift my body back and to the sides.

Figure 25.3: Don't Posture Up!

The over-the-shoulder belt grip is an advantageous position for your opponent, and it is critical that you do not waste your time or energy here (1). Remember, one of the goals of jiu-jitsu is not to tire, and there is no faster way to exhaust yourself in this guard than trying to pull back to posture out (2). Think of conserving your energy when you have to get out of tough situations! This will have the added benefit of exhausting your opponent as he fights to retain control.

Closed Guard

25-4 CLASSIC OPENING ON THE KNEES

This is the first guard opening I teach my students, and it is probably the one I have used the most. It is very simple, but do not make the mistake of trying to use your elbows to hurt your partner. This does not cause him to open his guard: it only gets him mad! Remember, you are not here to hurt your partners. Instead, use technical jiu-jitsu and preserve them. Change your angle to increase pressure on your opponent's locked feet and then move your body backward to generate opening power.

I begin in Paulo's Closed Guard with my right arm posting forward on his chest and my left hand grabbing his belt. The posting hand is important to prevent him from sitting into me or pulling me down to break my posture. My hand on his belt controls his hips to thwart any arm attacks or hip movement.

Angling slightly to my left, I draw my left hand back, hiding my elbow inside of Paulo's right knee.

Next I lift my hips high with my right leg and post my left leg to my rear left side. I make sure that I am always in balance between my knees. This posting action creates a more dramatic side angle to Paulo.

I lower my base as I pull my body toward my left knee.

To open the guard, I keep my left forearm on Paulo's knee and move my body backward. This action effortlessly opens Paulo's legs. As a side effect, my backward movement also creates an unfavorable angle for guard attacks from Paulo.

25-5 BLOCKING THE TRIANGLE

Whenever you open the guard from your knees, you must be mindful of your close arm and its relationship with the triangle choke. As you open the guard, always use your entire forearm and hand to block his inner thigh. Your opponent cannot get the triangle if he cannot use his leg. Also, keep your elbow tucked down under his legs to prevent him from pulling you into the submission.

Paulo has me in his Closed Guard with a cross-collar grip on my right lapel. Based on his grip, I post my right arm forward and stagger my left hand toward his hips.

Figure 25.5: Hand Block

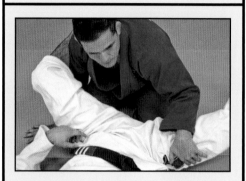

If I choose, I can also block the triangle by locking my left elbow to the outside of my left knee. This creates a very sturdy anchor. If Paulo decides to force my arm free by pulling with all his might, I simply will follow with my knee and crush his attempt. Once your arm is anchored here, do not allow your partner to muscle it free.

I step back with my left leg to change my angle with Paulo.

As I open the guard by moving my body backward, I make sure to hook the front of his thigh with my left hand while pressing downward with my forearm. I use my body weight behind my forearm to accomplish this pressure. Without trapping my right hand, Paulo will be unable to attempt the triangle choke.

25-6 FAILED TRIANGLE BLOCK

You are making a big mistake if you are only grabbing his pants with your inside hand. What do you think is stronger, your grip or his hips and legs? The hips and legs will win this battle every time, and in this case, the result is the triangle choke.

Paulo has me in his Closed Guard with the cross-collar grip. I am in perfect posture, angling my body away from his gripping hand.

I have started to angle my body to my left as I hide my left elbow inside of Paulo's right knee.

Unfortunately, I have forgotten to create downward pressure with my left forearm or to use my hand as a hook. Instead, I am only grabbing Paulo's leg with my hand. He takes advantage of my error by circling his knee over my left arm and onto my left shoulder. This puts me in incredible danger.

Now it is too late. Paulo has successfully trapped me in a tight triangle choke and I will be forced to tap.

25-7 OPENING WHEN OPPONENT HIDES BOTH ARMS

Oftentimes, an opponent will put his hands behind his head to prevent the standing guard pass. Although this effectively eliminates my ability to control his arms, it exposes him to a very obvious guard opening. If your opponent's hands are occupied, use this simple opening, and then, take advantage of his poor positioning.

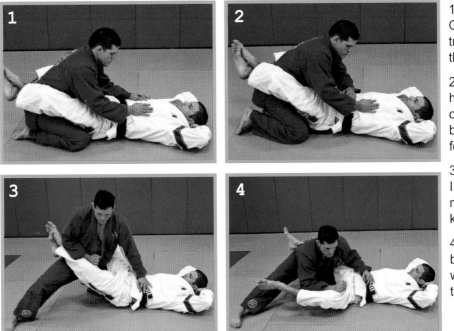

1) Paulo has me in his Closed Guard. To avoid having his hands trapped, he has decided to lock them behind his head.

2) With Paulo's arms behind his head, I will work the guard opening with impunity. I begin by blocking his hip with my left forearm.

3) While shifting to my right side, I elevate my posture and press my right forearm into Paulo's left knee.

4) Once again, I open the guard by moving my body backward while pressing Paulo's left knee to the mat.

25-8 BASIC SINGLE UNDERHOOK OPENING

The Basic Underhook Opening is a classic move taught in many beginning jiu-jitsu classes. Some think this move is too antiquated to be useful and others complain that this technique is a sure-fire way to get triangle choked. To all doubters I say this: if done correctly, your opponent will be unable to prevent the opening or triangle-choke you. The secret of this technique is not to hoist your opponent's leg to your shoulder. If you do this, you will die. Instead, keep your posture, and use your underhooking hand as a brace. Once this is in place, you can use your body movement to wedge his guard open. To me, this is a beautiful older-style technique that still works in the modern era.

Starting from Paulo's Closed Guard, I have my right arm forward with my left hand staggered back controlling the hip.

I change my angle by shifting my body to the left. As I do so, I place my left forearm on Paulo's right leg as I post my left leg to my side. My right arm posts on his chest to inhibit mobility.

As I try to continue the previous pass by pushing down on Paulo's leg, he resists and fights his hardest to keep his legs closed.

Instead of fighting against Paulo, I slide my left hand into the space between Paulo's right knee and my body. I make sure to stop as soon as my hand has cleared his knee. It is critical that I do not allow my elbow to pass the line of his leg.

Next, I step my left leg forward and rest my left hand on my knee. This movement locks Paulo's right leg in front of me.

I shift my weight back and easily pry open Paulo's Closed Guard.

25-9 BASIC UNDERHOOK PASS

This is the first guard pass you should learn in jiu-jitsu and it is important for many reasons. First of all, this technique introduces you to two of the most important aspects of passing: controlling the hips and stacking pressure. By grasping your opponent's leg with a deep underhook, you effectively negate his hip movement and control the direction of his guard. This action controls the fight for the passer. The stacking pressure further immobilizes your opponent as you make effective use of your own body weight plus the guard passer's best friend, gravity.

Use this guard pass throughout your development in jiu-jitsu; practice really makes perfect. Although some have decided that it is too dangerous because of the triangle choke, this is really an issue that can be negated by keeping your hips at an angle to diffuse the submission attempt. If you still do not believe in this technique, watch high-level black belt matches from champions like Roger Gracie and Xande Ribeiro and you are sure to see the efficacy of this move at the highest levels.

I have opened Paulo's guard and am ready for the pass.

In a swooping motion, I circle my right hand under Paulo's left leg until it reaches the mat. To protect against the triangle choke, I keep my posture low with my hips angling toward my rear left side.

I scoop Paulo's left leg to my shoulder by stepping forward with my right leg while lifting with my right arm. Once again, I keep my head upright and my left elbow hidden to prevent Paulo from pulling me into the triangle choke.

I grab Paulo's right lapel with my right hand. A thumb-inside grip gives me control of his upper body and threatens the choke. He cannot escape because I have trapped his hip by locking my right elbow and knee over it. My left forearm continues to prevent the triangle.

I jump up to my toes and begin driving Paulo's leg toward his head and right side. I make sure that my right elbow is pointed down to prevent Paulo from escaping.

Utilizing the power of my hips and legs, I drive off the mat with my toes while driving my core into Paulo's left leg. This causes his leg to clear my head without giving up hip control.

I maintain my current grips to take the Side Control position.

Closed Guard

25-10 BEATING THE BLOCKED HIP

Now that you are successful with the Basic Underhook Pass, it is important to look at one of your opponent's most natural and basic defensive techniques. After being passed several times with this technique, it is highly likely that even the newest student will begin pushing off your hips to prevent you from completing the pass. This straight-arm defense can be frustrating, even for the more advanced students. However, it is also easily defeated if you keep your wits about you. The trick is not to drive your weight onto his stiff arm; this only serves to keep your hips elevated, increasing the likelihood of a guard recovery. Instead, change your angle so that your knee slides inside of his stiff arm. This change of angle deflects his arm away from your hip and if done correctly, will result in the trapping of your opponent's pushing arm.

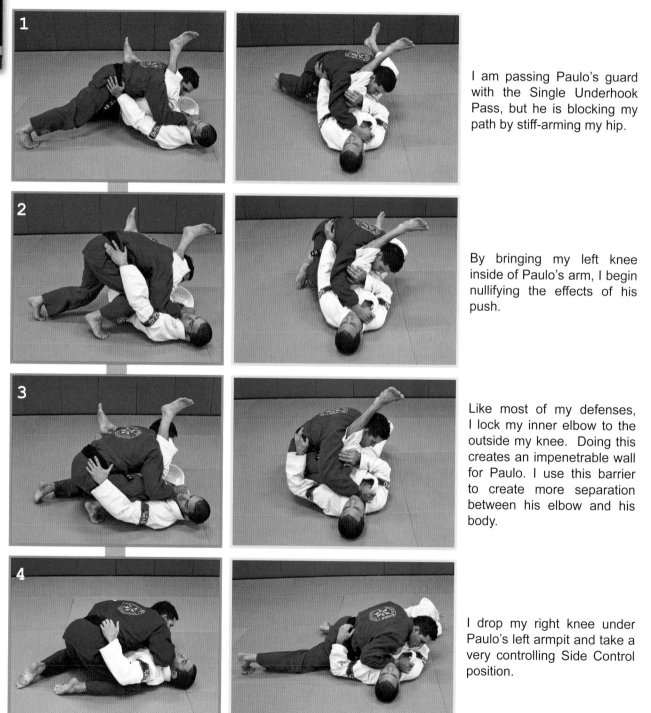

1 I am passing Paulo's guard with the Single Underhook Pass, but he is blocking my path by stiff-arming my hip.

2 By bringing my left knee inside of Paulo's arm, I begin nullifying the effects of his push.

3 Like most of my defenses, I lock my inner elbow to the outside my knee. Doing this creates an impenetrable wall for Paulo. I use this barrier to create more separation between his elbow and his body.

4 I drop my right knee under Paulo's left armpit and take a very controlling Side Control position.

25-11 BASIC UNDERHOOK PASS VARIATION

Oftentimes, a savvy opponent will escape his hips to the side when you attempt this pass. Not only will this change the angle to your pass, but it will also put distance between your body and your opponent's hips. If you try to force the original pass from this awkward position, you are likely either to assist his escape or to feed yourself into one of his attacks. To avoid this problem, regain control of his hips by flattening out his posture. By circling to flatten your opponent, you will create the perfect angle to control his hips and hop over to pass with this variation.

I attempt the Basic Underhook Pass, but Paulo manages to escape his hips to his left and slide his left leg between both my legs.

I drop both my hands to the mat in front of Paulo's hips.

With Paulo's hips locked in place, I can walk easily to my right to flatten him to his back. It is critical that I flatten his back to the mat.

Springing off my toes, I drive my hips high off the mat. While my hips elevate, I shove Paulo's right leg underneath me until it clears both my legs. It is important that I keep my shoulders tight to him throughout this action.

Having cleared Paulo's legs, I drop my hips on top of his and take the Side Control. Also, by keeping his legs pointed away from me, I inhibit his possible escape.

25-12 DOUBLE UNDERHOOK PASS

The Double Underhook Pass is a great companion to the classic Single Underhook Pass because it follows the same philosophy. Unlike other variations of this pass, I do not suck my opponent's hips onto my lap and clasp my hands together. I have faced many flexible guard players that make this difficult to achieve. My Double Underhook Pass uses one arm the same way as the Single Underhook Pass while the other arm blocks the opponent's leg and recovery. The secret to this technique is keeping your arm locked to your opponent's leg instead of reaching for the collar. By reaching, you may open your elbow and increase the chance of your opponent's escape. You may ask, "Saulo, how do I finish the stack if my arm is locked to his leg and I cannot pull my body into his?" The answer is simple. Finish by thrusting your hips to drive his leg away from you and you will not even have to worry about a grinding stacking pressure. The power of this technique is in the hips.

I have circled both my arms under Paulo's legs to attempt the pass. He is resisting by driving both his feet downward.

Circling my body to the right, I drop my left palm to the floor, letting Paulo's right leg fall to the mat. I continue to circle until I have Paulo's left leg on my shoulder. Once again, I use my body movement, not strength, to secure the leg.

I drop both my knees close to Paulo's hips to secure his leg. My right hip controls his hip for added control.

To clear Paulo's leg, I drive into him with my hips while propelling myself off my toes.

With Paulo's legs on the opposite side, I am clear to take control of the Side Control position.

25-13 DOUBLE UNDERHOOK PASS VARIATION

When passing with the Double Underhook Pass, look for this variation to present itself. Regularly, your opponent will keep his legs open while driving his legs and hips downward to prevent you from getting into a stacking position. As always, do not fight his momentum. If you feel his legs pushing to the mat, let them go. Give way to his force and take the opportunity to hop over his guard as his legs harmlessly fall to the mat.

Once again, I am double underhooking both Paulo's legs and threatening the pass. To defend, Paulo is trying to drive his heels to the mat while sliding his hips back.

This time, I decide to use a faster pass. I initiate it by pressing down on Paulo's right inner thigh with my left forearm.

Unexpectedly, I jump my left foot over Paulo's right leg while pushing downward with my left hand.

I land in Side Control while retaining control of Paulo's hips.

25-14 COMBAT BASE TO BASIC PASS

The Combat Base to Basic Pass is a vital technical series that everyone must master. First of all, let's discuss the role of the Combat Base. In this situation, I begin on my knees and open the guard into a kneeling Combat Base. Whether I am in a standing or kneeling Combat Base, the principle is the same. My forward leg serves as a wedge that inhibits my opponent's mobility and prevents him from closing the guard. To prevent my opponent's attack, I bind my forward elbow to the knee. This way, if my opponent pulls my arm, my knee follows in a pressuring fashion.

This pass is also the first time I introduce leg-on-leg trapping. Pay careful attention to using your forward leg to trap your opponent's bottom leg until you have managed to scissor your rear leg free. If you forget to do so, your opponent will more than likely lock the Half Guard position.

I have opened Paulo's Closed Guard and I am ready to pursue the guard pass.

While pressuring Paulo's left leg down with my right forearm, I penetrate my right knee to the inside of his legs, locking my elbow to my knee. This great defensive posture is the Combat Base position.

Immediately, I pressure forward with my knee, driving my weight onto Paulo. He reacts by trying to push my knee away from him.

Going with the direction of Paulo's pushing energy, I slide my knee to the right, flattening his left leg to the mat. Meanwhile, I continue to drive my hips forward.

I use my right hook to trap Paulo's left leg while cross-facing him with my right arm.

Pushing down on Paulo's right hip, I scissor my legs to my right to pass his guard.

To establish Side Control, I slide my left knee upward to block Paulo's hip and prevent the guard recovery.

Figure 25.14: Knee Detail

It is important to push your knee to the outside and not forward. Pushing your knee forward will only result in a battle of strength and we do not want that. Instead, slide your knee outward and use your hook to trap the leg. This hook is important if you want to finish this pass. Without it, your opponent will likely recover Half Guard and perhaps even Full Guard.

B. PASSING THE GUARD FROM STANDING

Standing passes offer their own risks and rewards that set them apart from passes on the knees. As for the risks, standing itself is a tenuous process where your balance will be constantly tested. Because you are upright and your base is high, the guard player does have some high-percentage sweeps at his disposal. Due to the distance between your opponent's body and yours, submissions are limited, but still they can happen from time to time, and there are a few to be wary of. The reward for standing passes is that you can generate a great deal of leverage with the assistance of gravity. Practice standing passes often and learn the balance it takes to adjust when your opponent attacks a sweep or submission. Once you get this down, your passing skills will go to another level.

25-15 BASE WARM-UP

If you have never practiced a standing guard opening or pass, I recommend trying the following warm-up. Start with your knees a little more than shoulder width apart and lock your elbows to your thighs. Sway your body from side to side while keeping your posture upright, and adjust your balance so that you feel rooted to the mat. As you get more comfortable, step back and mimic the standing guard opening while keeping the same balance and posture. This is a great way to loosen your body and develop your standing balance.

I begin standing with my feet a little more than shoulder width apart. Bending at my knees, I lean forward until my elbows lock just inside my knees.

Without moving my feet, I lean my hips to my right. While in this position, I can feel my body compensating as my weight shifts over my right foot.

Swaying back to my starting position, I square my hips again.

Next, I move my hips to my left. Once again, I wait a moment to acquire my balance.

Returning to the center position, I begin pushing my right arm forward as if to break open the guard. Notice my right elbow retains its contact with my knee.

While keeping my elbows locked to my legs, I step back into an athletic posture with my left leg. This simulates the guard opening posture.

25-16 STANDING CORRECTLY VS. INCORRECTLY

The ability to stand while your opponent has you locked in his Closed Guard is a skill that will take some practice to perfect. Always remember, while you attempt to stand, your opponent is constantly trying to attack and to knock you off balance. With this knowledge, you have to look at standing as a series of techniques built to defeat all your opponent's attempts at disruption. I recommend practicing this series as a drill until you can fluidly move from your knees to your feet without feeling the off balancing effects of your opponent.

As an exercise, study both the good and bad posture of this technique, paying special attention to how I lift my legs without toppling over. Again, the secret is in creating the ideal angle.

GOOD POSTURE:

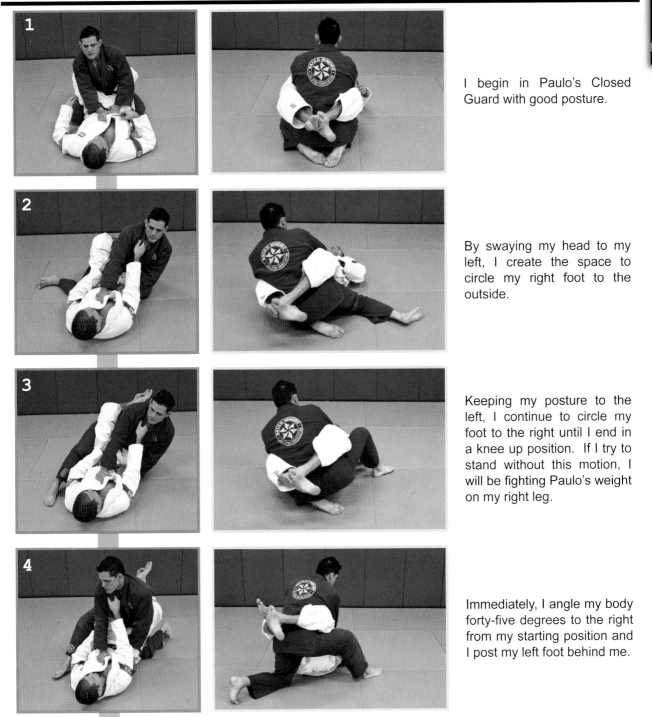

1 I begin in Paulo's Closed Guard with good posture.

2 By swaying my head to my left, I create the space to circle my right foot to the outside.

3 Keeping my posture to the left, I continue to circle my foot to the right until I end in a knee up position. If I try to stand without this motion, I will be fighting Paulo's weight on my right leg.

4 Immediately, I angle my body forty-five degrees to the right from my starting position and I post my left foot behind me.

While keeping my hands in posture, I drive off the mat with my left toes to come to my feet.

Finishing the position, I square my hips to Paulo as I make sure to keep my body in perfect alignment.

POOR POSTURE:

Paulo has me in his Closed Guard. My posture is down instead of to the side, and I am trying to use strength to get my right foot upright.

Because my posture is so far forward, Paulo simply pulls on my lapels as he bucks forward with his legs to break me down.

Although I have my right knee off the mat, I have not turned my body enough to drive my posture to a forty-five degree angle. Without this angle, I am imbalanced to my left side.

Pulling forward and to the right, Paulo frustrates my posture as he breaks me down toward my left side.

25-17 STANDING OPENING WITH HIP PRESSURE

The standing posture is an incredible platform for opening your opponent's Closed Guard. This guard-opening technique works because of the convergence of several principles. First of all, your opponent is carrying his bodyweight on the strength of his locked legs. Secondly, the strength it takes for you to stand in his Closed Guard is less than what it takes for him to keep his legs locked. In other words, gravity is not fighting against your ability to stand as much as it is fighting against his ability to hold on. Finally, you assist gravity by pushing his hips down while pulling your body back to open the guard. This intensifies the load on his legs until his lock hits the breaking point.

I am standing in Paulo's guard and in a great position to open his legs.

Keeping my hands posted forward, I step back with my left foot to create the perfect angle to open.

I drive my posture back by pushing off with my hands while driving my hips into Paulo's locked legs. His lock cannot withstand the pressure and it easily releases.

To stabilize the position, I drop my base down by bending at the knees while moving my right knee between Paulo's legs. Now, I can begin passing from the Combat Base position.

25-18 DEFENSIVE SQUATTING & STANDING OPEN

Although jiu-jitsu is epitomized as flowing and beautiful, it is also an art that takes a certain level of conditioning and stamina. In the course of guard-passing, you will get tired at some point. Do not panic, just transition into this defensive technique and then pursue your opening and pass. The trick is learning where you can safely wait to recover your stamina. This is where proper conditioning and mat time will be of assistance. Do not just stop anywhere! You may have to work a little, especially if you are exhausted, but you have to get to the defensive squatting position before you catch your breath. To fail to do so will increase your chance of being swept or submitted.

I begin already standing in Paulo's Closed Guard. At this point I am tired and in need of a moment's rest.

To rest, I drive my rear down toward the mat while locking my elbows to my inner knees. This traps both Paulo's legs and inhibits his hip mobility. I keep my head back to prevent chokes, as well as maintain my posture.

Paulo tries to counter by wiggling his hips back. This action is incredibly difficult while I have my elbows and knees trapping his legs.

In desperation, Paulo opens his legs to force the action. This is the perfect time to pull my posture back. By doing this, I prevent Paulo from resecuring the Closed Guard.

Without delay, I move my left knee forward to act as a wedge against Paulo's guard. Once again, I am in a safe Combat Base positioning.

25-19 OPEN WHEN OPPONENT HIDES ONE ARM

This is my favorite standing opening series. By trapping my opponent's arm underneath my own, I am able to safely stand without threat of the Underhook Sweep. In addition to this, by keeping my opponent's arm as I stand, I am able to prevent him from scooping his hips into a more comfortable attacking position. Practice this technique often because it is very dominant once mastered.

Paulo has me in his Closed Guard with both my knees on the mat. My left hand is posturing forward with my right hand holding Paulo's left sleeve.

To setup my standing posture, I first push Paulo's left arm under my left.

I clamp down on Paulo's left arm with my elbow while swinging my posture to the left. I do not release either of my grips.

Next, I raise my right knee off the mat as I change my angle forty-five degrees to my right. This standing method is always the same.

Driving off the mat with my left foot, I rise to both feet.

I posture up, thrusting my hips forward while standing upright. At the same time, I must release my left hand lapel grip and move it to his knee.

To pressure Paulo's lock, I step my left foot back while pressing downward on his knee. This creates wedging pressure against his legs.

I push my hips back until Paulo's legs blow open, leaving me in a great position to begin my pass.

Figure 25.19: Forget to Trap the Elbow

When attempting this pass, you must always have your opponent's arm trapped underneath your own. Failing to do so will allow your opponent to move his arm to disrupt your posture (1). If he manages to bring his hand behind his head, you will not have the control to complete this pass and you will have to transition to a different technique (2).

25-20 OPEN AGAINST LONG LEGS

Sometimes you get to the standing position and your opponent is so strong and lanky that all your previous efforts to open his guard have failed. For these select few opponents, use the following technique. As you posture back, forego your grips on his legs and body and double up your grip on his knee. Next, pursue a motion similar to the classic standing opening, but concentrate both your hands into a downward push on his knee. Even the longest legs will be unable to maintain the lock as you localize intense pressure against his knee.

Already standing in Paulo's guard, I am in a great position to open his guard. However, his long legs are troubling me and making previous opening techniques more difficult.

To combat the length of Paulo's legs, I release both my hands from his body and place them on his knee. As I do this, I step back with my left foot to create a side angle.

To open his legs, I simply drive both my hands downward while moving my hips back.

25-21 ARMPIT GRIP OPENING & BRIDGE DEFENSE

The Armpit Grip Opening is another useful technique that has to be a part of every grappler's tool-box. That this move is incredibly effective without the gi only solidifies its place of importance. Much of the strength of this technique comes from the fact that it is a hybrid of standing and knee openings. Through the seamless changing of levels, you are able to maneuver your knee between his legs and wedge his guard open. Some important factors for success in this technique are to block the use of his arms with your hands, to keep your forward foot flat so that your knee can easily slide between his legs, and to block his bridging attempt with your arm once you have unlocked his feet.

I begin inside Paulo's Closed Guard with both my knees on the mat.

As I lower my posture, I block both of Paulo's arms by pushing my hands into his biceps. I keep my elbows down to prevent him from circling his hands to the inside to escape. At this point, I have prevented his ability to choke me with either hand or attack my arms.

While standing my right knee off the mat, I change the angle of my body to the right.

Similar to my standing opening, I drive my left foot off the mat to come to a standing position.

5

I square my legs to Paulo while continuing to press my body weight into his biceps. He reacts by climbing his guard higher to either regain control or attack a double armlock.

6

Bringing my right forearm down on Paulo's hips, I block his upward hip thrust and negate any possible sweep or attack. At the same time, I maneuver my right knee between his legs to prepare for my guard opening.

7

While keeping my right heel flat to the mat, I drop my base until my left knee touches the mat. This drives my right knee upward between Paulo's legs.

8

To open Paulo's legs, I thrust my hips backward while I keep my knee in place to act as a wedge.

Figure 25.21 Bridge Sweep Block

Sometimes a savvy opponent will try to bridge into you while you are attempting this pass. To do so, he will have to push off the mat while driving his hips into you. If you still have your hands in your opponent's armpits at this point, you may be swept off balance. This is why I use either one or both arms to brace into my opponent's hip (1). This action will negate the effects of the bridge while actually setting up an even easier opening (2).

1

2

25-22 OPENING AGAINST DOUBLE UNDERHOOKS

The double underhooks position is a popular defensive strategy in MMA that is still seen from time to time in jiu-jitsu practice. Whenever my opponent gets the double underhooks from the Closed Guard, I think one of two things: he is trying to stall to recover energy or he is trying to get my back. In either case, my aim is to prevent him from achieving his goal. To eliminate the chance of him taking my back, I block his hips with my legs while using my posted arms to frame his body underneath my own. Regarding his recovery, I immediately stand so he will have to use more strength just to hold on to me. Strategy is important, so focus on eliminating his technical goals while being mindful of his endurance and physical status.

Paulo has me in his Closed Guard with both his hands clasped together underneath my armpits. He is hoping to use his hip mobility to escape to my back. I have pulled my right knee forward to block his left hip.

To initiate my escape, I keep both my hands on the mat on either side of Paulo's shoulders. Then, I raise my left knee close to Paulo's right hip to block his movement.

From here, I step forward with my right foot to block his left hip and rise to a standing position. I pinch my knees together to further impede Paulo's movement.

Lifting with the power of my legs, I stand straight into posture. It is very important that I do not lift Paulo's weight with my back. Once here, I move both my hands to his shoulders and keep my angle slightly forward to prevent him from taking me down.

Now, I let gravity do the work for me. I push downward on his shoulders to amplify the effect of his weight and gravity pulling him to the mat. I finish in a great position to pass the guard.

Figure 25.22: What Not to Do

When you are passing the guard, you always have to be in control of the situation. Never give your opponent the tools to disrupt your progress or to gain the advantage. When your opponent has the double underhooks, it is pertinent that you do not expose an arm. If you decide to use an arm to push yourself free (1), you are likely to have your back taken (2). Remember, your opponent does not have very many weapons from this position. If you play it safe without exposing yourself, you will assuredly come out on top.

26-0 CORE OPEN GUARD PASSES

The Open Guard is one of the hardest positions to deal with in jiu-jitsu. The two biggest variables are spatial awareness and defeating your opponent's legs and hips. For this section, I have asked my partner to take up a basic Open Guard so that I can show how to defeat his space and legs with three of the most common Open Guard passes and their variations. These three passes, the Leg Rope, Knee Cross, and Torreando, represent a complete system of general Open Guard-passing and they are key to a complete top game. That they will be used throughout the coming sections only adds to their importance.

26-1 LEG ROPE FRONT

Anytime you secure your opponent's legs together, you will be in a much greater position to pass the guard. The Leg Rope Pass uses such a technique. This pass gets its name from how you intertwine your outside arm around your opponent's legs. However, the name only references how you will complete the pass. The real attention should be on how you drive your hips onto your opponent's legs and hips to neutralize his mobility. Once you have mastered this weight distribution, you will find that your arms only serve as a block and that your focus should be on your body, not your arms!

I attempt to pass with the Double Underhook Pass, but Paulo manages to escape his hip and block my shoulder.

Instead of fighting for my original pass, I change my grip by wrapping my right arm around his left leg and blocking his left leg with my hand. This entwines Paulo's legs and keeps his knees together in the Leg Rope position.

I drive my shoulder and torso onto Paulo's left leg while spreading my legs wide for stability. By keeping on my toes, I increase the weight on his legs.

To begin the passing transition, I reach my left hand over Paulo's left shoulder.

I throw my right leg upward to escape Paulo's legs.

Continuing my momentum, I scissor my right leg backward and switch my hips to face Paulo.

I grab under Paulo's left leg and drive him to his back to stabilize the Side Control.

26-2 LEG ROPE BACK

Sometimes your opponent is able to frustrate your previous pass attempt by impeding your route with his bottom leg or hip escaping slightly. This should be of little concern for you. The true test for any passer is the ability to pass to either side instead of insisting on a more difficult pass. This pass is a great example of changing sides to overwhelm the guard player and possibly set up the Back position.

Once again, I am in the Leg Rope position and I am threatening the pass.

Instead of reaching my left hand over Paulo's shoulder, I place it on the mat in front of his left shin.

With my left hand in place, I can release my leg rope and secure a grip on Paulo's back.

I begin circling to my right side while using my left hand to pin Paulo's left leg.

I continue to circle until my left foot has cleared both Paulo's legs. It is important that I keep my legs posted away from him to prevent him from hooking them.

Once I have cleared the legs, I can safely secure the Side Control position.

26-3 LEG ROPE SIDE SWITCH & SMASH

Sometimes when you attempt to pass with the Leg Rope, your opponent will open his legs to prevent the pass. This is the perfect opportunity to switch sides. You have to understand that as your opponent gets comfortable in his positioning, it will be harder to pass his guard. This is why I like to change to the other side. First off, this usually catches your opponent off guard. Secondly, it results in the control of his legs and hips, which makes passing a breeze. Just remember one important aspect; when you change sides, you have to use your free hand to grab the bottom leg and pull it until your opponent's legs are clear to the opposite side.

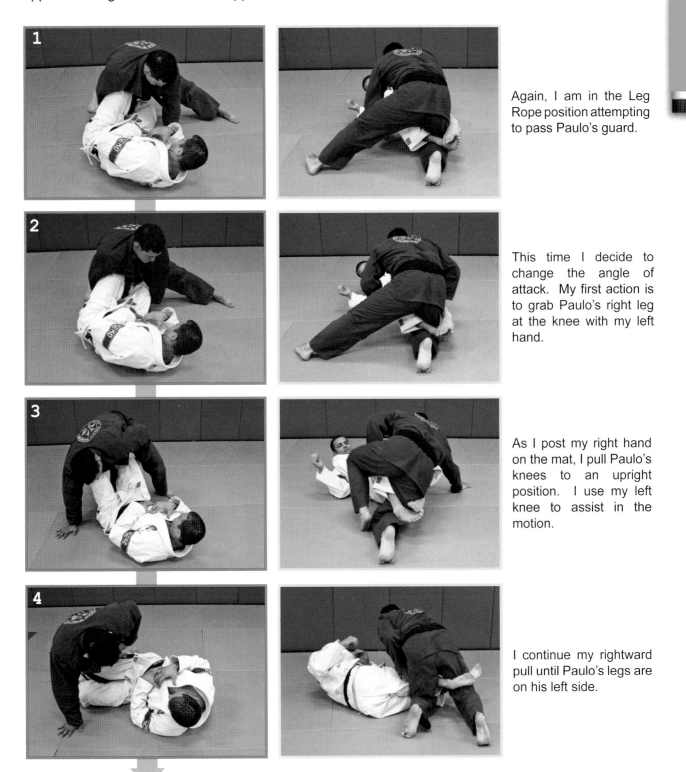

Again, I am in the Leg Rope position attempting to pass Paulo's guard.

This time I decide to change the angle of attack. My first action is to grab Paulo's right leg at the knee with my left hand.

As I post my right hand on the mat, I pull Paulo's knees to an upright position. I use my left knee to assist in the motion.

I continue my rightward pull until Paulo's legs are on his left side.

Keeping on my toes, I sprawl my left hip onto Paulo's collapsed legs, pinning them to the mat and freeing my right foot. My left hand goes to the mat behind his hips to prevent his hip escape.

To begin my transition to Side Control, first I cross-face Paulo with my right arm.

While my cross-face forces Paulo's head away from me, I step my left leg free of his legs and drive my left knee into his hip to prevent his guard recovery.

Figure 26.3 Freeing the Leg

I have moved Paulo's legs to his other side, but I have not been able to free my right leg.

By lifting my leg directly upward and slightly behind me, I am able to slide my leg free easily.

Now, I can step my leg back over the top of Paulo's to resume my pass.

26-4 KNEE CROSS PASS

The Knee Cross or Knee Slide Pass is a tournament-proven technique and one of the most dominant forms of guard-passing. There are two important aspects that will greatly boost your learning curve with this technique. First, do not try to penetrate the knee straight toward your opponent's navel. Instead, drive into your opponent's thigh and then away from his body. By driving into his thigh, you will push his leg to the ground, making it easier for you to step over with your outside leg. As you angle your knee out, you will notice that you have greater body control with your hip-to-hip pressure. The second important aspect is how you use your inside arm. As with many techniques, close this elbow to your body and thigh. This will prevent your opponent from penetrating his knee to escape. Focus on your knee slide and your near-side elbow and you will see great results in your Knee Cross passing.

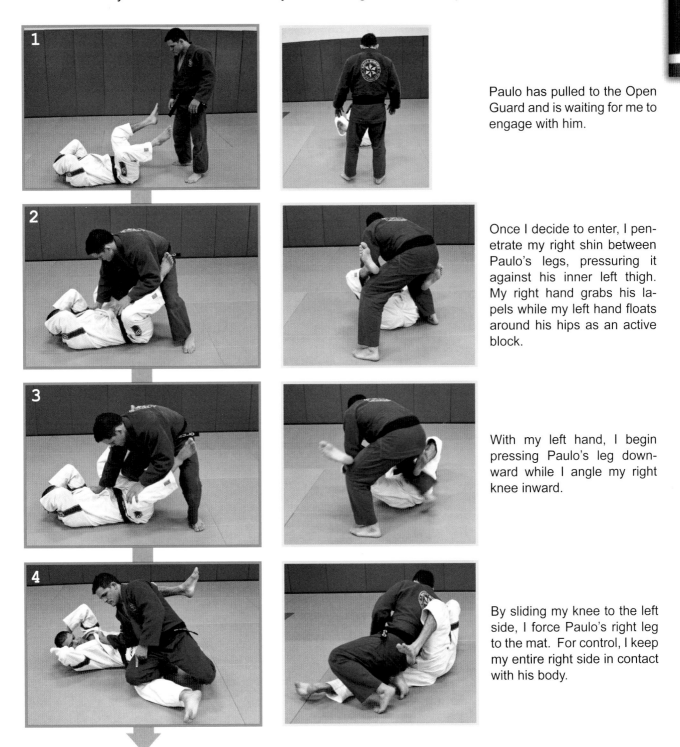

Paulo has pulled to the Open Guard and is waiting for me to engage with him.

Once I decide to enter, I penetrate my right shin between Paulo's legs, pressuring it against his inner left thigh. My right hand grabs his lapels while my left hand floats around his hips as an active block.

With my left hand, I begin pressing Paulo's leg downward while I angle my right knee inward.

By sliding my knee to the left side, I force Paulo's right leg to the mat. For control, I keep my entire right side in contact with his body.

As I continue to slide my hips to the mat, I secure Paulo's right arm with my left hand and I begin my turn into the Side Control position. I pull up with my right hand to keep Paulo flat on his back.

I finish my turn and secure Side Control.

26-5 KNEE CROSS AGAINST LAPEL GRIP

Sometimes, an experienced opponent will sit-up and grab your lapels to impede the progress of your Knee Cross Pass. This should be expected so do not worry! The only thing you have to do is stop your previous knee slide and lift your opponent's bottom leg off the mat. Doing so will reflatten him as his legs lift upward and your knee pushes him backward. This also diffuses the power of his lapel grip. If you insist on the previous pass without taking the time to flatten him, you are begging to be swept or have your back taken.

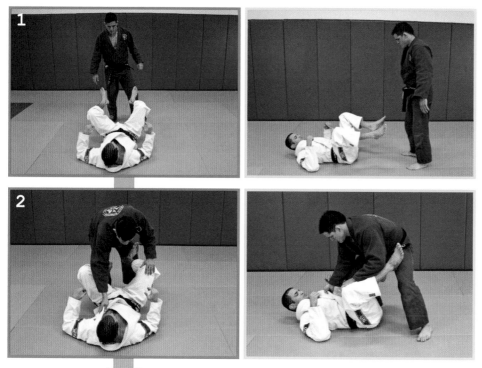

Once again, Paulo has pulled to the Open Guard and is waiting for me to engage with him.

This time, I enter with my right leg between Paulo's legs. I grab his left lapel with my right hand and his right knee with my left hand.

To avoid Paulo's blocking right foot, I push down on his knee while stepping my left leg back to clear his hook.

Once his leg is clear, I step my left foot to the side of his right leg. Paulo reacts by sitting into me on his right side and feeding my lapel between my legs.

Lifting with my left arm, I move Paulo's legs back to the center while driving my right knee forward. This action flattens him, taking away his angle to attack. My forward knee pressure keeps Paulo on his back.

Instead of continuing to push my knee forward, I lift my hips and point my knee to the left.

I slide my right knee to the mat while keeping hip-to-hip contact with Paulo.

With my right leg almost free, I push Paulo's left shoulder to the mat to flatten him.

I finish the pass by turning into Paulo and taking the Side Control.

26-6 ANGLE CHANGE TO KNEE CROSS PASS

If you are becoming a Knee Cross Pass master, it is likely that your opponent will adjust to shut down your favored side. In the following example, Paulo uses his shin block to keep distance and beat me to the punch. As you practice, you will notice that your opponent often gets his knee in front of your abdomen as you pass. The solution to this problem is changing the angle. When your opponent creates a formidable wall, simply go around it by changing the pass to the other side as you pull him out of his comfort zone.

Paulo has me in his Open Guard with his left hand in a cross-collar grip and his left shin acting as a shield block.

I avoid the position by stepping up to my feet while angling my body to the right. This eliminates the threat of the choke.

In one motion, I push Paulo's left knee to the mat while stepping my right leg over it.

Cutting my left knee to the side, I slide my body onto Paulo's hip as I drive toward his side.

Finally, I turn into Paulo to establish the Side Control position.

Open Guard

26-7 TORREANDO & APPROACH

The Torreando or Bull Fighter Pass is one of the most widely used passes in jiu-jitsu. Most people like this maneuver for its speed and relative safety. Because you are on your feet when doing this pass, you can move at a much faster pace than other guard passes where one or both knees are on the mat. This speed is often the determining factor in success. In addition, because you are far in front of your opponent's hips, you do not have to worry as much about submissions. Once you learn to avoid or anticipate collar chokes, arm and collar drags, and leg picks, you will become a very potent threat with the Torreando Pass.

For the following technique, it is important to practice with the action-reaction principle. In so doing, you will learn the correct timing. In this case, the time to execute the pass is when you enter, push into your opponent with your forward shin, and your opponent pushes back. Once you feel your opponent pushing, you give way to his force and pass his guard. This idea of releasing pressure by going with the strength is crucial not only to the Torreando, but to all of jiu-jitsu.

Paulo is in the Open Guard as I approach to engage with him.

I establish the standing Combat Base position with my right shin pushing into Paulo's left thigh.

Using my body movement, I drive Paulo's legs to the left while continuing my shin pressure.

As Paulo begins to resist against my forward pressure, I pull my right leg back while pushing his legs to my right. This opens up the perfect path to his side.

I take a big step with my right foot and consolidate the Knee-on-Belly position.

26-8 TORREANDO AGAINST ONE HOOK

This Torreando variation is great against opponents who have good foot movement, hooks, and Spider Guards. The goal here is to isolate one of your opponent's legs and then pass with the Torreando. As with the previous technique, the time to execute this pass is when your opponent resists your pressure. In this situation, you will use forward shin-to-shin pressure.

Paulo is in the Open Guard as I approach to engage with him (1).

Instead of driving my knee between Paulo's legs, I make shin-to-shin contact with my right leg. While I am doing this, I grip both his legs for control (2).

I move my left hand to Paulo's left ankle and push his leg to my left to free my legs (3).

From here I can easily slide my left leg forward into the Knee-on-Belly position (4).

26-9 TORREANDO W/ HIP CONTROL DRILL

This is one of the newest and most popular ways to pass the Open Guard. At the heart of it, you are posting on your opponent's pelvis while staying on your toes. This drives all your weight onto his body and completely petrifies his hips. Now to complete the drill, all you have to do is move from side to side while using your free hand to deflect or remove the foot that gets in your way. For best results, practice this Hip Control Drill from side to side until you can easily pass to either side without changing your grips.

I begin in Paulo's guard with both my knees on the mat. My left hand is posting on his hip while my right hand is floating inside his left knee.

2

3

4

Jumping to my feet, I create a tripod between my posted arm and my outstretched feet. This action drives all my weight onto Paulo's hips and inhibits his mobility.

While moving to my left, I grab Paulo's right foot with my right hand.

I push his foot down to remove the hook.

5

6

7

With his blocking foot out of the way, I can continue circling to my left.

Keeping my grips, I collapse my body into the Side Control position.

Starting from the beginning position, I prepare to pass the other side with the same grips.

8

9

10

I begin circling to my right, making sure that my legs are out of Paulo's hooking range. Once more, I make sure that all my weight is driving into Paulo's hips.

This time, Paulo's left leg is in my way, so I clear it by pushing it down with my right hand.

Having cleared the block, I can safely finish my pass by taking the Knee-on-Belly position.

26-10 TWO-ON-ONE LEG PASS

The beauty of this technique lies in its simplicity. Often enough when passing, students tend to overcomplicate an uncomplicated matter. This is where a pass like this is great to reset your clock and understand that sometimes the most effective move is the easiest one! The principle of this pass is to control your opponent's inside or bottom leg and elevate it away from you to control the guard. Your opponent cannot easily defend if you properly pull and then push his leg while circling to his side. Simple yet devastating!

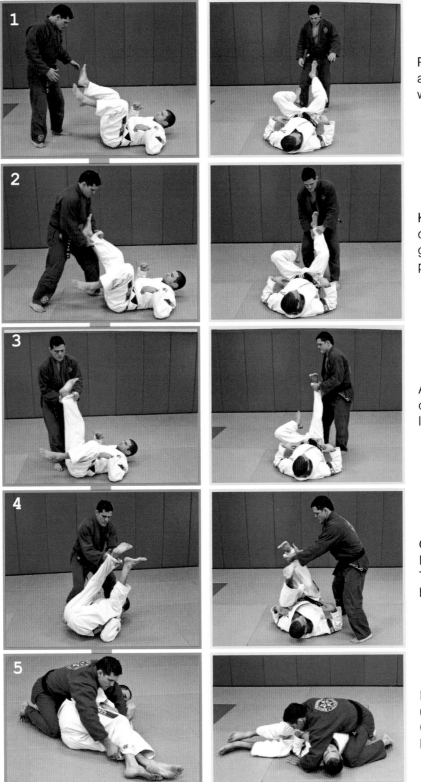

Paulo is in the Open Guard as I approach to engage with him.

Keeping my left leg to the outside of Paulo's legs, I grasp the end of his right pant leg with both hands.

As I step my body next to his controlled leg, I lift Paulo's leg to straighten it.

Once Paulo's leg is straight, I begin pushing it forward. This drives both his legs to his left side.

I continue pushing the legs until I have ended in Side Control with both of Paulo's legs on the opposite side.

27-0 BUTTERFLY GUARD PASSES

The Butterfly, or Hooks Guard, is one of the most classic sweeping platforms in jiu-jitsu. To beat this guard, you must learn to distribute your weight effectively and move in and out of different passing techniques. A great way to look at passing this guard is to focus on the hook that sweeps you and the arm that your opponent needs to control the sweep.

The following section provides great examples of how to defeat the sweeping hook, maintain balance, and dominate through your opponent's Butterfly Guard.

27-1 POSTURE & BALANCE

The first time you jumped in a higher-ranked student's Butterfly Guard, it is likely you were easily controlled and swept at will. This is due to lack of familiarity with the position. Take the time to play with the following two positions and learn to ride the Butterfly Guard and use your hips to squash your opponent's control.

LATE HOOKS DRILL:

This is a very useful drill. Let your opponent pull you forward and elevate your hips with his hooks. Then, play with your balance and see if you can use your arms and hips to stay balanced above him. Have him lower you and repeat the drill as often as it takes for you to get comfortable with stabilization.

Paulo has me in his Butterfly Guard with both his hands underhooked, grasping my belt.

With a rocking chair motion, Paulo falls directly back and lifts me with his hooks. To prevent the sweep, I post both my hands on the mat next to his shoulders.

Finally, I kick my heels to my head as I push my hips toward his body. At this point, I feel relatively safe as I ride the motion of his sweep.

WET BLANKET DRILL:

This time, the drill is the exact opposite of the Late Hooks Drill. Instead of allowing your opponent to pull you forward, anchor your hips downward while spreading your base wide. Doing so will make your hips feel much heavier, negating the guard player's ability to lift you up. Practice this move at full speed. One partner drives his weight down and the other tries his hardest to lift with the hooks.

Again, Paulo has me in his Butterfly Guard with both his hands underhooked, grasping my belt.	This time, I prevent the sweeping motion by turning my knees to the outside and flattening my hips to the mat. This creates a heavy "wet blanket" sensation on Paulo's hooks as my hips and body sag downward.	Even if Paulo pulls with all his might, he cannot lift my grounded hips off the mat.

27-2 FLAT BUTTERFLY–WALK-AROUND PASS

When faced with a good Butterfly Guard, a great primary objective is to flatten your opponent. By flattening the guard player, you can better control him while minimizing the leverage of his basic sweeps. This Walk-Around Pass is a great basic-level technique against the Flattened Butterfly. Focus on controlling one hook while isolating the other with your heavy hips. Stay on your toes as you walk around his guard and you are on the way to dominating the Flattened Butterfly!

Paulo has me in his Butterfly Guard, but I have managed to flatten him to his back. This puts me at an advantage to pass his guard. I keep my knees pressing forward with my elbows tight to Paulo's hips to block his movement.

2

As I straighten my right leg, I shift all my weight onto my right hip, driving downward on Paulo's left hook.

3

Reaching with my left hand, I grab Paulo's right ankle to control his other hook.

4

With control of Paulo's right leg, I can lift my body off the mat, moving my hips over Paulo's right knee. I keep on my toes to drive my weight into his lower abdomen.

5

Once I have circled past his legs, I insert my left knee in front of Paulo's left hip to prevent his guard recovery.

6

Finally, I climb Paulo's body and establish the Side Control position.

Figure 27.2: Flat Butterfly Leverage

It is important to realize that your opponent is not in the best position to lever a sweep (1). Although there are some exceptional athletes, like Fernando Terere, who can have success from here, I would not recommend this guard position for the average student. With his body flat, it is the guard player's quadriceps muscle versus all your weight and leverage (2). There is no momentum in this sweep; therefore, it is easily stopped.

27-3 WALLID ISMAEL VARIATION

This is another great variation for passing the Flattened Butterfly. Made famous by Wallid Ismael, this is a hands-free pass that utilizes the legs to isolate one hook and then step over it to pass. The mobility to kick out a hook and place both knees in front of the other is integral for this pass as well as others.

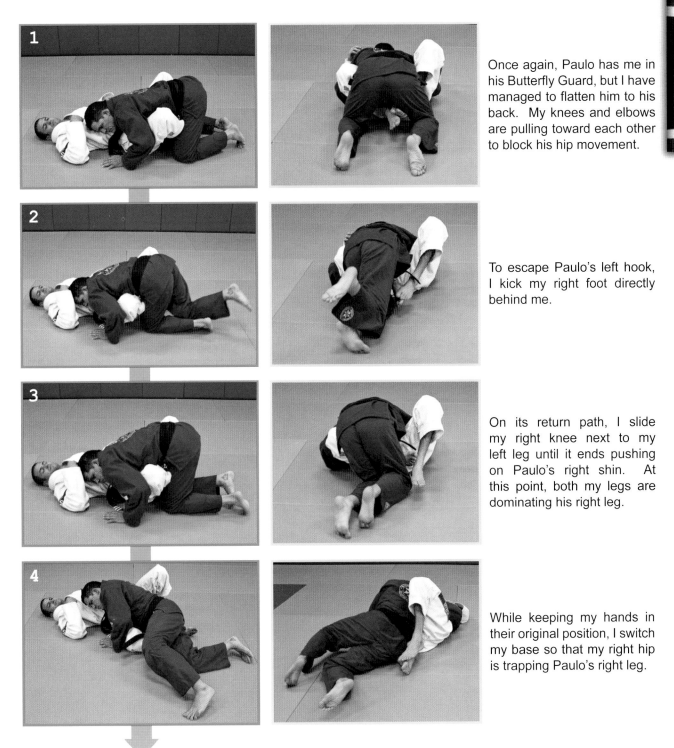

1 Once again, Paulo has me in his Butterfly Guard, but I have managed to flatten him to his back. My knees and elbows are pulling toward each other to block his hip movement.

2 To escape Paulo's left hook, I kick my right foot directly behind me.

3 On its return path, I slide my right knee next to my left leg until it ends pushing on Paulo's right shin. At this point, both my legs are dominating his right leg.

4 While keeping my hands in their original position, I switch my base so that my right hip is trapping Paulo's right leg.

I step my left leg over the top of Paulo's left knee as I thrust my hips square onto his leg.

Stepping my right leg free from his guard, I finish in Side Control with my right knee pressing into Paulo's hip.

27-4 WRAP-THE-LEGS PASS

Wrapping the legs is a great strategy for passing the Butterfly Guard. By wrapping the legs, you force your opponent's knees together, dramatically reducing the efficacy of his position. However, similar to Leg Rope passes, it is your body that will pin the legs and do the work to control the position. A common error is to get your opponent's legs wrapped and try to pass without pinning his legs with your shoulder and body. This will only result in guard recovery and frustration, so make sure you pin those legs with your weight, not just your arms!

Paulo has me in his Butterfly Guard, and this time he is sitting upright. This gives his attacks a higher chance at success.

Immediately, I hug both of Paulo's legs together, locking them to each other at the knees.

I feed Paulo's left pant leg to my left arm to get an even tighter lock on his legs. While I do this, I move my head to the center to control his centerline.

Using my right shoulder, I manage to shove Paulo's legs toward my left.

Next, I switch my base onto my right hip as I pull Paulo's legs away from my left leg. If my leg gets stuck here, I can simply lift it upward while I move his legs to my left.

Once Paulo's legs are clear, I can easily assume the Side Control position.

27-5 HAND PLANT PASS

Really, the Hand Plant Pass is a two-for-one deal. In one step, you effectively block his sweeping motion as well as pass the guard. By planting your hand inside one of his legs, you create a block for that side's hook sweep. Even if he tries to force the sweep, your arm will prevent him from getting the necessary leverage. In addition, your block perfectly sets up the angle and side to which you will pass. As with all these passes, always align your body with your head and legs as you pass, and keep your head lower than your opponent's to disrupt his posture.

Paulo has me in his Butterfly Guard and is controlling with an over and under grip. He is in a great position to sweep me.

To negate the power of Paulo's guard, I circle my left hand over his right arm, and inside his right leg. Meanwhile, I plant my right hand on the mat for a base.

I continue this motion until I have my left hand planted on the mat between Paulo's legs.

As I drop my hips even lower, I move my right hand to block Paulo's left hip.

While posting off my left hand, I sprawl my legs away from Paulo's feet. By keeping my hips high, I create the necessary space to push his left leg to my left side.

With Paulo's left leg clear, I can drop into the Side Control position. I keep my left knee tight to his left hip to prevent his guard recovery.

27-6 LEVEL CHANGE PASS

If you find that you are continually swept by your opponent's Butterfly Guard, consider changing your level to pass. By jumping to your toes against an opponent in good posture, you can effectively nullify his forward hook, and pass easily to his side. Notice that in the following technique, my hips and legs move up and away from Paulo's hook, making his forward hook completely harmless to me. Remember, just as you change levels for effective takedowns, you can also do the same for passing!

Paulo has me in his Butterfly Guard and he has perfect posture to attempt a sweep.

Immediately, I ground my hips to the mat. This makes my body feel much heavier than it is and buys me time to set up my pass. I keep my left hand on his right knee as my right hand takes an over-the-shoulder grip.

I jump to my feet while pressing down on Paulo's right knee. My hips are high so that my body and legs clear his left leg.

To maneuver around Paulo's left leg, I cross-step my left leg in front of my right.

Now I step my right foot toward Paulo's head to get to his side.

To flatten Paulo, I drive into him with my left arm and shoulder. I must push Paulo onto his back if I want to pass into the Side Control.

I stabilize the position with the cross-face control.

27-7 FORWARD KNEE-PRESS PASS

The Forward Knee-Press Pass is an important technique because it introduces your forward leg as a passing factor. For this example, my opponent has double underhooks and I can pass to either side. By pressing your front knee into your opponent's hook, you can drive his knee inward and open up his side for the pass. In addition, you create an angle to escape your back leg as you push your knee inward. Smashing the leg away from you with your knee is a preliminary step for many other hip-switching passes, so you must master it at this basic level first. Practice this move to either side until you are comfortable with this movement.

Paulo has me in the Butterfly Guard with both underhooks. He is pulling my body forward to prevent me from basing low.

Lifting my right knee off the ground, I step forward and block Paulo's left leg.

As I stand to both feet, I grab low on Paulo's back with my right hand while grabbing his left knee with my left hand.

Combining pressure, I drive my knee into Paulo's left thigh while pushing his knee to the floor with my left hand. The weight of my attack smashes both of his legs together and clears the way for the pass.

While continuing to press down on Paulo's knee with my left hand, I drop my body down into the Side Control position.

27-8 PASSING THE CROSS-GRIP

Although the cross-grip can feel quite daunting and there are certainly a myriad of sweeps and attacks from the position, it is also easy to defeat with the Forward Knee Press. The trick to this pass is twofold: change your levels to reduce your partner's control and use the Knee-Press Pass away from the side he is facing. If you pass toward his face, you are likely to be swept or have your back taken.

Paulo has me in a very strong Butterfly Guard position. He has successfully arm-dragged my right arm and taken an over-the-shoulder grip to prevent me from pulling my arm free. From here, he is threatening to sweep or take my back. I press down on his right knee to prevent him from turning into me.

Just like the previous position, I step my right leg close to Paulo's upper thigh. This prevents Paulo from taking my back or sweeping me to the left.

In one motion, I press inward with my right knee, step my left leg back, and push down on Paulo's left knee with my left hand. Once again, this has the effect of smashing his legs together.

By crossing my left foot in front of my right, I can use my back leg to block Paulo while releasing my front leg.

I step my right leg toward Paulo's head and take the Side Control position. From here, I can attack his exposed left arm or transition to even better positions.

27-9 FLOATING HIP-SWITCH PASS

Once you have mastered the Forward Knee-Press and its variations, it's time to move on to an even more dynamic pass – the Floating Hip-Switch Pass. Essentially, this pass has all the same criteria as the Forward Knee-Press, except this time you are accomplishing everything while airborne. While elevated, use the Late Hooks Defense to posture on your hands and prevent the sweep. Then, bring one knee forward like you would in the Knee-Press Pass and pressure it into your opponent's knee. In one motion, drive your knee inward while switching your hips in the air. This will free your other leg and create a powerful driving motion. If done correctly, you should fall safely into the Side Control. This switching motion is advanced, but also very useful for passing the guard at the highest levels.

1. Paulo has me in the Butterfly Guard with both underhooks. He is pulling my body forward to prevent me from basing low.

2. In an explosive motion, Paulo falls to his back to attempt a sweep. As my feet leave the mat, I place both my hands near his shoulders to maintain my balance.

3. Once elevated, I climb my left knee toward Paulo's right while extending my right foot back.

4. To escape Paulo's hooks, I start driving my left knee inward by his right knee as I lift my right leg to the sky.

This action clears my right leg as my left leg drives Paulo's legs to his left.

Finishing my fall, I land in a great position to take the Side Control.

27-10 FLOATING HIP-SWITCH AGAINST PANT GRAB

When you practice jiu-jitsu, always be prepared to face a smart opponent. In this case, my opponent is aware of the previous pass and grabs my pant leg to prevent me from committing to the Hip-Switch Pass. If I go for the previous pass anyway, I am likely to be swept. To defeat this grip, I must always pass toward my opponent's underhook and circle my trapped leg over my opponent's to set up the hip switch. Once I manage to get my trapped leg on top of my opponent's, I can use the previous technique to free my legs and slide safely to Side Control.

This time, Paulo has me in the Butterfly Guard and is grabbing my left leg to prevent me from walking around his guard.

In an explosive motion, Paulo falls to his back to attempt a sweep. He lifts with his hooks and left arm to get me airborne. As my feet leave the mat, I place both my hands near his shoulders to maintain my balance.

To escape Paulo's grip on my right knee, I scoot my left knee forward while pointing it to the inside. As I do this, I circle my right foot counterclockwise until my shin traps both his ankles.

I thrust my hips into Paulo while falling to my left side to break his grip.

My thrusting motion has also pushed Paulo's legs away from me as I fall into a Side Control position.

27-11 THE STAR PASS

Some techniques are poetry in motion, and the Star Pass is one of those techniques. The timing for this technique is critical. Begin this pass the moment your opponent has your hips elevated and your posture down as he tries for the Basic Butterfly Sweep. Your success with this technique will depend on your ability to post your forehead and hand on the mat for a base, climb your knee high, and feel when your opponent has reached the zenith of his hook extension. Once you feel that he cannot stretch his hook any farther and your weight is sagging into his leg, extend upward into a modified headstand to escape his hook and pass the guard. It is important to have a solid base to prevent your opponent from pushing you over, so make sure that your arm and head can withstand his potential onslaught.

Paulo has me in his Butterfly Guard. I can tell from his over-and-under arm position that he is likely to attack with the Classic Butterfly Sweep.

2

As Paulo tries to pull me into the sweep, I dive my body downward to base out while I grasp his back with my right hand.

3

I am too late and Paulo manages to lift my body off the mat with his left hook. To buy myself some time, I post my forehead on the mat for balance and place my left hand in front of his right knee. I step my left leg far to my left for base.

4

Paulo continues to pull on my belt while lifting with his hook. If I stay here, I will be swept.

5

As Paulo reaches the pinnacle of his movement, I use my head and left arm to lift my legs into a headstand. In one motion, I lift my left leg free and push my right knee inward to remove his hook.

I switch my right hip all the way through as I fall onto Paulo's left side.

Once on the mat, I block Paulo's hip escape with my left knee as I achieve the Side Control position.

27-12 TRANSITION TO MOUNT OFF PASS

As with the previous technique, the goal is to make your opponent pay for trying to sweep you. This technique works great in conjunction with the Star Pass because you pass to the other side and can take advantage of a mounting alternative. Pay attention to your hips when practicing this move. It is the power of your hip switch that will allow you to get your leg between those of your opponent. Do not try to force the move, just rotate onto your hip as you get elevated to squash his leg. Believe me, your hip on hook pressure will kill his leg and leave you in the best position to take the Mount.

Paulo has me in his Butterfly Guard. I can tell from his over-and-under arm position that he is likely to attack with the Classic Butterfly Sweep.

Once again, Paulo falls to his right side to initiate the Classic Butterfly Sweep. I delay the sweep by placing both my hands on the mat and posting my left foot to my side for base.

3 By angling my right knee toward my left side, I am able to switch my hips to the right. This action forces Paulo's left leg to the mat. I land with my right knee deep between his legs and my left leg to the outside.

4 Facing Paulo, I lift up on his right arm and insert my left knee into his armpit. I keep my hips low to prevent his hip-escape movement.

5 To secure the mount, I step my right leg over Paulo's left hip. It is crucial that I have my left knee in his armpit as I transition. If this is not secure, he will be able to recover Half Guard as I attempt the Mount.

27-13 STAND-UP WHEEL PASS

The Stand-Up Wheel Pass is a great variation to the standard Wheel Pass from the knees. Think of this move as a pass where you pull your opponent to where you previously were. I know this sounds confusing, so I'll use the example of the Butterfly Guard sweep. Theoretically, both of these moves work on the same principle. In the case of the Butterfly sweep, you hip-escape and sweep your opponent toward your previous location. It is the same for the Stand-Up Wheel Pass. The only difference is that you stand up and wheel your opponent to your previous location to pass the guard instead of sweep from it!

As an exercise, think of all the different types of movements that utilize this idea of pulling your opponent to where you were previously. You will be surprised to see how many techniques there are!

1 Paulo has me in his Butterfly Guard with both underhooks. I grab his left collar and right pant leg to defend his position.

Pushing off with my grips, I stand while making sure to keep my hips high and my legs far from Paulo.

I pull down with my right hand as I lift with my left to pull Paulo off balance to his left. By using his hips as an axis, I can easily manipulate his positioning with this steering-wheel-type movement.

As Paulo spins to a perpendicular position, I bring my right shoulder down on his chest.

Once I flatten Paulo, I maintain my grips to secure the Side Control position.

27-14 X PASS

The X Pass is a Torreando variation that works exceptionally well against the Butterfly Guard. To make the X Pass work, you must first exaggerate a pass to the other side to entice your opponent to overcommit to his defense. Then, as your partner moves to face you, change direction and move to his side. The X Pass gets its name from the way your forearms cross as you complete the pass. This arm position serves two purposes; it allows you to move from side to side without changing grips, and as you make the final cross position, it blocks your opponent from recovering guard.

I am standing in Paulo's Butterfly Guard, ready to pass with the previous technique.

As I step to my right, Paulo defends the Wheel Pass by hip-escaping to his right and posting his left hand on the mat. At this point, I do not have the angle to spin him to the mat.

Instead of fighting for the Wheel Pass, I step my right foot next to my left while my left hand pushes Paulo's right leg away from me. As I push his leg away, my arms cross into the X position. I must maintain this position throughout this technique.

I cross-step my right foot in front of my left to move to Paulo's right side.

I finish the pass on Paulo's side, ready to take the Knee-on-Belly position.

Figure 27.14: X Detail

By crossing my arms, I am able to maintain pressure on Paulo's shoulder and knee at the same time while my arms form a block (1). If I changed my grips to do the same thing, I would create too much space and Paulo would escape. This is why I like to use the X pass. It allows me a great deal of mobility without having to change my grips.

27-15 SHIN-TO-SHIN PASS

At the University of Jiu-Jitsu, there is a constant flow of information between students of all levels. I encourage every student to help his classmates and learn from them. Here, Diego Moraes and Joe Van Brackle introduce the Shin-to-Shin Pass. In this pass, you must press into your opponent's shin so that he resists, then you relieve the pressure, shuck his knee to his other side and pass. Your foot works as a hook over his shin and keeps him from recovering Half Guard. Practice this Shin-to-Shin Pass when your opponent plays an upright Butterfly Guard and your success of passing the Butterfly hooks will assuredly increase!

1

Diego gets a strong grip on Joe's knees by grabbing his inner pant leg.

2

Keeping his grips on Joe's knees, Diego inserts his knee in between Joe's legs. As he does this, he makes a hook with his right foot, blocking Joe's shin with his own.

3

Diego begins pushing his weight into him and moves his right hand to Joe's hip.

4

Diego posts his left leg out while he pushes Joe onto his back. He stays tight to him and closes the distance between their bodies.

Diego keeps his elbows tight and head close to the mat. His left hand continues to grip Joe's knee and will assist him in passing.

Diego lifts his hips and shoves Joe's knee away from him with his left hand. His head posts on Joe's body while he continues to grip his hip. This isolates Joe's hips and keeps him from hip-escaping back to the guard.

While he has his knee collapsing to the other side, Diego removes his shin block and circles his knee until it lands just below Joe's right thigh.

Diego adjusts his grips so that his left arm reaches under Joe's head and his right arm controls Joe's left arm. Diego's shoulder puts pressure on Joe's face so that he cannot turn back into him. He drops both knees to the mat and secures Side Control.

Figure 27-15: Shin-to-Shin Control

When Diego drops his right knee in between Joe's legs, he flexes his right foot to create a hook over Joe's shin (1). His knee on the floor posts for balance, which gives his hook the right amount of leverage to control Joe's leg. Even when Joe tries to lift his leg, Diego's hook over his shin and grip on his knee block Joe's leg from moving (2).

Spider Guard

28-0 SPIDER GUARD PASSES

The Spider Guard is one of the most popular open guards in use today. Whenever you are in someone's Spider Guard, you have to be aware of his control while staying mindful of your posture. If your head sinks down or your body moves too far forward, you can expect a lightning fast triangle choke or sweep. Therefore, always keep your posture as you begin to eliminate the grips.

To defeat this guard, I like to think about the perilous control that my opponent is using. Think about it. If he loses even one grip, he will have to transition quickly to something else or regain his control to avoid being passed. This is the dangerous nature of Spider Guard. With this in mind, always confront the spider hooks first and then put your opponent on the run!

28-1 BREAK & PASS

The Break and Pass is a simple and highly effective technique to pass the Spider Guard. Basically, swim your hands underneath your opponent's legs to avoid the control. Then, drive your forearms into his legs while pushing them effortlessly to the side. What I really like about this technique is that you do not have to completely break the grip to make this move work. Just clear your hands and propel your forearms into his legs to move him into Side Control. Likely, your opponent will continue holding on to your sleeves until he notices that it is too late. By then you have already passed!

Paulo has me in his Spider Guard. I immediately stagger my right leg forward to set up my defense.

Lifting both my palms outward creates the perfect angle to escape my arms.

I circle both my hands outside and then under Paulo's grips and legs. This neutralizes the effectiveness of his Spider Guard.

Next, I drive my right knee forward in a standing Combat Base as I stack Paulo's legs forward with my forearms.

Driving with both my elbows, I push Paulo's legs to his right.

I continue this motion until Paulo's legs are driven completely to his right.

To stabilize the position, I collapse my weight onto Paulo's hips.

SPIDER GUARD ❋ 265

28-2 LEG LASSO PASS

Oftentimes, an astute opponent will prevent your Spider Guard pass by looping his leg over one of your arms. This is an effective way to block your progress to Side Control as well as set up certain sweeps and attacks. To beat this guard, I do something a bit unorthodox. I give my opponent my back. Don't worry. I have zero intentions of letting my opponent take my back. I only use this technique to pressure his trapped leg and open him up for the pass. You'll see—almost every opponent will get greedy and try to take the Back when you turn. However, as he goes for the Back he removes your pass block. This is the perfect time to turn back and pass!

I have just escaped my right arm from Paulo's spider grip and stepped my left leg in front of his left hook. He reacts by lassoing his right leg over my left arm. His right leg now impedes my pass to his left side.

I rise to my feet to set up the pass. As I do this, I lean my body toward my left hip.

While posting on my left leg, I swing my right leg behind me.

4

Once I have completed my swing, I end faceup on top of Paulo's right leg and hip.

5

Sensing he can take my back, Paulo tries to swing his leg to the right to take the position.

6

Paulo has taken the bait. By attempting to take the Back, he has opened himself to an easy pass. As his leg clears my head, I turn to the left to face him. As I do this, I lead with my right arm going over his right shoulder.

7

I take the Side Control position with my right arm over Paulo's shoulder and my left hand blocking his hip.

Cross-Grip Guard

29-0 CROSS-GRIP PASSES

Beating the cross-grip can be a real nightmare, especially if you try to pass to the wrong side. When your opponent has you in his Cross-Grip Guard, he has dominated your entire side and is waiting for you to try to underhook his far leg with your free arm or step over it with your free leg. Both actions are traps. Always keep in mind that your opponent has a dominant grip and you may be giving him what he wants.

Instead of turning the position into a grip-fighting battle, conserve your energy and use the action-reaction principle to pass his guard. The following technique is the gold standard for dealing with the cross-grip using a minimal amount of effort and exposure.

29-1 SAME SIDE PASS

The Same-Side Pass is the go-to technique for dealing with the cross-grip. Remember, do not resist your opponent. Instead, flow with his movement and let that dictate how you pass. In the cross-grip situation, you dominate one side as your opponent controls your leg and pulls on your arm. Instead of feeding into his game by trying to pass to the other side, simply drop your weight over the dominated side and let his pulling action take you straight to Side Control.

Paulo has me in the Cross-Grip Guard. As an initial defense, I grab his left ankle with my right hand and insert my left knee between his legs.

Keeping both my hands inside his legs, I collapse my left shin onto Paulo's right thigh and drive my weight downward.

Next, I lock Paulo's leg in position with my left hook while my right elbow blocks his hip.

While keeping my left hook in place, I scissor my right leg backward to escape the guard. I must maintain this hook until my right leg is free. Otherwise, Paulo will transition to the Half Guard.

With my right leg free, I release my hook and take the Side Control position.

De La Riva Guard

30-0 DE LA RIVA PASSES

When De La Riva and others first began playing with this guard years ago, they caught everyone by surprise by taking their opponent's backs, sweeping, and attacking with omoplatas and triangles. Decades later, this guard is still very much a threat in the right hands.

To combat the De La Riva you must think of two things: controlling your opponent's pushing leg and escaping his hook. If you can control his pushing leg, you will able to buy the time to set up your escape; if you fail to do so, he can easily sweep you off balance. Escaping his hook is also essential. His hook serves to control, off-balance, sweep, and take the Back, so the earlier you rid yourself of this nuisance, the better.

30-1 UNLOCK & PASS

This is a very slow and methodical way to pass the De la Riva Guard. What I like about this move is that you are deliberately controlling your opponent as you set up and accomplish the pass. If done correctly, your opponent has very few options to defend, as he gradually feels his control waning away. The key to this move is in the squatting motion. Once you have squared yourself with your opponent and have locked your elbows to your knees, your forearms should be resting on top of his legs. As you squat, your forearms will naturally push his hooks downward until they are released.

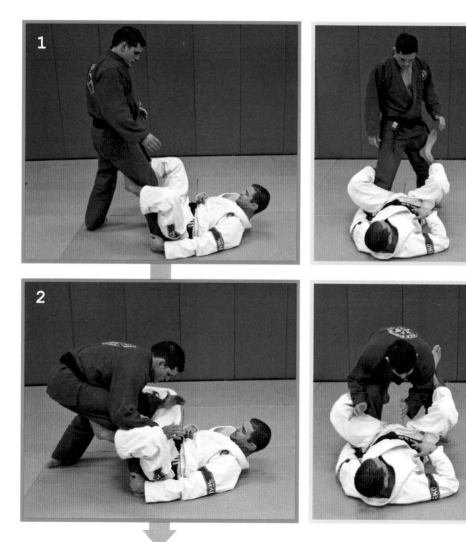

Paulo has me in his De la Riva Guard. I am standing in posture to prevent him from controlling my arm.

Keeping my right elbow locked to my thighs, I drop down to a standing Combat Base. My left forearm blocks his right thigh.

3 I step my left shin forward and lock my left elbow and thigh. At the same time, I sink deeper into my squat. This forces my forearms to lower Paulo's legs toward the mat.

4 Moving to my right, I slide my right knee onto Paulo's left knee. Meanwhile, my left arm hugs his body.

5 Using my right hook, I trap Paulo's left leg on the mat while I cross-face him with my right hand. My cross-face will prevent him from facing me.

6 I lift my left leg back to escape Paulo's guard.

7 I drive my left knee into Paulo's left hip and I take the Side Control position.

30-2 HOOK ESCAPE PASS

This is a wonderful technique that is much faster than the previous move. As with the previous maneuver, you have to control your opponent's pushing leg. Once you accomplish this, turn your trapped foot to the outside. This places an incredible amount of pressure on his hook and forces it to pop free. This is important for anytime you want to remove a hook so use this movement often! With the hook out of the way, collapse your weight and finish the guard pass as shown.

Paulo has me in his De la Riva Guard. My initial reaction is to control both his knees.

Pivoting on my right heel, I turn my foot 90 degrees to the outside. This angle change forces Paulo's hooking foot to pop off as my knee turns outward.

Continuing my motion, I drop my right shin on top of Paulo's left leg. I push his right knee away from me to prevent the possible block.

While trapping Paulo's left leg with my right hook, I cross-face him to gain control.

I scissor my left leg back to bring my hips to Paulo's left side. I must pressure with my cross-face and left hand to prevent him from turning into me for the sweep.

I hip-escape slightly to my right while pushing Paulo's leg away from me to take the Side Control position.

Figure 30.2: Poor Grab Defense

The De la Riva Guard can be a difficult position if you fight against your opponent's control. Remember, your left side is being dominated and that is what you have to escape (1). However, if you try simply to pull your leg free (2), you will bring your opponent with you and off-balance yourself. Body movement without proper technique and mechanics is useless. Learn how your opponent's body works, and use the proper angle to efficiently impose your game.

30-3 PASSING THE DEEP DE LA RIVA

Passing the deep De la Riva can be a tricky proposition for most. Obviously, your opponent is threatening to take your back as his hook naturally twists you in that angle. To beat this position, bring your forearm inside your opponent's pushing leg and sit back into the Reverse Half Guard position. Your forearm brace will have the dual function of preventing your opponent from circling his outside leg to take your back and keeping your opponent from locking a Half Guard as you pass. This movement works because you are not fighting his attempt to take your back. Instead, you are giving it to him, but on your terms, not his.

Paulo has me in his De la Riva Guard with his left foot feeding deep to my right hip. I have to be careful not to allow Paulo to take my back.

Facing Paulo, I bring both my forearms to the inside of his thighs.

I step my left leg back as my left arm prevents Paulo from moving his right leg. This will prevent him from taking my back as I pass his guard.

Next, I sit my right hip onto Paulo's left shoulder to inhibit his movement.

Simultaneously, I grab Paulo's right knee with my left hand as I place my left foot on his left knee.

Using my foot and hand in unison, I push Paulo's knee to the outside to free my right leg.

Having escaped my right foot, I safely transition into the Side Control position.

DE LA RIVA GUARD ✳ **275**

31-0 SIT-UP GUARD

The Sit-Up Guard is a De la Riva variation that is great for sweeping your opponent, taking the Back, and transitioning to a single-leg takedown. Personally, I love to pass this guard. Your opponent always feels open and you can move in and out of the following techniques to effectively dominate the pass. Just be careful of a couple things. You cannot let your opponent dominate your arms or you are going to get swept. Also, inhibit his movement by pressing slightly with your forward knee so he cannot slide his hips or stand up for the single leg.

31-1 STEP-AROUND PASS

The Step-Around Pass is a fast and simple way to pass the Sit-Up Guard. The goal of this pass is to free your trapped foot. Once you have escaped your foot, you pass the guard! To do so, apply pressure onto your opponent with your knee while pulling up on his outside knee. This will create the action for his reaction. When he pushes back in resistance, circle your trapped foot to the outside and step your other foot clear of his legs to pass the guard. Again, this movement makes use of the action-reaction principle, as well as the foot-circling movement that you mastered during your Spider Guard practice.

Paulo has me in his Sit-Up Guard and is controlling my lower lapels with his left hand.

Lowering my base, I reach down and grab Paulo's left shoulder with my right hand and his right knee with my left hand.

I pull up on Paulo's shoulder and pressure his right knee while slightly pressing my knee into him.

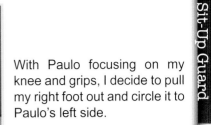

With Paulo focusing on my knee and grips, I decide to pull my right foot out and circle it to Paulo's left side.

My right foot lands close to Paulo's left side. As I do this, I continue to pull upward on his shoulder and push his knee to the outside. Once I escape my right foot, I nullify Paulo's grip on my lapel.

Next, I circle my left foot to Paulo's left side.

This puts me on Paulo's side.

While maintaining my grips, I press into Paulo until I have established a tight Side Control position.

Sit-Up Guard

31-2 UNDERHOOK TO MOUNT

Whenever I am passing any type of guard, I like to keep my mind open to taking the Mount position. It is easier to take the Mount from some guards. I feel the Sit-Up Guard Pass provides a very easy transition into the Mount. The important aspect of this position is how you change your angle to shift your opponent's energy. As you do this, notice you can underhook his arm much easier than if you tried it from the starting position. Like most of my techniques, the secret is always in changing the angle to take your opponent out of his game and creating the best leverage.

Paulo has me in his Sit-Up Guard and is controlling my lower lapels with his left hand. I place my right hand on his left shoulder.

I drop my base into a standing Combat Base, locking my right forearm and thigh.

After stepping my left leg over Paulo's right leg, I drop my left knee next to his right hip, and face his right side.

This angle change opens up the perfect space for me to underhook Paulo's left arm. As I get the underhook, I clasp my left hand over his shoulder, and drive him to the mat.

I have driven Paulo to his back and achieved the Half Mount position.

Lifting with my right underhook, I push Paulo's right arm upward and slide my right leg into the Mount position. I must clear this arm to prevent him from blocking the Mount.

31-3 UNDERHOOK TO KNEE-UP-THE-MIDDLE VARIATION

As a companion move to the previous technique, get used to alternating to the Knee-up-the-Middle Variation. Obviously, you want to have as many options as possible when passing in order to overwhelm your opponent's guard. You always want to lead him down a path where his reactions make it easier and easier for you to accomplish your goal. In the situation below, Paulo defends my Mount attempt by moving his hips, so I transition to the Knee-up-the-Middle Pass.

I have attempted the previous position and my right arm is already hooked under Paulo's left armpit.

This time, I decide to return to my feet and shift to a different pass.

I slide my right knee to the left, cutting it over Paulo's right hip.

As I continue sliding my leg, I drive Paulo onto his back. I keep my head on the right side of his, and I grip his right elbow with my left hand.

I pull up on Paulo's arm while sliding my right leg under his right armpit to secure the Kesa Gatame position.

32-0 REVERSE DE LA RIVA PASSES

Consider the Reverse De La Riva an extension of the De La Riva Guard. As you break the De La Riva hook by turning your foot and knee to the outside, it is natural for your opponent to assume this dangerous guard position. Notice that when he transitions into this guard, his hips will automatically shift slightly to the side. This is the direction in which to continue your pass and it is the same path you started when you broke the De La Riva hook. Do not hesitate! These guard passes should become an instinctive continuation of your De La Riva passes to keep your opponents at bay.

32-1 HIP SMASH

When using the Reverse De La Riva, your opponent must keep his inside knee elevated to block you from passing his guard. This should be seen as his first and last line of defense. Therefore, your job is to push his knee down to incapacitate his guard movement and then pass. To do so, do not just push or use your strength to rid yourself of his blocking leg. Instead, push down on your knee while moving to the side. Your sideways movement will cause his knee to follow you and create a better angle to collapse it to the mat. Once there, you will control his hips and pass his guard at will.

Paulo has me in his Reverse De La Riva Guard. I keep my posture forward with both hands on his knees to set up my defense.

I push Paulo's right leg to the mat as I drive my weight to my right.

Dropping my hips downward, I smother Paulo's legs and lock them in place. My left hand underhooks his right arm. At this point, I have completely dominated Paulo's Reverse De La Riva Guard.

REVERSE DE LA RIVA GUARD   281

To escape Paulo's legs, I sprawl my feet backward.

I finish by scissoring my left foot back into Side Control while cross-facing Paulo for control.

32-2 FLOATING PASS

Just as you can ride your opponent's sweep in the Butterfly Guard, you can also ride the Reverse De La Riva to pass the guard. This technique applies the same concept as the previous one. That is, squash his knees and you will beat the Reverse De La Riva. The key detail with this technique is to continually drive your hips forward. If you hesitate and shift your hips back, even for a second, your opponent likely will pursue the sweeps for which this guard is famous. So focus. Don't turn back. Keep driving your hips until you have smashed his legs and passed his guard.

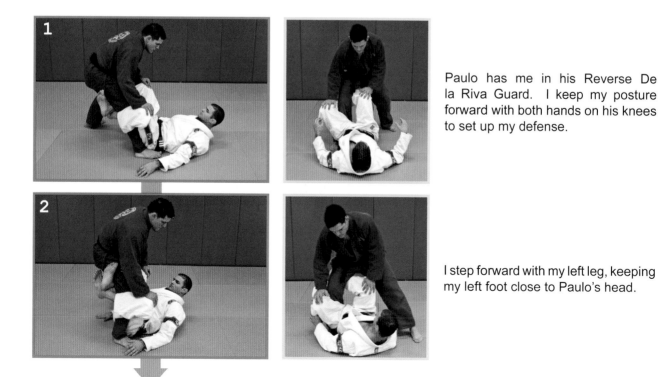

Paulo has me in his Reverse De la Riva Guard. I keep my posture forward with both hands on his knees to set up my defense.

I step forward with my left leg, keeping my left foot close to Paulo's head.

Without stopping, I drive my hips down and forward. This creates enough pressure to smother Paulo's right leg.

As I continue my forward hip pressure, I step over Paulo's head and drop all my weight onto his chest.

I look toward Paulo's knees to begin shifting my body onto its right side. I continue sagging my weight into him the entire time.

I drop my hip onto the mat next to Paulo and I am ready to transition to attacks or better positions.

33-0 INVERTED GUARD PASSES

The Inverted or Upside-Down Guard can be a difficult guard to face even for seasoned jiu-jitsu veterans. The problem when facing this guard is that forward pressure often results in triangle chokes, armlocks, and helicopter sweeps, while backward movement can end in a swift footlock or guard recovery. To stay safe, keep your hands outside his legs and try to put some distance between your legs and his body. Be especially careful if one of your legs is between his; he is likely to attack a sweep or submission.

33-1 HIP PASS

The first time I saw the Hip Pass used was when Rigan Machado passed Roberto "Roleta" Magalhaes's guard at the Pan-Americans tournament. At the time, Roleta swept everyone he faced and his guard was definitely one of the best flexible guards in the history of the sport. By using this move, Rigan was able to do something that few others have accomplished. He controlled Roleta's hips and top leg. When practicing this move, focus on walking your opponent's hip toward yourself and then sagging your hips onto his. In doing so, you will avoid the threat posed by his flexibility and movement while introducing your own control into the situation.

Paulo has rolled into an Inverted Guard. If he is strong in this position, he will be able to attack submissions and sweeps while defending the guard pass. For control, I grab his left hip with my right hand.

As I step back, I pull Paulo's hip toward me. This forces him onto his right side.

I sprawl my hips onto Paulo's upper left thigh as I secure his back with my right hand.

By stepping my right leg over to the left, I pass Paulo's legs and secure the Side Control position.

33-2 DANGER OF CIRCLING

I have seen so many people commit the mistake of circling inside the legs to pass the Inverted Guard. The problem is you actually can be successful doing this against less seasoned or flexible opponents and that builds a false security in this tactic. However, if you find yourself facing an expert of this guard, you are likely to pay with the following sweep or submission. Avoiding this is simple. Keep your arms to the outside and control the hips!

Once again, Paulo has rolled to the Inverted Guard (1).

Instead of grabbing Paulo's hip, I try to circle my arms inside his leg to secure the North-South position. This is a big mistake! (2)

Paulo makes me pay by lifting his right leg while grabbing my exposed arm (3).

I can do nothing to stop the momentum and Paulo rolls me toward my head to get the sweep (4).

34-0 PASSING THE X-GUARD

The X-guard is a modern guard that is known for incredible sweeps originating from the crossed-hooks control. To beat the X-guard you must first understand the dynamics of the hooks. The top hook pushes your weight backward while the bottom one pulls your leg forward. When done in conjunction, this creates an off-balancing sensation to the rear. In addition, the hooks easily can be extended to "split" the opponent off balance. Both sensations, splitting and off-balancing, often lead the guard passer to commit a grave error – grabbing the hooks to forcefully remove them. This gives the X-guard player everything he needs to sweep.

The following technical series addresses the necessary techniques to pass the X-guard with body movement. Remember, the power is always in your hips and legs, not your arms and hands.

34-1 BALANCE BALL BREAK & PASS

Before you hop into the X-guard to practice the pass, I recommend starting on a balance ball to get comfortable with the passing hip slide. As you practice, be mindful always to keep contact with your hips on the ball, just as you would against a live opponent. The balance ball makes a great practice partner and you may be surprised how well it mimics reality.

As an additional exercise, practice other guard passes, like the Reverse De la Riva pass, while working on the balance ball.

I start with a staggered stance on the balance ball. I must make sure both my hips are facing forward, even though one leg is in front of the other.

Leaning slightly to my right, I begin sliding toward my right hip, letting the ball pull my body sideways.

I make contact with my right hip and float on my right side as my feet move toward the mat.

Before the ball rolls me to my feet, I switch my hips and sprawl on the ball.

34-2 BREAK & PASS

The most effective way to break and pass the X-guard is with forward hip pressure. Because your opponent's legs are one of the strongest parts of his body, it does not make sense to push on them with weaker parts, like your arms. Instead, use your hips combined with gravity to smother his hooks and change the angle of attack. You will notice that as you slide your hips through, your opponent's hooks get weaker and weaker. This is because the optimal place to use the X hooks is from directly underneath. When your hips thrust through, his hooks move to the side, making them useless. This is an important concept to remember. There is always a maximum angle for any hook. Once this has been surpassed, the hook will always lose efficacy.

1 Paulo has me in his X-guard.

2 First, I square my hips so they are parallel to Paulo's. This changes the angle of the X-guard and already weakens his top hook.

3 Next, I begin sliding my hips downward and to my right. This hip pressure, combined with my angle, easily knocks Paulo's top hook free.

4 Continuing my hip slide, I lift my left leg over Paulo's head. I keep my entire left side in contact with Paulo's body to inhibit his movement.

X-Guard

My hips reach the ground with both legs on Paulo's left side.

Finally, I turn to face Paulo and establish the Side Control position.

Figure 34.2: Poor Strategy

Most people seem to think the secret to escaping the X-guard has to do with how you grip your opponent's leg to remove his hook. This could not be further from the truth. First of all, if you never change the angle of your hips, you will always be susceptible to being pulled off balance to your forward and rear (1). Secondly, grabbing the gi pants does nothing to alleviate this fact (2). In fact, once you grab your opponent, it is easier for him to sweep you forward or backward (3). This is especially valuable if you are fighting someone with an exceptional X-guard. Remember, treat every partner as if his X-guard is as good as Marcelo Garcia's, and use the correct pass to beat this position.

35-0 HALF GUARD PASSES

When using the Half Guard from the bottom, it is important to see it as an offensive position for attacking sweeps and the back. On the top, you have to see this position as halfway to passing the guard. Do not underestimate the power of this guard. In the right hands, it is very effective. However, remind yourself that you have gravity on your side and your proximity can make this position a nightmare for most.

When playing with this position, focus on three things: a flat opponent, base, and your opponent's underhooks. Ideally, you want control. To control, you need your opponent flat. If your opponent is on his side, he has the mobility and leverage for reversals. Your base is another aspect. Even while passing, you should be strong in your position. Never get careless with your positioning and compromise your ability to defend a basic bridging sweep. Finally, be aware of where your opponent puts his arm. If he underhooks your arm, he is trying to get posture to attack sweeps or take the Back. Likewise, if he underhooks your leg, he is seeking to change to a deeper Half Guard to trap you in a game of off-balancing reversals.

35-1 FLATTENING THE OPPONENT

When your opponent is on his hip in the Half Guard, he is in a great position to attack or take the Back. This side posture neutralizes the effects of many of your passes, so this should usually be addressed before you pass. Use the following technique to flatten your opponent and then set up the pass. You will find that flattening your opponent gives you so much more control over his Half Guard, and your passing percentage will assuredly increase.

Xande has me in a strong Half Guard position. He is postured on his side and is threatening a sweep with his left underhook.

First off, I drive my left knee into his right hip.

Next, I step my right foot away from me to the right.

As I collapse my right knee forward, I flatten Xande to his back.

HALF GUARD ❋ **289**

35-2 STRAIGHT LEG PASS WITH KNEE BLOCK

Switching the base is a technique that you must practice to master passing the Half Guard. By switching base, you change the angle so you can escape your leg at an opposing angle to that of your opponent. This is favorable when passing because it makes it difficult for your opponent to secure your leg while you maneuver for its escape. The following pass is a great example of how to use the low switched base to set up a kick to free the leg. Use your arm to pull up on your opponent's top leg and then kick forward and back for the instant escape!

Xande has me in his Half Guard, but I have managed to flatten him to his back. My left arm cross-faces him to prevent his hip escape or inside turn.

I switch my weight onto my left hip and slide my left leg underneath Xande's right leg. At the same time, I grab Xande's left knee and pull upward.

As I pull on Xande's knee, I kick my right leg forward.

To free my leg, I kick my leg backward. My left leg and hip prevent Xande's legs from following mine as I kick my right leg free.

I establish the Side Control position.

Figure 35.2: Don't Fight It!

One thing I do not like to do is have a tug-o-war battle as I try to escape the Half Guard. If my opponent is hell bent on locking onto my leg, all the pulling in the world is not going to make my job any easier, especially if I am pulling without establishing a good position (1). Once again, focus on your positioning and body angle to minimize your workload when passing the Half Guard.

35-3 BASE-SWITCH PASS WITH SHIN

I have been doing this pass for years, and it is still as effective today as the day I started using it. The trick with this technique is to insert your free shin in front of your opponent's bottom shin while escaping your hip into his armpit. This does two things. It creates a wedging pressure against your opponent's bottom leg and it inhibits your opponent from using his near-side arm to escape or sweep. To finish the pass, pull on your opponent's top leg with your hand while pulling with your trapped leg. Your wedged shin will prevent his legs from following and your leg should effortlessly slide free.

Xande has me in his Half Guard, but I have managed to flatten him to his back. My left arm cross-faces him to prevent his hip escape or inside turn.

Pushing off with my feet, I stretch my hips upward to escape my right knee. As I do this, I begin angling my left knee toward Xande's inside hip.

As I fall back to the mat, I slide my left shin in front of Xande's hips while grabbing his left knee. My shin will serve as a wedge throughout this guard pass.

Using countering movements, I push with my wedging shin and knee grip while I pull with my leg to release my right foot.

I step my right foot back and take the Reverse Kesa Gatame position.

35-4 BLOCKED ARM PASS

This is a variation of the previous pass, and it works on the same principle of using the shin wedge to free the leg. The only difference is that this time your opponent is reaching under your armpit to regain control with an underhook. This is the perfect timing to trap his arm and switch your hips for the pass. Beware. This technique works because you have already flattened your opponent and he is trying to get an underhook and escape to his side. Do not attempt this technique on an opponent on his side; this could end in a sweep or with your back taken. Instead, flatten your opponent again and then continue with this technique.

Xande has me in his Half Guard and is attempting to underhook my right arm.

I reach my left arm over Xande's shoulder to trap his arm while I straighten my left leg for counterbalance. I make sure to have a strong grip on Xande's belt before I proceed.

As I switch my hips to the left side, I wedge my shin in front of Xande's right hip. Then I grab his knee with my right hand.

While pushing with my hand and shin, I pull my right leg free, scissoring it behind me.

I reflatten Xande by pushing his knee toward his left side while I establish the Side Control position.

35-5 XANDE'S FLATTENING PASS

Xande's Flattening Pass is a great example of putting all the previous techniques together into one pass. In this situation, my brother is passing me while I have the deep underhook and side posture. To beat my posture, Xande will combine two different flattening techniques, the cross-face and sideways movement. Once he turns my head and forces me onto my back, he inserts his shin and completes a variation of the Blocked Arm Pass.

I have Xande in my Side Control. I am on my right side with a strong underhook.

Xande blocks my left hip with his right elbow, sets in a strong cross-face, and drives me to my back.

To escape his right knee, Xande switches onto his left hip, sliding his left leg under my right hip. Then, he pushes off with his hands slightly to pull his knee free.

By pushing on my knee and hip-escaping at the same time, Xande is able to pull his right leg free as he kicks it behind him.

Finally, Xande faces me to finish the guard pass in Side Control.

35-6 SHIN SLIDE PASS

This is my favorite passing series against the Half Guard because it provides options for the passer. At the heart of this pass is the shin slide. By sliding your shin across your opponent's hip line, you can control his body while changing the angle to pass. If you decide to continue to Side Control, the shin will act as a wedge to free your trapped leg. If mounting is your preference, the shin will work to free your trapped leg to the ankle and then you can step over into the Mount. This is a powerful passing series, but you must trap your opponent's head or underhook him while you pass. Otherwise, your opponent will take your back as you transition into the pass.

TO SIDE CONTROL:

1 — Xande has me in his Half Guard.

2 — Switching my hips slightly to the left, I create the necessary angle to lift my knee free. Notice that I lift my knee free by driving my hips upward.

3 — Next, I penetrate forward into the Half Mount position and underhook Xande's left arm. Xande knows he is in danger of being passed, so he locks his legs tight to stall my progress.

4 — I slide my shin forward until it blocks both Xande's hips.

To free my trapped leg, I pull on my foot while keeping Xande's legs in place with my shin. This wedge action makes it easier to free my leg.

I finish in the Side Control position.

TO MOUNT:

As I slide my shin across Xande's hips, I decide to change my angle to transition to a different position.

With Xande's hips pointed to his left, it is easier for me to slide back into the Half Mount position, and work my leg out. My arm keeps the underhook to prevent Xande from blocking my leg with his left arm.

I slide my right leg free to take the Mount position.

35-7 ESGRIMA PASS

The Esgrima or Underhook Pass should feel very comfortable for those that are on their way to mastering the Knee-Cross Pass. Essentially, this pass works on the same principle to slide the trapped leg free. The only difference is this pass begins with a tripod-like posture as you drive your forehead to the mat on the same side as your body while underhooking your opponent's far arm. This forehead posting and underhook are two very important aspects. First, the forehead will act as a point for you to keep your balance as you drive your hips to the sky to free your knee. Your arms will be preoccupied so you must get comfortable with posting on your forehead. Secondly, your underhook will be your protection against your opponent taking the Back. So keep your head planted and your underhook tight and you should have no problem passing with the Esgrima Pass.

Xande has me in his Half Guard and is blocking my cross-face attempt with his right arm.

I drive my weight onto him as I underhook his left arm. My right hand grabs high on his collar to secure the underhook.

I move my head to the right side of Xande's and grab his right knee with my left hand.

4

Driving off my toes, I lift my hips high off the mat. My arm acts as a brace, keeping Xande's legs in place, while I tripod off my feet and forehead. The upward movement of my hips frees my knee from his legs.

5

Once my knee is through, I grab Xande's right arm at the elbow while stepping my left foot forward for base.

6

As I drive my knee outward, I make hip-to-hip contact with Xande. I pull up on his elbow to keep his back flat to the mat. He tries to defend by tightening his grip on my foot.

7

Placing my left foot on Xande's left knee, I kick backward while scissoring my left leg forward to escape the Half Guard.

8

I continue to pull Xande's right arm upward to take the Kesa Gatame position.

35-8 ESGRIMA MOUNT

In this technique, Xande demonstrates how to use the same Esgrima Pass to take the Mount position. How Xande uses his shin to push my hips clear to the other side is of special importance. To do so, he must drive his shin along my hip line until his knee makes contact with the mat. At this point, he will easily free his leg and take the Mount position.

So far, Xande has followed the steps of the previous technique to pass my guard with the Esgrima. He has a deep underhook and has freed his knee from my Half Guard.

Xande decides to change to a different pass than before and places his left foot on the mat in front of my right knee.

Pushing off with his toes, Xande lifts his hips high above me while angling his right knee slightly to the right.

As he drives off the mat with his left foot, Xande slides his right knee along my hips until his right knee touches the mat next to my left hip. This action turns my hips from my right side to the left.

Once Xande's right knee hits the mat, he flings his right foot outward to escape the Half Mount position.

Finally, he assumes the Mount position and is ready to continue his attack.

Figure 35.8: Hip Detail

It is important to drive your knee and shin along the hip line to turn your opponent's legs to the other side. If you try to drive your knee forward to pass, you will not have the body positioning to do so. Learn to cut your knee toward his hip and you will always have control of your opponent's movement (1). Once you have his hips pointed away from you, you will be in the perfect position to pass to an even better position (2).

35-9 FREDSON ALVES' ESGRIMA PASS

This is a variation of the Esgrima Pass for which my good friend, Fredson Alves, is known. Fredson likes to trap the far triceps and then drive his elbow down to create pressure against his opponents. This is one of those occasions where it is acceptable to allow your opponent to get onto his side. Because your forearm impedes his progress and your arm is underhooking, you do not have to fear him coming to his knees or taking the Back. The secret is to pressure his body with your forearm while you slide your knee free.

Xande is in my Half Guard and has secured an underhook on my left arm. As always, I block the potential cross-face with my right hand.

To initiate the Fredson Alves Esgrima Pass, Xande cups my left triceps while driving his forearm inward and onto my chest. Xande then pressures his forearm onto my chest.

Next, Xande steps out with his left foot while he pushes my right knee down with his left hand. This frees his right knee.

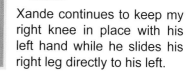

Xande continues to keep my right knee in place with his left hand while he slides his right leg directly to his left.

He will continue his slide until his left leg is free from my Half Guard.

To finish, Xande turns into me to take the Side Control position.

35-10 WHIZZER ARMBAR FEINT PASS

This is a particularly tricky move that I like to use to get the pass. If your opponent manages to get a deep underhook while you are passing, you should immediately whizzer, or overhook, his arm. This will prevent him from taking your back. Then, slide your posture back while closing your elbow to your body to put pressure on your opponent's elbow. For some, this pressure will be enough to get the tap. However, if he doesn't tap, use his moment of trepidation to pass the guard as he tries to understand what is happening to his arm. This is a perfect example of using distraction to accomplish your goal.

Xande has me in his Half Guard and is already in a great side posture with a deep underhook.

To defend the underhook, I circle my right arm around his left to establish the whizzer. This will block Xande from taking my back.

3

I continue feeding my arm until I can grab Xande's right lapel with my right hand.

4

Next, I step my left leg to my rear left while I push on Xande's right knee. This creates armlock pressure on his left arm.

5

I free my right knee and begin sliding it directly to my left.

6

My slide continues until my leg is free. It is important that I maintain cranking pressure on Xande's arm as a distraction.

7

Finally, I turn into Xande to take the Side Control position.

35-11 THE OPPOSITE SIDE PASS

The first time I used this pass was when I faced the Half Guard master, Roberto "Gordo" Correa. I knew when I got into his dangerous Half Guard I had to change the angle to successfully deal with his guard. By switching to the opposite side, I was able to kick my leg free while eliminating all of his control.

When you practice this technique, focus on the entry. You want to have your opponent on his side when you launch your leg over. This will make it difficult for him to follow as you move in the other direction. In addition, push off the mat with your free arm to add more propulsion to your leg as it crosses his body. Doing this will reduce the chance that your opponent will take your back as you move to the opposite side.

Xande has me in his Half Guard and is already in a great side posture with a deep underhook. My weight is too far forward and he is in a great position to attack my back.

I post my left hand on the mat while grabbing the small of his back with my right hand in an over-the-shoulder grip.

Pushing off the mat with my left hand, I launch my left foot toward Xande's left side. This gives me the momentum and distance to clear his legs.

As I land on the opposite side, I brace my left hand against Xande's right knee to prevent him from turning into me.

5

Once I feel safe, I move my left hand to Xande's right hip. I brace against his hip while hip-escaping to my right to free my leg to the ankle.

6

To free my ankle, I press my left foot on Xande's left knee to create a counter pressure to my pull.

7

I continue this push and pull until I safely free my left foot. Once again, I maintain control of Xande's right hip to prevent his escaping movement.

8

To complete the technique, I square my hips to Xande and take the Side Control position.

35-12 OPPOSITE PASS AGAINST UNDERHOOK

This is a very useful variation of the Opposite Side Pass to use when your opponent has underhooked you and achieved a strong side posture. Before passing, reach over his underhooked arm and secure the belt at this elbow level. Then commit to the Opposite Side Pass. When you land, you will contort your opponent's arm in a bent armlock. At this point decide either to pull up for the submission or to use the distraction principle to pass the guard.

Xande has me in his Half Guard and is already in a great side posture with a deep underhook. My weight is too far forward and he is in a great position to attack my back.

This time, I lock my right arm over Xande's left elbow and grab toward his lower back. At the same time, I sink my weight back.

Posting off my left hand on the mat, I stretch my left leg and drive my hips high to my right side.

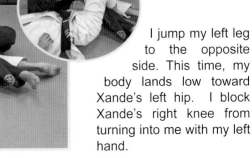

I jump my left leg to the opposite side. This time, my body lands low toward Xande's left hip. I block Xande's right knee from turning into me with my left hand.

Once I feel safe with my balance, I move my left hand to Xande's right hip.

Bracing with my left grip, I hip-escape to my left to free my right foot.

As I free my foot, I keep pressure on Xande's right hip to prevent him from turning into me.

I finish by turning into him to take the Side Control position.

35-13 OPPOSITE-SIDE PASS TO MOUNT

Xande's version of the Opposite-Side Pass to Mount is one of the highest percentage techniques for taking the Mount from the Half Guard. Notice as he switches to the opposite side, he does not try to step all the way to the Mount. Although this is possible, it is also a lot riskier because your opponent can lift his knees and recover the guard in transition. Instead, he pulls my knees toward him and mounts my legs. From here, Xande has the security to sprawl his legs free and slide to the Mount without worry of my guard recovery.

1 This time, Xande is in my Half Guard. He is already basing his left leg away from his body to counter my side posture. To set up his pass to the opposite side, he sits down on my left thigh.

2 Xande swings his left leg toward my left side. As he does this, he grabs my right knee with his left hand.

3 As Xande's hips fall to the mat, he uses the momentum of his swing to pull my right leg toward him.

4 Changing directions, Xande steps his left leg over my legs and locks his left thigh to the back of my knees.

While sprawling his hips down, Xande manages to spread both his feet outward. This escapes his leg from my Half Guard control.

Keeping his hips heavy, Xande slides his right knee in front of my lower abdomen.

To finish passing to the Mount, Xande simply slides his left knee past my rear while squaring his hips with mine.

Figure 35.13: Step Back Detail

Xande has reached the opposite side of my Half Guard and is in control of my right knee. He must pull my knee toward him to set up his transition.

Notice that he continues to push my knee down as he steps on top of them. Xande does not try to step onto my torso.

Once on top, Xande locks his legs close to my knees and drives his hips down for control. Note that he does not try to step all the way to the Mount; instead, he plays a game of inches to ensure he does not lose control during the transition.

35-14 HALF MOUNT PASS

The Half Mount is one of those in-between positions in which everyone finds themselves from time to time. Although this is a dominant position for the top person, it can be a difficult lock to break if you are not using the correct technique. To break the Half Mount, use the same principle as the Knee Cross Pass. Point your leg to the outside and slide your knee away from your opponent. Once your knee touches the mat, you have reached the optimal angle to sprawl your leg free and take the Mount.

After trying to pass Xande's Half Guard, I have ended up in the Half Mount position.

Immediately, I drop my left knee under Xande's rear to lock him in this position. As I do this, I begin angling my right knee to the outside.

3

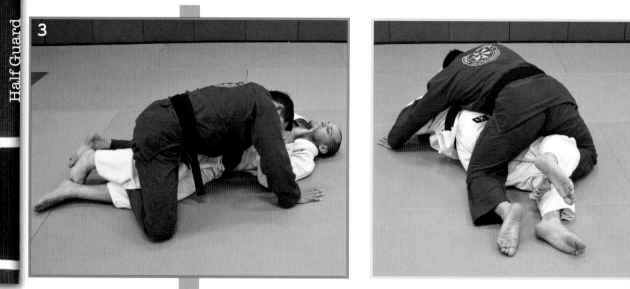

Once I have turned my knee to its utmost extent, I drop it to the mat next to Xande's knees.

4

Because I have created such an extreme angle with my right knee, it is easy to kick my right leg free.

5

I slide my hips and knees upward to take the Mount position.

35-15 HALF MOUNT TO KNEE CROSS

As a rule, if there is a mounting option when passing the guard, there is always a Knee Cross option. For this variation, post both your hands on your opponent's chest to block his movement and then stand upright to put distance between your hips and his. Change the angle by driving your knee to the other side and pass with a Knee Cross variation.

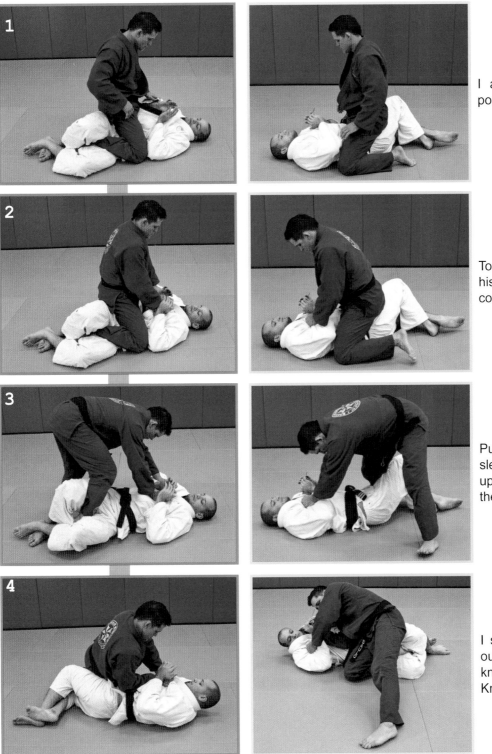

1

I am in the Half Mount position on top of Xande.

2

To control Xande, I grab his right sleeve and left collar.

3

Pushing off Xande's sleeve and collar, I stand up to change the angle of the pass.

4

I step my left foot to the outside and slide my right knee to the left to use the Knee Cross Pass.

Half Guard

As I keep hip-to-hip contact, I slide my right leg free. I must spread my legs wide in case Xande tries a last-ditch reversal.

Facing Xande, I block his left hip with my right elbow and establish the Side Control position.

35-16 DEEP HALF—LEG PULLOUT

The deep Half Guard happens whenever your opponent underhooks one of your legs while securing your other leg in his Half Guard. This is an advantageous position for your opponent because he can affect your balance by altering your center of gravity. Obviously you have to get out of this dangerous situation and this is a great first-line escape. The technique is simple and effective; point your toe and pull up fast to escape the deep Half Guard.

Xande has me in the deep Half Guard. With his hips underneath my own, he is in a superb position to attempt some sweeps.

While keeping my left arm posted on the mat away from Xande, I point my right toes to the mat.

I pull my leg straight up to escape the lock. This is only possible because I keep my toes pointed and I pull in the same line as my shin.

To clear my leg, I step it behind me.

Keeping Xande's right arm between my legs, I take the Side Control position.

COMMON MISTAKES:

Bear Crawl:

Xande has me in the deep Half Guard (1). I try to turn to All Fours and bear crawl forward to escape (2). There is no reason for him to let go at this point, so he keeps his legs locked and waits for me to tire. If I continue, he likely will go out the back door and take my back.

Flexed Foot:

Xande has me in the deep Half Guard. My right foot is bent upward (1). I attempt the pullout technique, but the angle of my foot prevents its escape. I should have my toes pointed at the mat instead of upward (2).

35-17 HALF BUTTERFLY HIP-SWITCH

Sometimes, your opponent will use a hybrid guard, like the Half Butterfly Guard. With his hook in place, your opponent has a greater ability to lift your hips. This makes him a threat for sweeps and guard replacement. To pass this position, I adhere to the same hip switch principle as I do when passing the Butterfly Guard. The hip-switch is effective because you push your knee into your opponent's to drive his hook downward. Then, you can switch your hips to clear both his legs.

Paulo has me in his Half Butterfly Guard and has a deep grip on my left thigh.

To initiate my pass, I lift my right knee close to Paulo's left knee.

Using the power of my hips, I turn my right knee to the inside until Paulo's left knee crashes on top of his right and my right hip makes contact with his.

As I push Paulo's left leg down with my left palm, I swing my left leg toward my backside.

Once my left foot makes contact with the mat, I start sliding my right leg to the same side.

I take the cross-face grip and establish the Side Control position.

35-18 OPEN HALF GUARD HIP-DRIVE PASS

In this technique, Xande showcases the effectiveness of switching his hips to pass the open Half Guard. Because my left shin and right heel are trapping him in my open Half Guard, Xande switches his hips to change the angle and to create acute pressure on my top leg. This hip pressure forces my bottom leg to the mat and opens up a clear path for his knee to slide over my foot. From here, there is nothing to stop him from reaching the Side Control.

I have Xande in my open Half Guard. Neither of my legs are locked, and I am using space and my left shin to prevent him from getting too close to me.

Sensing that my knees are too close to each other, Xande sprawls onto his toes and drives his hips into my top knee. As he does this, he grips his right hand on my back and his left hand pushes down on my right knee.

Still, my legs are bothering Xande, so he switches his weight onto his right hip to unhook my bottom and top legs. This hip-switching movement is key to many guard passes.

His hip-switch has forced my left foot to the mat and he uses this as the perfect time to slide his right leg over my right leg.

Xande continues his slide until his right leg has escaped my Half Guard. His hip-to-hip pressure stifles my ability to escape.

To finish the position, Xande turns into me to establish the Side Control.

Figure 35.18: Hip Switch Detail

Anytime you are dealing with a tough open Half Guard or Butterfly Guard, you must have a tight posture to your opponent (1). You should be able to try the hip switch to remove his hooks or blocks. By changing your body angle, it becomes very awkward for your opponent to hold you in his original position (2). In most cases, this type of fundamental movement results in your hips slicing through his defenses. To reach the highest levels of guard-passing, master this movement.

35-19 OPEN HALF GUARD LEMON SQUEEZE PASS

Although this pass is very common when passing the open or closed Half Guard, it is seldom done properly. Some people correctly lock their hands under their opponent's rear and sprawl their hips back, but they fail to create the best angle to escape their leg. To do so, walk your legs in the direction of your trapped leg. This will push your opponent's Half Guard to its breaking point. Once you can walk no farther, then you can escape by clearing your leg. Your opponent will not be able to follow you due to his flattened position and locked hips.

As I attempt a guard pass, Paulo decides to transition into an open Half Guard to defend.

While I drive my left shoulder onto Paulo's left hip, I scoop my left arm under both his legs. He reacts by closing the guard.

My right hand scoops under to grip my left wrist. This binds Paulo's legs together.

Staying on my toes, I begin walking my body to my right. By clasping Paulo's legs and walking mine toward them, I put a tremendous strain on his lock.

Once I have walked as far as I can go, I break the lock by kicking my right foot to the right. Paulo cannot hold his lock against my pressure and angle.

Immediately, I kick my right leg back in the direction of my left leg. This clears my legs from Paulo's guard.

With both feet on the same side, I drive my right knee into Paulo's hip to prevent his escape, and establish the Side Control position.

The Black Belt's Focus: SUBMISSIONS

"There is no doubt that armlocking is a dangerous business."
— Neil Adams, 1981 Judo World Champion

5-0 ACCEPTING DEFEAT IN TRAINING

I think jiu-jitsu is the only martial art where you must continually accept defeat. You have to recognize at that moment, that another man is better than you. I think for a man, this is hard to accept. Although it is very difficult, you really need to let it go and understand that this is something that will happen frequently. I prefer for it to happen in the academy, rather than in a tournament or the street. So, in the academy, I train like it is a place of learning, and I tap.

Personally, I always have been a competitive person, but I have also had to check my ego. I have had to remind myself that I am at the academy to learn and not to compete. The time to compete always comes, and the academy is rarely the place for this.

5-1 ACCEPTING DEFEAT FOR THE UPPER BELT

Tapping is a difficult concept to wrap your mind around, especially if it is an upper belt tapping to a lower belt. To these students, I say set your souls free. I believe that jiu-jitsu is a samurai art. So as a samurai, your job is to pass your knowledge to the lower belts. As a purple belt, your job is to be soft with someone lower than you. This is because you want to make the lower belt feel better and allow him to see his progression. The way that he will feel progression is when he starts to bite you, and this is a good thing because he will owe his progression to you. Therefore, you are not going to battle the lower belts, you are going to bring them with you. It is the same for white belts. Sometimes they cannot see that upper belts help them and their egos become bigger than themselves. They think they can pass this guy and they do not need the upper belts any more. This is the point where they start to regress.

When I train, I tap to lower belts from time to time. Everyone does. The important part is bringing your students with you, not fighting them to keep your superiority. If you do not help them, you will never create the image of yourself in your students.

5-2 SUBMISSIONS AS A TOOL

I believe that tapping is a great way to train healthily and prevent injury. Once the mistake is made, there is no return, so tap! There is no level of toughness that can undo mistakes. If you understand this, it doesn't matter if you are strong enough to hold off the armbar or can squeeze your neck so tight to avoid the choke. It doesn't matter because the mistake is already made. You already failed. If you fail, just start over. It's that easy.

It is better to tap many times, train hard, and have a safe learning experience than not to tap once and suffer injury and time away from the mats.

5-3 FLOWING AND SUBMISSION

You must be able to flow with your submission attacks. The guy who is just using his strength to roll people over doesn't trust his jiu-jitsu and has already failed to use it properly. Flowing and adaptation are so important. If you just hold the position, you eventually will find yourself in trouble. That is why I tell my guys not just to hold the position, but to *feel* it. This is a very different concept.

There is no holding the Side Control or holding the Mount. There is only feeling the Side Control and *feeling* the Mount. If you are holding the Side Control and your opponent starts to turn, you should not be forcefully holding onto him to back him up. Instead, you will feel where to adjust and if he turns, you have other options—the Back, choke, and so on. You must always adapt so that you are one step ahead. Once your opponent thinks about turning, you are already moving to take his back. Your opponent isn't even thinking about defending yet because he is still caught up in his turn. Now he is one step behind you in his thinking and this is dangerous in the submission game.

5-4 STRENGTH AND THE END GAME

The submission is the only time that you ever need strength. This is because once you have caught the submission, you still have to squeeze. The squeeze takes strength and stamina and this is the only time when you really need some muscle while you are rolling.

In contrast, some say you should never use strength. The truth is you need some strength. The strength only comes out at certain, specific times – not to get out of trouble, not to defend, not to play the guard, but only to finish the submission at particular times.

Helpful Submission Tips

- Release your ego. Always tap! Tapping prevents injury so you can train tomorrow.

- Never forcefully hold down your opponent. Use his movement to transition to submissions.

- Use strength where it is necessary, like the end game, not to defend, to set up submissions, or to play the guard.

- Learn what is needed for each submission, whether it be leverage, angle, or movement. Each type of submission has special mechanics.

Saulo assists his student with a submission.

Photo: Catarina Monnier

Leticia Ribeiro practices controlling the submission by securing a Kimura lock and slowly finishing her partner.

5-5 BUILDING YOUR TOP GAME TO THE TAP

I always tell my students that the ultimate goal is the submission. But, let's go step by step. Let's first pass the guard, transition to the Knee-on-Belly, take the Mount, and then start your submission. The Mount is the biggest proof that all your opponent's defensive skills were beaten and that you passed through his entire game: his guard, his Half Guard, his Side Control defense, his Knee-on-Belly defense, everything. If you can beat your opponent's entire game, the submission should come easily.

Once you have a dominating game and it is time to finish the submission, pay attention to the smallest details about the position you hold. Some submissions require speed while others require aggression and timing. Focus on these details as you proceed through the rest of this text.

With submissions, it is important to differentiate between types because each kind of submission has a different treatment. With chokes, you deal a lot with wrist control and body adjustment. With armlocks, it is movement. When you deal with armbars, you talk a lot about hip control and the ways to tie up someone. Focus on the mechanics of the movement and you will master the submission.

5-5 POSITIONAL CONTROL AND SUBMISSIONS

Most instructors do not spend enough time talking about the importance of keeping the position and defeating your opponent's defense. I see submissions as the result of certain situations where you are in a completely advantageous position and you can choose the proper way to make your opponent give up. This means I can choose to be fast and precise, or to be rough, or I can choose to be slow and to give him some hope. I can choose my objective and then apply my submissions to that platform.

5-6 TOP SUBMISSIONS AND THE BLACK BELT

For most students, the submission is their favorite course to study, but it is also one of the smallest parts of the jiu-jitsu game. When you consider the time spent sparring and competing, the smallest percentage of that is the finishing submission. A good analogy for this is surfing. Most surfers dream of big tube rides and carves, but the majority of their time is spent paddling. So, what is more important to learn, paddling or aerials? For the lower belts, it is best to learn the foundation of jiu-jitsu as presented in this book. The submissions from the top are the end of the road, just as aerials are for surfers.

The black belt student should be well rounded in his jiu-jitsu skills by this point and the top game is the place where he can dominate with submission attempts. He must learn two aspects of this game: to flow between submissions in order to overwhelm his opponent and to direct his opponent into his submission. Dominate the position and submit!

As with all dominant positions, the secret to submitting someone while on his back is controlling the position. Use your heels as hooks to maintain the position and attack his neck and arms to keep his focus away from escaping. This is a very important aspect to controlling the Back. If your opponent is worried about the submission, he cannot focus on your legs. Also, keep your chest glued to his back and anticipate his movement to prevent him from scooting out or driving away to escape. First master the control and then focus on the submissions! You will have a higher rate of success and ground domination.

Drill this position by assuming the Back with your opponent facing up. Practice by trying to maintain the position against an escaping opponent and by trying to submit a defensive opponent. Both drills will give you a Back attack game that is stifling and frustrating to escape or survive!

36-1 GETTING THE COLLAR: BOW & ARROW CHOKE

The bow-and-arrow choke is my go-to submission whenever I have the Back. When practicing, be aware of two things. First, your opponent always will try to block your hands from entering into the choke, and second, your choking pressure must be strong because your opponent often fights for his life to prevent from tapping. This technique is successful because of how it treats these tangibles. By contorting your attacking hand into a knife position, you can minimize its profile as you slide it down your opponent's jawline. This allows your hand to penetrate his defense while sliding into a tight choke. To create maximum choking pressure, change your angle so that you are perpendicular to your opponent. From this position, you can make alternating pressures—one pressure pulls on the choke and his leg while the other pushes his torso. In doing so, you create a maximum choking pressure with minimum effort. This is the goal of jiu-jitsu.

I have taken Xande's back and have both hooks in for control.

Grabbing his right collar close to the neck, I cut the slack for my approaching left hand.

As Xande raises his hands to defend the choke, I use a monkey paw grip next to his ear to enter into the submission.

I slide my monkey paw grip along the ridge of his neck until my right hand can feed my left hand his left lapel. This approaching grip is important; by using it, I can slide my hand right underneath his defense.

Once my left hand secures his lapel, I reach my right hand down to his knee.

To finish the choke, I move my body perpendicular to Xande's to create the maximum choking angle as I drive down with my right leg and pull up on the choke and knee grip. This creates the bow-and-arrow motion for which this choke is known.

Figure 36.1: Choking Detail

Remember, whether you are in the guard or the Back, you should always feed your other hand the choke (1 and 3). This is because you can get a choke much tighter, and faster, if you feed the collar. Specifically with the choke from the Back, get used to working in small spaces as you slide in your choking hand (2). Your opponent does not want your hand there, so you have to make it the smallest target possible. This is why you hide your fingers in a monkey grip and use your hand as a blade that slices into choking position.

36-2 ARMBAR AGAINST CHOKE DEFENSE

Whenever your opponent lifts one arm to defend the choke, he is exposing himself to this easy armbar. You will be surprised at how often this armbar presents itself because many students believe this is a safe posture. The key point to this technique is to secure your opponent's arm with the figure-four lock and then to push him to the mat as you slide your hips out from underneath him. Be prepared: your opponent likely will try to resist. But instead of losing the position, feel the control of the figure-four-lock and steer your opponent into the armbar submission.

I have Xande's back with both hooks in for control. This time, he has his right arm elevated to begin his defense.

As I attempt to set up the previous choke, Xande blocks my approaching hand with his left hand.

Instead of fighting for the choke, I secure his right arm with my right.

Next, I grab Xande's right wrist with my left hand and secure the figure-four lock.

Pivoting my hips to the right, I let Xande's body fall into the space I previously occupied.

Xande completes his fall, and my right leg slides down his belt line.

I throw my left leg over Xande's head.

While keeping consistent downward pressure on both legs, I fall back, pulling Xande's arm into the armbar with my falling body weight.

36-3 ARM & COLLAR CHOKE

The arm-and-collar choke is a tricky choke variation that works great when your opponent has an arm lifted in a choke-defense position. However, this technique also works just as well if you have an over-and-under grip from the Back. The reason this choke works is simple. Defensively, most jiu-jitsu players are concerned about the choking hand. Offensively, they are taught the choking hand is always the one that comes over their arm. By getting a deep collar grip with the underhooking arm, your opponent is likely to dismiss this as not a real choking attack. This is the trap—once you get your hand deep enough, simply pull your opponents arm in front of his neck to sink in the tight arm-and-collar choke. The choke should have the same pressure as the head-and-arm or triangle chokes.

I have Xande's back with both hooks in for control. Once again, he has his right arm elevated to begin his defense.

Noticing that Xande's left hand is low, I grab his left lapel and feed it to my approaching right hand.

I feed a deep collar grip to my right hand.

With my collar grip in place, I grab Xande's right elbow with my left hand.

To finish the choke, I drag Xande's elbow onto his face while pulling with my choking hand. This simple choke comes on fast and strong.

36-4 EZEQUIEL CHOKE FROM THE BACK

The Ezequiel or sleeve wheel choke from the back is one of the most high-percentage attacks from the Back . Originally popularized by Ezequiel, a judo and Brazilian jiu-jitsu practitioner, it has continued to evolve into a highly effective submission that can be utilized from the over-and-under back grip. Remember to feed your front hand all the way to your opponent's collar bone to ensure an easy feed for your back hand. To create that intense choking pressure, bring your rear hand completely around your opponent's head until you can clamp down on your own forearm. From here, your opponent will have no recourse but to tap.

Xande has my back and I am defending my right side by lifting my right arm to my ear.

Realizing I am in a compromising position, Xande feeds his right arm under my armpit and cups my left shoulder with his hand.

Tightening his hold, Xande grabs his left sleeve with his right hand. His grip should be with four fingers inside the sleeve.

Xande begins wrapping his left arm around my head to increase choking pressure.

To finish the choke, Xande grabs his right forearm with his left hand while slightly angling to his right. The choke is incredibly tight as it completely wraps my head.

37-0 THE MOUNT

Like submissions from the Back, your ability to submit from the Mount will depend on your experience controlling the position. To start, think of the Mount as having two variations: the High Mount and the Low Mount. Both are effective platforms for submissions, but they also offer their own costs and benefits.

The High Mount occurs anytime you are postured high on your opponent's chest. This is a great position to attack armlocks and cross lapel chokes, but you have to have your hips ready to ride out his defensive bumps or else you will lose the position. Also, get used to deflecting your opponent's pushes and grips as you dominate the position. Many of the following submissions work well when your opponent tries to defend the High Mount so take advantage of his movement and end the match with a submission.

The Low Mount is the position where your hips are tight to your opponent's and your legs are usually grapevined or locked underneath his. This forces your chest into your opponent's and can cause a very claustrophobic feeling for him. This is a great beginner Mount because often it is much more difficult to escape than the High Mount. The S-Mount is a great defensive position to catch your breath, but can also be used offensively with the Kata Gatame and sleeve wheel chokes.

Drill this position by starting on the top of the Mount and having your partner do everything he can to escape the position. Your only goal is to maintain both the High and Low Mounts and diffuse his escape attempts. Once you are comfortable maintaining and transitioning between the Mounts, add some of the following submissions into the mix until you have a well-rounded attacking Mount.

37-1 THE AMERICANA

The americana, or ude garame armlock, is likely to be the first submission you will learn from the High Mount position. This move is introductory by nature for a couple of reasons. First of all, the bent armlock is a great submission technique that exerts an extraordinary amount of pressure on your opponent's shoulder and elbow. Secondly, you do not have to change positions, as you do with the armbar. This makes it a "safe" attack for many beginners who have not overcome their fear of losing position. Finally, the entry into this technique teaches you how to use your bodyweight, instead of your arm strength, to isolate your opponent's arm. One more thing, do not confuse "introductory" with "low-percentage." This is a highly effective attack that you should use throughout your jiu-jitsu journey.

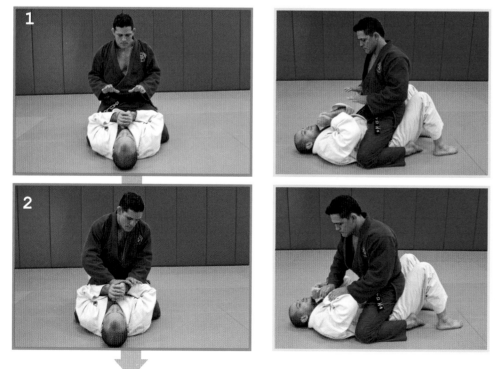

I have Xande in the High Mount. He has his hands tucked toward his face to defend a possible choke.

To set up the americana lock, I place my right hand on his right wrist and my left hand on his right forearm.

Using my body weight, I drive Xande's right arm to the mat. My right elbow locks tight to his neck. It is important that I only use my bodyweight; the strength of my arms alone is not enough to isolate his arm.

I place my left hand on the mat palm down behind his tricep to set up the lock.

Sliding my left arm under Xande's right triceps, I secure a figure-four lock on my own wrist. Both of my grips should be five-finger grips with all digits on top.

To apply the armlock, I start sliding Xande's right hand toward his hip. This is the paintbrush technique of the americana.

Once I can no longer slide his hand any farther, I lift his elbow upward to finish the armlock. Xande feels quick pain in his right shoulder and is forced to tap out.

37-2 MOUNTED ARMBAR

The armbar from the Mount, or Juji Gatame, is a classic attacking position in jiu-jitsu. However, it is also a position that is lost as the opponent escapes his elbow during the attack. To alleviate this risk, always control your opponent's elbow. In this technique, you will begin by controlling your opponent's elbow with both hands and then with your body weight. This dominates the elbow and drives into an attackable position. Master the elbow control and you will see your armbar success go through the roof.

I have Xande in the High Mount. He tucks his hands toward his face to defend a possible choke.

First, I slide my left arm between Xande's arms and trap his left triceps.

Then, I move my right palm on top of my left hand and push Xande's left elbow to the inside.

The strength of my arms is not enough to keep Xande's arm in place so I drive my bodyweight onto his elbow to prevent him from clearing his elbow.

5 While maintaining constant pressure on Xande's left elbow, I shift my body to a perpendicular position to attack the armbar. To lighten my right leg, I lean my body to the left.

6 I swing my right leg over Xande's face to get to the armbar position. Because my body is angled to the left, my leg swings over easily.

7 To finish the armbar, I secure his arm to my chest, fall back, and hyperextend his elbow joint by thrusting my hips. I must be sure to keep my knees tight to each other and his thumb pointed upward to prevent his escape.

Figure 37.2: Perfect Armbar Posture

Just as there are many details to achieve the armbar position, there are just as many to finish the submission. As a recap, remember to tighten your knees together. This closes off space and secures your opponent's body. Be sure to keep your hips tight to your opponent's armpit. If you fail to do this, his arm can easily slip out of the hold. Keep his wrist vertical with his thumb upward. Aligning the wrist prevents your opponent's rollout escape. Finally, grab at his wrist and thrust with your hips. His wrist is the end of the lever and your hips are the fulcrum, so get used to using efficient positioning when attacking the armbar submission.

37-3 EZEQUIEL

The Mount

The Ezequiel is one of the most famous and infamous chokes from the Low Mount position. Named after the Brazilian judo and jiu-jitsu player, Ezequiel Paraguassu, the Ezequiel has become famous for its direct choking action. The goal of this technique is to use your arms and head positioning to trap your opponent's arms so that you have complete reign over his neck. To attack the neck, slide the blade of your hand along your opponent's jawline, just as you do in other chokes. Finish by continuing this penetration until your hand meets your forearm. This move can and should be done in this clean and effective manner. However, some students like to use their knuckles to enter into the choke, or they pull back to put pressure on their partner's trachea. This is not our goal. Remind yourself, do you want your jiu-jitsu to be clean and beautiful or dirty and hard? This is a great move, but it should be done in a way that preserves your partners and friends; injury is unnecessary!

This time I have Xande in the Low Mount to counter his hip bumping movement. Both my arms are forward for stabilization.

While keeping my hips pressuring into Xande, I slide my left hand under his neck.

Next, I grab my right sleeve with my left hand. I grip with my four fingers to the inside of the sleeve.

With my fingers tight like a blade, I circle my right hand in front of Xande's throat.

Keeping my posture low, I feed my right hand to my left forearm. By encircling Xande's head, I have secured a very tight and effective choking technique. He will tap as I feed my right hand deeper.

AGAINST TOUGHER OPPONENTS:

This time, Xande is being more difficult, and I do not want to give him as much space as the previous technique. Therefore, I hug his head with my left arm and drive my head to his left side. I keep my right elbow pinched down to the mat to block him from using his left arm.

While blocking Xande's view with my head, I grab my right sleeve with my left hand. I continue to use my right elbow to block his left arm.

Next, I pressure my head into Xande's to open up his neck. Then, I begin circling my right hand in front of his throat. Because everything has been hidden and tight, he has a very limited response.

As I move my choking hand deeper toward my left arm, I pivot my head to the side of the choke for increased tightness. Xande is forced to tap immediately.

37-4 KATA GATAME

The Kata Gatame, or head-and-arm choke is a perfect attack whenever your opponent attempts an elbow escape. If you catch your opponent early as he tries to push on your knee, you will have a clear path under his armpit into the head and arm position. The key to this position is actually getting his arm into position. To do so, alternate between walking your hand on the mat and straightening your arm. Every time you straighten your arm, you lever your opponent's arm closer to the attack. Simply continue this process until you have the choking position and then finish this calculated attack.

I have Xande in a High Mount. To initiate an elbow escape, he pushes down on my right knee with his left hand while his right forearm braces against my hips.

Instead of trying to remove his grips, I decide to slide my right hand under his left biceps.

The Mount

As I slide my right arm through, I cross-face Xande with my left hand. I keep both my palms flush with the mat.

Next, I pull on the mats with my fingertips until both my hands are fisted. This tightens both my controls.

By lifting my right elbow and walking my hands farther, I am able to propel Xande's left arm skyward.

With Xande's arm elevated, I slide my right arm deeper underneath his triceps.

To get Xande into position, I straighten my right arm while posting my hand on the mat. My elbow drives into his arm and forces it to cross his centerline.

Locking my hands together to the left of Xande's neck, I drop my head to the mat and trap his left arm across his neck and face. To finish, I contract my biceps and pectorals while driving my head into him to get the tap. He taps due to pressure on his carotid arteries on both sides.

37-5 PALM UP/PALM DOWN CHOKE

The classic palm up/palm down cross choke is a favorite technique for many jiu-jitsu players. Most opt to learn this position because it is seen as much easier to achieve compared to the palm up/palm up variation. This is because the top hand can enter anywhere near the neck as long as there is a collar or shoulder to grab on to. The trick of this position is molding the blades of your hands and wrists to your opponent's jawline to effectively block his carotid arteries. Then, the process of curling your hands and touching your elbows to your ribs only increases the choking pressure for this highly successful submission.

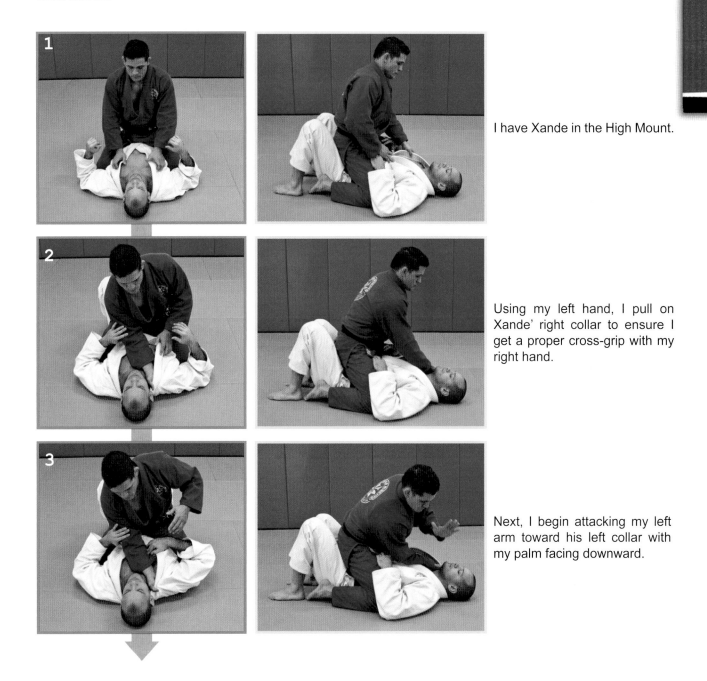

I have Xande in the High Mount.

Using my left hand, I pull on Xande' right collar to ensure I get a proper cross-grip with my right hand.

Next, I begin attacking my left arm toward his left collar with my palm facing downward.

Figure 37.5 A: Choking Angle

Note that as my second hand enters, I contort the blade of my wrist and hand to mirror the shape of his neck (1). This level of adaptation is important when dealing with chokes. I must make my physiology match that of my opponent to create a snug-fitting choke. By doing this, I will have a very tight choking position once I secure my second grip (2).

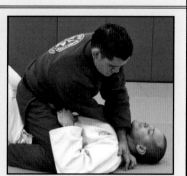

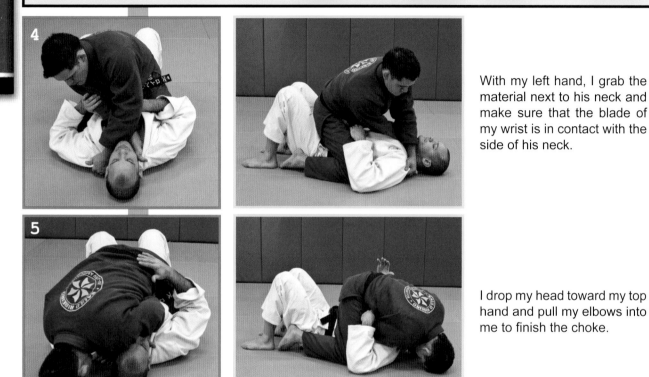

With my left hand, I grab the material next to his neck and make sure that the blade of my wrist is in contact with the side of his neck.

I drop my head toward my top hand and pull my elbows into me to finish the choke.

Figure 37.5 B: Choking Close-Up

Once you have the cross-choke in place, be sure to keep your elbows tight to your side and be confident in your base (1). As you drop your weight forward, use the pressure of your body mass to control the position while you draw your elbows toward your body (2). This choke does not have to be an instant tap, but your opponent will not last long if done properly.

37-6 PALM UP/PALM UP CHOKE

The reason most people have not mastered this choke is because they are using the wrong entry. The usual mistake is that they try this technique as a first option and get blocked. Once blocked, they give up on the technique and move into something else. Instead of missing this important choke, just change your entry! Begin by attacking with the palm up/palm down choke. When your opponent goes to defend, use your choking hand to drive his defensive hand away from his neck. This will open the necessary space for the choke and lead to a successful submission. Practice this move in conjunction with the palm up/palm down choke until you have become a cross-choke master!

Once again, I have Xande in a High Mount. My right arm is cross-gripping his right collar, and he is trying to defend by holding onto my arm.

As I begin to attack the palm up/palm down cross-choke, Xande prepares his defense.

Xande prevents my left hand from gripping by blocking my incoming arm.

The Mount

I counter this movement by returning my left hand to my inside and opening my right elbow toward Xande's head. This forces his left hand upward and creates a perfect space for an attack.

To capitalize on Xande's gap, I slide my left hand underneath his left arm to achieve the cross-collar grip. Both my palms are facing upward.

To finish the choke, I must always lean my head toward the top hand. In this case it is the right hand, so I collapse my head over Xande's right shoulder until it posts on the mat. Then I pull my elbows tight to my ribcage and await his tap.

Figure 37.6: Space Detail

When your first hand enters into the choke, it is vital to drop your elbow onto his body (1). With your elbow on his chest, he cannot block the choke (2). If you fail to do so, a seasoned opponent will swim his hand to the inside and block your first grip (4). This will greatly reduce the effectiveness of any choking technique.

37-7 TRIANGLE CHOKE

The triangle choke is another attack that is a great asset to your Mount submission game. When attacking this position, do what should now come naturally. You do not need to confuse your game by trying an awkward set up. Instead, push down on one of your opponent's hands while trapping his other and pulling down on his neck. This should feel very familiar to the basic triangle set up from the guard. Remember, if the technique works great in one situation, the leverage and mechanics should be present in others.

Xande has me in the High Mount.

I try to defeat Xande's upward advance by bracing my right forearm against his hips and tucking my left elbow inward. Unfortunately for me, I have not been able to get to a side posture. He reacts by pushing my left wrist into my body.

While pressing my arm into me, Xande leans to his left and lifts my head off the mat with his left hand.

This creates the perfect angle for Xande to step his right leg over my left shoulder in a near triangle.

Xande circles his right foot toward his left knee and clamps his shin with his left hand.

Leaning to his right, Xande creates the necessary angle to lock his triangle. If Xande tries to do this without the angle, his own weight and leg will block him from locking the hold.

To finish the submission, Xande rotates back to a square position and pulls up on my head while squeezing his knees together.

37-8 S-MOUNT CROSS CHOKE

Whenever you use the S-Mount, your goal should be to overwhelm and defeat your opponent. This is not a resting position–it is a submitting one. The S-Mount occurs anytime you go from a square mount to a perpendicular one. This sets up the perfect angle to attack the armbar and cross choke in rapid fire until one finds success. In this technique you can go for the straightforward cross choke. The trick to this technique is in how you enter your choking hand. Note that you slide your hand over your opponent's face until you reach the collar. This allows you to peel away his defensive hand until you can get a clean collar grip. If you try to grab straight for the collar, he is likely to block it and you will have to go for the armbar.

I have Xande in the High Mount position. He has reacted by keeping his hands high to protect his neck.

Using a low lapel grip, my right hand opens up Xande's lapel to the outside. This forces his left hand to the outside and opens a path for my initial grip.

I maneuver my left hand to the open left collar to grab a cross-collar grip. This time my initial grip has the thumb inside with four fingers on top. I lift my right hand to threaten the cross-collar choke.

Next, I slide my right knee under Xande's left armpit and face him at a perpendicular angle. Now, he must worry about a possible armbar attack.

I place the back of my right hand on Xande's forehead and slide it toward his neck.

This moves Xande's defense down until I am able to grasp his gi on the right side of his head.

To finish the choke, I sink my elbows toward my body and drive my head toward my top hand. Xande taps out from this surprising technique.

37-9 S-MOUNT ARMBAR

As previously discussed, the S-Mount is a wonderful position for attacking submissions. Because you have so much control over your opponent's upper body and arms, the armbar is always a great go-to attack. The trick of this position is learning to move in and out of choke attempts and armbars. For instance, if your opponent manages to escape his elbow, go for the choke because his neck is now exposed. If your opponent tries to turn away from you to defeat the choke, take the armbar as his arm becomes exposed. Drill this series often until you can seamlessly blend the two attacks.

Xande has me in the High Mount position. He is gripping my right lapel with his left hand, just below my arms.

Pulling my lapel with his left hand, Xande penetrates his right hand underneath my arms to establish the cross-collar grip.

Next, Xande moves his left hand to my elbow and forces it down while he slides his left knee under my shoulder. Once there, he prevents my escape by driving his chest into my arm.

With my right arm trapped, Xande grabs my left elbow with his left hand and pulls it to him while he circles his right leg under my triceps. His legs now form the S-Mount position.

Xande drives his weight forward and to the right to lighten his left leg.

Then he steps his left leg over my head to achieve the armbar position.

To finish, Xande falls back to submit me with the S-Mount armbar.

37-10 KATA GATAME TO EZEQUIEL

Even when you are close to finishing your opponent, you need options in case your opponent can weather your submission attempt. This is where combinations come into play, and the Kata Gatame to Ezequiel is a perfect one to master. In this technique, moving from the Kata Gatame to the Ezequiel makes sense; to defend the Kata Gatame, your opponent must make space between his own choking arm and neck. When he makes this space to survive, fill it with the Ezequiel choke!

As an additional exercise, outline other complementary submissions that work well together and play off of the opponent's defense. Next, create your own combinations and drill them until you can freely flow between them. Your game will skyrocket as you become a submission master!

Xande has me in the Kata Gatame from the Low Mount. I am defending by pushing into my right arm with my left. This opens my right carotid artery.

Instead of forcing the Kata Gatame, Xande grabs inside his left sleeve while I am preoccupied with defense.

Xande circles his left arm over my head until the blade of his wrist reaches my throat.

To finish the Ezekiel choke, Xande drives his choking hand toward the mat to create an incredible choking pressure.

37-11 COLLAR CHOKE DRILL

This is an excellent drill to learn the necessary body movement to transition from the Mount to the Seated Mount to the Back. The icing on the cake is this ends in a very tight submission. Repeat this drill often until you are lightning fast on your transition. You should not even have to think when you do this move! Regarding the lapel choke, it is important always to pull your opponent toward your choking arm. This will lock him into the choke and prevent him from escaping the choking angle.

I have Xande in the High Mount with my right hand gripping his left collar.

Xande tries to bridge into my arm to roll me, but I lift my hips, and he safely moves to his side.

I drop my body into the Seated Mount. My right foot is locked to his hip and my left shin is tight to Xande's back.

Next, I pull Xande to his right while I penetrate my left knee to his left shoulder.

I continue this motion until Xande ends on his right side. This gives me the perfect opportunity to get my second hook to control the Back.

To tighten the choke, I swing my left arm under Xande's armpit and place the back of my left palm behind his head. I pull my posture back to increase the choking pressure and he is forced to tap.

38-0 SIDE CONTROL

Most of the time, you will find yourself in the Side Control after passing the guard. Passing the guard can be difficult against an opponent of equal skill, therefore Side Control often becomes a stalling position for the person on top. This is why I emphasize building your game from survival to submissions. Now that you have practiced jiu-jitsu in this bottom-up style, you should have no concern about losing this position and passing the guard again.

Of course, the goal of this position is control and then submission. You control the Side Control with hip-to-hip pressure and the blocking action of your body. I like to use as much of my body as possible for control because that leaves my hands open to attack my opponent. If all you are doing is holding on to your opponent, it is highly unlikely that you will accomplish any meaningful attack.

As a drill, I recommend starting on the top of the Side Control with both hands behind your back until you are used to using your body weight and positioning to dominate the position hands free. Once you have accomplished this, move to the following submissions to add depth to your Side Control game.

38-1 KIMURA

The Kimura from Side Control is a great example of using your opponent's defense against him. Instead of seeking out the submission, I allow my opponent to get an underhook and try to bridge me off of him. This should expose his arm to the Kimura every time because my weight is evenly distributed on him. Once again, timing is everything and you have to recognize the moment to switch your hips. Practice with a compliant partner until you can safely read his body language and tension. As you feel his tension build and his legs move into bridging position, prepare your hip-switch and then beat him to the punch as he tries to explode you off him. Then, make your partner pay for his over exuberance with a perfect Kimura lock!

I have secured the Side Control position and Xande is trying to escape with his left arm underhooking my right armpit.

As Xande tries to push me off with his arm and defensive bump, I grasp his elbow with both arms and change my base to the Reverse Kesa Gatame. It is important that my left arm wraps over Xande's left triceps.

Driving off my right foot, I use my weight to push Xande's arm back to his body.

Then, I grab his wrist with my left hand and secure the figure-four hold. Xande defends by grabbing onto his own belt.

To break Xande's defensive grip, I glue his arm to my body and pull back with my body to clear his grip. The power of my body weight easily rips his arm clear from his body.

Next, I drive Xande's wrist to the mat on his left side.

I switch my base again so that I am on my right hip.

As I lean toward my right, I lighten my left leg so that I can lift it over Xande's head.

Once I have Xande's head locked, I lift his left shoulder off the mat and push his wrist downward to secure the Kimura lock. This is a painful shoulder lock, and he has to tap immediately.

38-2 WALK-AROUND ARMBAR

Whenever your opponent reaches over your near-side shoulder, realize he is trying to pull you over in a reversal. However, he is also leaving his arm open for attack and you should make him pay for his mistake. The walk-around armbar is the perfect submission for this situation because you completely dominate his arm with your entire body as you methodically progress to the armbar position. The key is using both your arms to trap his arm and pinching your head to his wrist to prevent him from rolling his arm free. With his arm trapped, move your body forward to create the best angle for your hips to enter and sit back for the submission!

I have Xande in the Side Control position. This time, he is reaching over my left shoulder to pull me into a reversal.

Sensing Xande's ambition, I clasp my hands together underneath his armpit and pull his tricep toward my body. As I do this, I change my angle slightly to the left to set up the following transition.

With a large step, I bring my left leg deep to Xande's left side.

Pushing off with my right toes, I swivel my hips slightly to my left while driving downward with my head.

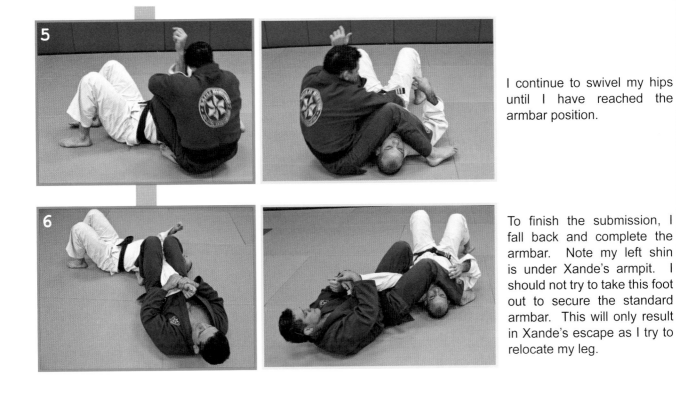

I continue to swivel my hips until I have reached the armbar position.

To finish the submission, I fall back and complete the armbar. Note my left shin is under Xande's armpit. I should not try to take this foot out to secure the standard armbar. This will only result in Xande's escape as I try to relocate my leg.

38-3 ROYLER'S ARMBAR

When I first started training with Royler Gracie, this was probably the submission that he caught me with the most. Anytime I was under Royler's Side Control or North-South and I tried to grab an over-under grip from the bottom, it would be an instant armbar. This move is simple and effective at the highest levels. The important detail of this technique is how you switch your inside hip to the mat to make the necessary space to slide your inside knee into armbar position. Do not try to pull your inside leg over your opponent's body; just trap his arm under your armpit, squeeze your knees together and lift your hips to hyperextend the elbow.

I have Xande in the North-South position. Xande has his right arm under my right arm and his left arm in front of my left.

Side Control

As I transition to the Side Control, I trap Xande's right arm and drive my weight toward his legs. This allows me to control Xande's arm, control his body, and lighten my left leg.

To secure the armbar position, I step over his head with my left leg.

I begin falling back, making sure to trap Xande's right arm under my armpit.

To finish the lock, I pull my right knee upward and secure it with my right hand while driving my hips upward.

38-4 SPINNING ARMBAR

In this technique, your opponent reaches over your outside shoulder to pull you into a reversal. Although he may think that he is avoiding the walk-around armbar, actually he has set himself up for the smooth transitioning spinning armbar. Because his reaching arm is far from his neck, you have plenty of space to step over his head and spin to the armbar. Once again, use your head and shoulder to control the arm and angle your body to the side to lighten your leg for the step-over attack.

A great drill for this technique is to start in Side Control and have your opponent expose his arm. Do the spinning armbar, finishing the submission on the other side from which you started. Continue by having him expose his arm and repeat this process from the alternate side. Again, it is pertinent to develop an automatic transition, so make your drills count!

I have Xande in the Side Control position. His right hand is gripping over my left shoulder in an attempt at a rollover reversal.

Keeping my base centered, I grip his left elbow with my left hand. I need to have my arm under his elbow for this to be effective.

To isolate his arm, I pull my posture upward to separate his arm from his body. I pin his wrist against my shoulder and head for added control.

Next, I lean to my left to lighten my right foot.

In one motion, I pull Xande's shoulder to lift him to his side while I stand my right foot.

With Xande postured on his side, I can step my right leg over his head. I keep my lower right leg glued to the middle of his back.

I pivot my hips to the right until I am facing the opposite direction. As I do this, my left leg slides in front of Xande's face while my right knee falls behind his left armpit. I grab his belt with my right hand to prevent his escape.

I fall to my rear in control of the armbar position. I make sure that my legs are tight and my knees are already pinching together.

To finish the armbar, I fall all the way to my back and hyperextend his elbow by thrusting my hips upward.

38-5 FAILED SPINNING ARMBAR

If you fail to control your opponent's arm with both your neck and body weight, you are giving him too much space for a potential escape. In this scenario, I have failed to control the arm and wrist and there is a lot of space between my opponent and myself. This is all my opponent needs to circle his wrist inside and escape the armbar.

1) I have Xande in the Side Control position. His right hand is gripping over my left shoulder in an attempt at a rollover reversal.

2) Although I have gripped Xande's arm and pulled it up for control, I have mistakenly started to scramble to his other side to finish the attack. Xande senses my inexperience and braces against my left hip to block my movement.

3) As I continue to rush to his left side, Xande stalls my progress by keeping my hips elevated with his blocking arm, while turning his wrist downward to free his elbow.

4) Finally, he completes his arm rotation and escapes his arm. My hips are still elevated high off his body and Xande is in a great position to attempt an escape.

38-6 SPINNING ARMBAR TO KIMURA

If your opponent manages to escape his wrist from the spinning armbar, do not give up on the position! Instead, maintain your control over him and change your grips to the figure-four lock. From here, gently torque his wrist using the turn of your body to secure the Kimura. Pay attention to your legs; they will block him from moving with you to alleviate the shoulder pressure.

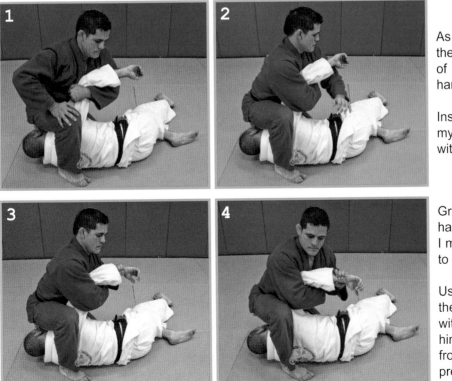

As I am stepping over to complete the spinning armbar, I lose control of Xande's wrist as he points his hand toward his body (1).

Instead of controlling his elbow with my left arm, I change so I secure it with my right (2).

Grabbing Xande's wrist with my left hand, I secure the figure-four hold. I make sure to glue Xande's elbow to my body (3).

Using my body movement, I turn to the right to crank Xande's shoulder with a Kimura lock. My legs keep him in place and prevent him from following me to release the pressure (4).

38-7 STEP-OVER CHOKE

This is my favorite submission from the Side Control and I have caught many guys in this position before. The step-over choke should feel like an effortless trap when perfected. By taking a loose collar grip and giving your opponent a little space, he will often react by turning into you to escape. This is the perfect time to spring the attack! Block his outside arm with your hand and lean toward his legs to lighten your front leg. Make sure that he cannot return to his back or pursue you any further. Then, step over his head and apply downward pressure on his head while you pull up on the choking hand. Once trapped, your opponent will have no other option but to tap!

I have Xande in the Side Control position and I am grabbing his collar behind his head with my right hand.

Lifting off my knees, I open some space between me and Xande.

Xande takes the bait and turns into me to attempt an escape. I begin my attack by cupping Xande's elbow with my left hand. I do this so Xande cannot return to his back.

Then, I lean my body toward Xande's hip to lighten my right leg. As I do this, I start to set in the choke.

To finish the choke, I pull up on my choking hand while anchoring my right leg into the mat. Xande is completely trapped and has no other option but to tap.

SIDE CONTROL 357

38-8 BREAD CUTTER CHOKE

This is a classic choking technique from Side Control, but it is also a move that is seldom done correctly. Most people tend to trap the near arm and fight for the choking grip. Although this is not wrong, it is inefficient. In this version, I trap the near-side arm at the triceps and then try to get a cross-face grip. Because, my opponent does not wish to be cross-faced, he will put the back of his head on the mat. This opens his neck for the choke. From here, I quickly take the bread cutter choke position, but I do not try to fight my elbow to the ground to submit my opponent. Instead, I pull up on his elbow to drive him into the choke. Once my opponent is pushed to his side, I use downward pressure on my choking hand to finish the submission.

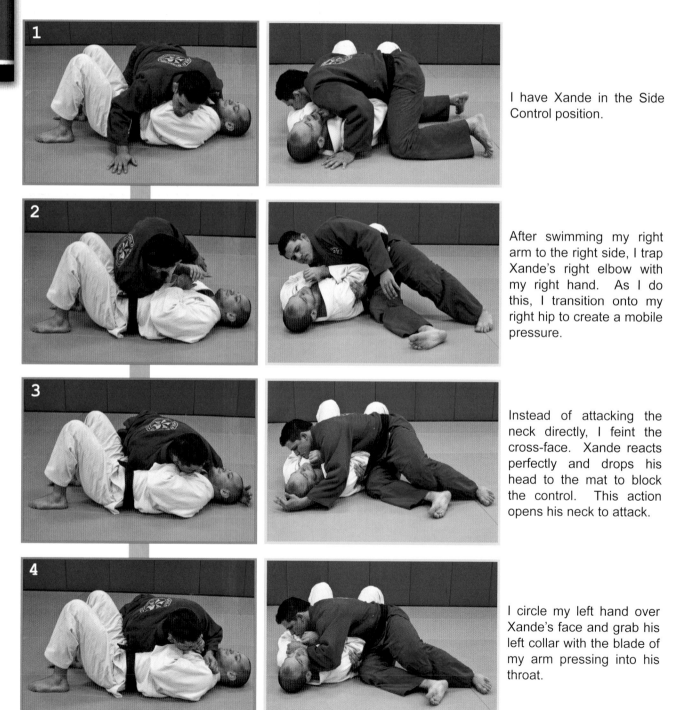

1 I have Xande in the Side Control position.

2 After swimming my right arm to the right side, I trap Xande's right elbow with my right hand. As I do this, I transition onto my right hip to create a mobile pressure.

3 Instead of attacking the neck directly, I feint the cross-face. Xande reacts perfectly and drops his head to the mat to block the control. This action opens his neck to attack.

4 I circle my left hand over Xande's face and grab his left collar with the blade of my arm pressing into his throat.

5

I initiate the choke as I drop my elbow toward the mat. Most guys will tap at this point.

6

Xande is able to withstand the choking action, so I lift his right shoulder off the mat as I drive down with the choke to create even more choking pressure. At this point, even Xande's strongest defense crumbles and I force him to tap.

38-9 BASEBALL CHOKE

The baseball choke is a submission that gets its name from how the attacker grips the collars as he would hold a baseball bat. This is a highly effective submission that has caught many good jiu-jitsu players, including me in the 2001 Mundials. The power of the technique comes from the spinning motion that tightens this nooselike choke. However, this move can be very difficult to set up against an aware opponent. If you try for this move directly, your opponent is likely to prevent your grips or pull down on your elbow to prevent the choking pressure. This is why I like the following setup. By shifting your body toward your opponent's head, you will give him the feeling that he can push you off him. As he tries to do so, he opens his neck for your second grip. From here, his arms are out of defensive position, and you can easily circle his body to finish the submission.

1

I have Xande in the Side Control position. My right hand has a loose collar grip with my thumb on the inside of his lapel.

2

As I shuffle my body to my right, Xande naturally reacts by extending his arms to push me away from him. I allow him to assist my side movement until I get to his head.

Side Control

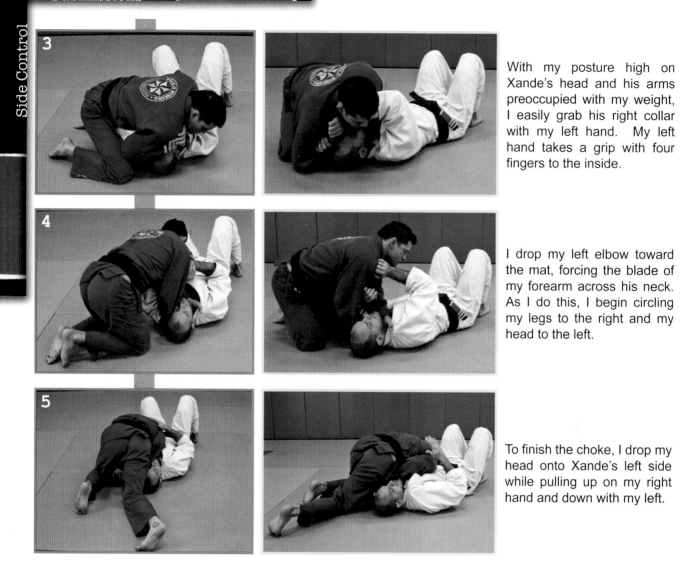

3 With my posture high on Xande's head and his arms preoccupied with my weight, I easily grab his right collar with my left hand. My left hand takes a grip with four fingers to the inside.

4 I drop my left elbow toward the mat, forcing the blade of my forearm across his neck. As I do this, I begin circling my legs to the right and my head to the left.

5 To finish the choke, I drop my head onto Xande's left side while pulling up on my right hand and down with my left.

39-0 TURTLE TOP

To master the Turtle position is to master your weight distribution on top. The student on bottom must feel constant pressure on his hips or else he will easily escape or reverse the position. Once again, use your hip-to-hip pressure and mobility to stay a step ahead of your opponent and use the clock choke position and back attacks to finish the match.

To gain comfort in the Turtle, first drill movement around the Turtle, asking your partner where he feels you are lacking pressure. This will help you alter your weight and angle as you get comfortable on top. As your movement gets better, try some positional drills. Start with your opponent on the bottom and ask him to escape, then try your hardest, using technique and movement, to prevent him from changing positions. If he does get to his back, make sure your hips follow him into Side Control. Once you can dominate the position, add submissions into the drill to round out your skills.

39-1 CLOCK CHOKE

The clock choke is a popular way to attack the Turtle position, but it is an attack that is often practiced inefficiently. Most jiu-jitsu practitioners are taught to circle around their opponents like the hands of a clock. The idea is that the circling motion tightens the choke as you continue to circle farther and farther. Although this is not incorrect, it is antiquated. The chief problem with this method is it does nothing to inhibit your opponent from following as you walk your feet to the front. This is your opponent's instinctive defense to unravel the choking pressure. This version addresses this missing piece by driving your opponent onto his shoulder to immobilize him. Once here, simply drive your hips forward to complete a very tight choke. Notice that this version gives you greater control and contact while efficiently finishing the submission.

Xande is in the Turtle position with me on top. I am in the process of attacking his neck with my left hand while my right hand blocks his hip. This is important to keep him from rolling to escape.

As my left hand gets a good grip on Xande's right collar, my right hand grips his right knee.

Using my bodyweight and mobility, I pull Xande toward his left elbow. This completely breaks down his posture.

To finish the clock choke, I scissor my right leg through, driving my hip into Xande's shoulder while I pull up on the choke. My right hand blocks his hip to prevent his escape.

Figure 39.1: Choke Details

The clock choke is not about how much you can run around your opponent to get the tap. It is about placing your hip on his shoulder and breaking his posture to the mat. When you are in position, look at his left elbow; it is all that is keeping him upright (1). If you pull him toward his forearm's dead angle, you are sure to bring him down (2). Once there, it is simply a matter of driving your hips onto him to keep him there and creating the optimal amount of pressure (3).

40-0 HALF GUARD

Originally thought of only as a passing position, the top Half Guard has recently transitioned into an attack position as well. The key to Half Guard submissions is the ability to move between passing principles and submissions. Remember, you always want your opponent relatively flat and you should never forego control for a reckless submission attempt. Instead, use your base and pass attempts to set up the following two submissions to create a diverse top Half Guard game.

40-1 BRABO CHOKE

The Brabo choke is a submission that I first saw used by my good friend and jiu-jitsu phenomenon, Leonardo "Leozinho" Vieira. Since then, it has become the staple move for submitting an opponent with an offensive Half Guard. When attempting this choke, it is often easy to get the lapel grip, but difficult to pull your opponent's arm across his body to finish the choke. This is because you need to bait him into giving you his arm. To do so, attack the cross-collar choke. If your opponent fails to defend it, you will finish the submission. In all likelihood, a good opponent will defend with his outside hand to block the choke. This is the perfect moment to trap his elbow and pull his arm across his neck. To finish the submission, drive your body weight onto your opponent's shoulder and triceps as you pull up on the choking hand to create a very tight choke.

When practicing this move, it is important to get a lot of feedback from your partner. Ask him if the position feels like a neck crank or a choke. With this information, alter your angle and pressure until you master the feeling of the choke. The reason I say this is because the choke is much tighter than the crank and you always need to focus on the best technique.

Xande is in my Half Guard and is grabbing my lower left lapel with his right hand. My side posture indicates that I hope to sweep or recover the guard.

In one motion, Xande sets in a deep cross-face while stretching my left lapel.

Once he has pulled the slack out of the lapel, Xande feeds the lapel to his left hand.

Next, Xande drives his right hand to the inside toward my head.

Xande then feeds the lapel to his right hand and releases his left. As he does this, he drops his right shoulder to produce acute pressure on my chest.

With his left hand free, Xande attempts the cross-choke as he reaches for the cross-grip on my left collar. I defend by pushing his arm away with my left arm.

I just fell into Xande's trap. He seizes the opportunity and grabs my left elbow with his left hand.

8

Xande finishes the choke by pulling my elbow across my neck and dropping his weight onto my triceps. He increases his choking pressure by pulling slightly on the choking hand while sprawling his hips low. This choke is very tight and it forces me to tap.

Figure 40.1: Choking Details

The mechanics of this choke are very simple. As Xande crosses my arm downward, a combination of my left arm and his right lapel close my carotid arteries by pressing into them. However, Xande's left arm is not strong enough to hold my arm in place, so he has to drop his body weight to secure the position.

40-2 BRABO TO STRAIGHT ARMLOCK

Sometimes your opponent will push off the mat with his arm to relieve the Brabo's choking pressure. This is the perfect time to move to a straight armlock attack. Simply pull up on the elbow, using your body as a fulcrum to get the straight armlock submission. If your opponent is abnormally strong or resistant to this technique, then transition back to the Brabo choke to get the finish. As with all submissions, your aim is to overwhelm your opponent with attacks while using the least amount of energy.

Xande has me in the Brabo choke position, but I am pressing off the mat with my left hand to relieve the pressure.

Instead of giving up on the position, Xande grabs my left wrist with his left hand.

He extends it outward to get a very fast straight armlock. He uses his body as the fulcrum to attack my elbow joint.

41-0 GUARD TOP

At some point, most beginners will try to submit their opponent from within his guard. Although this is usually a mistake that leads to chokes and armbars, there are situations in which it is practical. The trick is going for submissions that do not lead to the attacker getting submitted!

The following attack is a great example of a submission that originates from within the guard and has a high chance of success if used correctly. However, do not utilize this move in lieu of learning proper guard-passing skills. This move is a great technique, but you will have many more submissions available to you once you learn to pass the guard.

41-1 STRAIGHT ANKLE LOCK

Of the few submissions available from the top, the straight ankle lock is by far my favorite. However, I like to do the straight ankle lock a little different. In contrast to others, I do not intend on finishing the first ankle that I attack. Because I know that my partners are very good, I anticipate their defenses when I set up the submission. As my opponent sits into me to defend the ankle, I change to the other leg. This results in my opponent's body angling to the wrong side, giving me the perfect angle to finish an easy ankle lock.

Drill this move often and pay attention to how I immobilize my opponent's feet by never letting them touch the mat. This isolates him, and prevents him from effectively coming into me with a defense.

I am in Xande's Closed Guard with both my hands posted in his armpits.

Driving off my hands, I stand up in his guard. At this point, Xande thinks I am going to try to wedge open his guard to attempt a pass.

As I bring my right knee in to wedge open Xande's guard, I step my left foot to the outside and begin falling to my back. I grab both of his knees for control.

I trap Xande's right foot and slide my right knee high to the inside to secure the ankle lock.

This causes Xande to defend and he sits into me to relieve the tension on his outstretched ankle. This is when I go for my real attack.

As Xande sits toward his right side, I switch my left knee to the middle and begin turning to my right.

7

I have wrapped Xande's left ankle with my right arm. I place my right foot on his hip and I continue to turn to my right side. This creates the perfect foot-locking angle because Xande's body is overcommitted to my left side.

8

I lean completely onto my right side and arch my back to finish the straight ankle lock. The fulcrum is my forearm and the lever is my shoulder pushing his foot downward. The lock itself hyperextends Xande's ankle joint.

Figure 41.1: Both Feet Up Detail

When you are switching from one side to the other, you must control both his ankles. The reason is quite simple; if you keep both your opponent's feet off the ground, they cannot stand up or easily sit into you to defend. This is a great way to frustrate your opponent and set up your next leg attack or transition back to the pass.